TAILWIND
BOTH WAYS

Photo by Watt M. Casey, Jr.

TAILWIND BOTH WAYS

A Cowman's Chronicle

LAURENCE M. LASATER

BRIGHT SKY PRESS

BRIGHT SKY PRESS

Box 416
Albany, Texas 76430

10   9   8   7   6   5   4   3   2   1

Library of Congress Cataloging-in-Publication Data

Lasater, Laurence M., 1941–
    Tailwind both ways : a cowman's chronicle / by Laurence M. Lasater.
        p. cm.
    ISBN 978-1-933979-09-0 (jacketed hardcover : alk. paper) 1. Lasater, Laurence M., 1941– 2. Beef cattle—Texas. 3. Cattle breeders—Texas—Biography. 4. Beefmaster cattle—Texas. I. Title.

SF194.2.L37A3 2008
636.20092—dc22
[B]

2007035848

Book and cover design by Isabel Lasater Hernandez
Edited by Dixie Nixon

Printed in China through Asia Pacific Offset

Written for my family

and

for those men and women worldwide

who work hard every day in the cattle industry,

with little payment or recognition.

CONTENTS

With Isabel, J.C. holding Luke, Leslie, Watt, Lorenzo, Beau and Annette

Our family at the Adolphus Hotel, Dallas, Texas, September 24, 2004, at Dad's induction into the Texas Heritage Hall of Honor

AUTHOR'S PREFACE

Annette recently commented that in no other career could we have become acquainted with the remarkable people we have known in forty years in the cattle business. She is absolutely right. I have lived a life of high adventure, surrounded by the kindest and most interesting, as well as some of the smartest and most honest people in the world. I have traveled extensively, done and seen everything I wanted to at least once. Just like the old-timers, we have lived periods of heartbreak, disappointment and financial stress interspersed with days of beauty, joy and perfection. Our wonderful family life has more than cancelled out any setbacks, and I am grateful for that and many other blessings.

Many people have suggested that I write a book, especially my friend Guillermo Osuna, saying that I have an unusual feel for the business. After thinking about it for several years, I decided to accept their good advice. Many of the stories from Annette's well-told book, *Two to Mexico*, are repeated here. Marcos Giménez, my collaborator on the Spanish version of *The Lasater Philosophy of Cattle Raising*, pointed out, in his introduction, that my role in the four-generation history of the Lasater family, to date, was to translate the genetic and ethical legacy of the family into business reality. I am one of the few large-scale, registered producers who do business on leased land and borrowed money. Many of the outstanding people and interesting experiences we have had resulted from operating under such pressure for so many years.

Those who are close to me know that I love scrapbooks. I selected the photographs in this book from several hundred of my favorites. I started this book Saturday, October 30, 2004, the month I turned 63, and our youngest grandson, Luke Laurence Hernandez, turned one year old. We also had our 43rd bull sale. In December 2004, we celebrated our 40th wedding anniversary and our 40th year in business.

The fifth generation is now in charge. Our son, Lorenzo, is doing the hard work, and our son-in-law, J.C., a banker, is counting the money. Our daughter, Isabel, who designed this book, has her own business, INK Design Group, and is in charge of our company's public relations. Leslie is president-elect of the Junior League chapter in San Angelo. The sixth generation—Watt, Beau and Luke—are off and running, and like all good patriarchs, Annette and I are enjoying the show.

Throughout, there have been failures and disappointments, including numerous experiences with incompetence and criminality that are not mentioned here. Their telling serves no purpose. This book was written out of my love for the cattle business, my admiration for many of those in it, and my gratitude for the fulfilling life I have lived. I hope you enjoy it.

PART I

CHAPTER 1

THE HERITAGE

Some years ago, standing in front of the Alamo, next door to the Menger Hotel in San Antonio, Texas, I noticed the Menger Bar sign showing that it was established in 1859. As I read it, I realized that not only had Teddy Roosevelt recruited the Rough Riders there, but also that all my ancestors in the cattle business and heroes such as Charles Goodnight had undoubtedly passed through there as well.

In the families of Ed C. Lasater, J.A. Matthews and George Reynolds, the pioneer legacy is not something of academic interest, but rather a commandment to "go and do likewise." Ed C. Lasater and George Reynolds are featured in *The Trail Drivers of Texas.* Sallie Reynolds Matthews, my maternal great-grandmother, in her book *Interwoven* tells the story of the settling of Shackelford and Throckmorton Counties. Her husband, J.A. Matthews, took a trail herd to Nevada at 19 years of age. My brother Dale's book, *Falfurrias,* tells of the founding of Brooks County by our grandfather, Ed C. Lasater.

In 1997, our generation of Lasaters established a niche at the Texas and Southwestern Cattle Raisers Museum honoring Ed C. Lasater and his sons, Tom (my father) and Garland (my uncle). In addition to their many other accomplishments, the sons carried on and bequeathed Ed C. Lasater's priceless legacy of integrity to our generation. This legacy has enabled me to do business successfully on a handshake basis around the world. When I received the Beefmaster Breeders United Breeder of the Year award in 2000, I said truthfully that I accepted on behalf of my father and grandfather, who did most of the hard work.

In 2004, Tom Lasater was inducted into the Texas Heritage Hall of Honor, having been nominated by Nolan Ryan. He joined Watt Matthews, John Armstrong, Dolph Briscoe, Jr., and Charles Goodnight, among others. My entire family attended on behalf of the Lasater clan, with our son, Lorenzo, and me representing the fourth and fifth generations of ranchers in our family. The sixth generation (Watt, Beau and Luke) was also present and is ready for action.

The seed for this book was planted that day in front of the Alamo. I realized that my generation of ranchers, born between 1937 and 1950, have had experiences similar to those of the pioneers we admire and emulate. Some of us have lived through drought, fire, flood, market breaks, bank failures, cattle theft, trail drives, screw worms, and Indian fights as well as all the daily hardships—exhaustion, searing heat, bitter cold.

Our generation, which grew up admiring the courage, integrity, fortitude and entrepreneurship of those who had gone before, has had to witness the beginning of the decline of the great U.S. cow-calf industry. In this book, you will meet dozens of individuals and families who have the values of the pioneers, and who share my grief over the slow death of our beloved industry, along with the precious traditions and values that are an important part of America's story.

When Annette and I moved our family to San Angelo, Texas, in 1972, my grandmother, Ethel Matthews Casey, approved, saying that outside Shackelford and Throckmorton Counties, only Tyler, Graham and San Angelo were suitable places for us to live. Her brothers, my great uncles, Joe and Watt Matthews, always told me of their pasturing cattle on a pretty ranch near "Angelo" that had a nice creek running through it.

In the late 1980s, I was pasturing cattle with David Krieg and Ben McCulloch on the Mustang Ranch in Concho County. Whenever we worked cattle, Ben's wife, Ann, always prepared a delicious lunch. One day before lunch, I was sitting on their sofa with Ben's dad, Mr. H.E. McCulloch, who was about 90 years old, sometimes lucid and sometimes not. He was telling me the ranch's history and how different people had cattle there around 1920. As we looked out the window at Mustang Creek, an eerie feeling came over me as I realized this was the place where Uncle

Watt and Uncle Joe had pastured cattle 60 years earlier and had remembered fondly.

The first trail herd came through Fort Concho (San Angelo) in 1865, and 21-year-old George Reynolds was with the herd, representing his family. I have leased numerous ranches along their probable route from Fort Concho to the cavalry post near Santa Fe. Many times I have wondered on which side of a certain hill they passed, or where they had crossed a certain draw as they ground their way 500 miles from Central

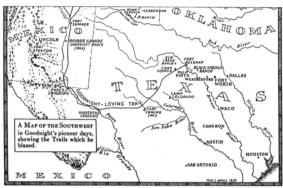

Map showing the Goodnight-Loving Trail passing by Fort Concho (San Angelo).

Texas to Eastern New Mexico. I have always been aware of following trails that previously have been trod.

In addition to the pioneer legacy, another priceless aspect of my heritage is the genetic legacy of our Beefmaster cattle. I have traveled all over the cattle world. Everywhere I have visited I have been told that our bulls sired the best calves. I have been told this even on ranches using genetics from well-known producers with other breeds of cattle.

Cattle are a perishable commodity on a moving stage. They have to be financed, fed, cared for and delivered to market. The money collected and the bankers paid. Vast amounts of capital are employed. The original word for capital was cattle (livestock).

People in our industry have a profound spirituality due to working with the forces of nature. We have a living awareness of those who have passed before, and a sense of the joy that awaits us when we all are reunited across the Great Divide.

The "Family Cow Outfit" on the Lasater Ranch. On horseback: Sally, Tom, Laurie, Dale and Lane. Standing in front: Brian and Alan.

CHAPTER 2

GROWING UP ON
THE LASATER RANCH

I was born at the Nix Hospital in San Antonio, Texas, on October 21, 1941, the eldest of the six children of Mary Casey Lasater and Thomas Miller Lasater of Falfurrias, Texas. My parents, founders of the Beefmaster breed of cattle, were both very dynamic; they were a great team, highly educated and united in their ambition to raise a fine family, establish a great ranch and leave the world a better place. They had some failures, but also great successes. This story focuses on the successes.

Falfurrias was founded in 1904 by my grandfather, Ed C. Lasater. His ranch

My first horseback ride with Dad in 1942 in Falfurrias.

there grew to 350,000 acres. The area is flat, sandy, hot and infested with brush—an extremely harsh environment, which probably accounts for the fact that Beefmasters and other American breeds originated in that area as ranchers sought cattle that could thrive under such conditions. The culture is a mix of Texas and Mexico, of which the inhabitants are very proud.

My childhood experiences were typical of those of all first-borns. I was the beneficiary and the victim of my parents' ideas and campaigns such as no movies, cokes or candy until six years of age. I also received the best they had to offer at the peak of their powers, for which I will always be grateful. My experiences and outlook are probably characteristic of those of any oldest sibling. I felt obliged to take the lead in many situations, and my younger brothers and sister, Dale, Lane, Sally, Alan and Brian, humorously referred to me as "king of the royal mountain," a favorite game we played. My second brother, Lane, wrote my epitaph when he said, "You patrol the high ground ruthlessly."

Spanish was nearly a native language for me. Both Mother and Dad spoke it well, and all the cowboys and maids in South Texas were of Mexican origin, so it was spoken every day. I was called Lorenzo as a child in South Texas, and again twenty years later, as a grown man in Northern Mexico. The Hispanic language and culture have been key ingredients in our lives. My business has taken me to Mexico and Central and South America, where I have always felt comfortable with the customs and liked the people, who reciprocated the feeling.

Grandparents

I did not know my grandfathers, but both grandmothers were present. Dad's mother, Mary Miller Lasater, the second wife of Ed C. Lasater (his first family having died of various frontier illnesses). Dad was born in 1911, the youngest of five children; his father was born at the time of the Civil War.

I remember Dad's mother, Maya, to whom he was close, very well. She lived across the way from our little cottage on the original family ranch at La Mota, five miles from Falfurrias. We used to go walking together and she called me her *compadre,* a word I have always loved. I can still remember when she died in the mid-1940s. My brother Dale and I were together in Mother and Dad's bed when they came home with the news.

• • •

"Just sweeten it, Tom."
—*Ethel Matthews Casey*

Mother's mother, Ethel Matthews Casey, was the daughter of J.A. and Sallie Reynolds Matthews of Albany, Texas. Grandmother was an important influence in our lives, not only as the daughter of pioneers but also as an arbiter of culture. I have numerous first-edition books, many signed by the author, dating back to the 1940s, that were gifts from her.

I never knew Grandmother's parents, Sallie Reynolds Matthews (Other Mama) and J.A. Matthews (Other Papa) who married on Christmas Day, 1876, in the Barber Watkins Reynolds House. The house is still there at Reynolds Bend on the J.A. Matthews Ranch at Albany, Texas, in the bend of the Clear Fork of the Brazos River.

Both great-grandparents have always been a presence in our lives—Sallie, through her pioneer chronicle, *Interwoven,* of which this book is a descendant, and J.A. through his legendary status as a trail-driver, pioneer and philosopher, as well as founder of the Lambshead Ranch. With five daughters, he was experienced in dealing with prospective suitors. His normal opening gambit was usually, "Young man, what is your approximate annual income?" My favorite of these anecdotes concerns a young suitor who came to the house wearing a handsome pair of slacks. Other Papa asked him what they cost. The young man, not wanting to lie and not wanting to reveal the true cost, picked a middle figure. Without hesitation, J.A. replied, "Order me two pair."

Grandmother Casey was part of our lives until her death in 1985. As she approached 100 years of age and became enfeebled, I began writing her a letter each month as a means of doing something for her. My uncle, Watt Casey, told me that she had my most recent letter in her little bag of treasures when she died. Being a ranch woman, she was an active participant in our family life. Dad used to take her and us children horseback riding. In our family, the cocktail hour was sacrosanct, and although "Mrs. C.," as Dad called her, was of the generation of women who did not smoke or drink, she would enjoy a scotch and water and a Lucky Strike cigarette, if offered. When it came time for a refill, her inevitable response was "just sweeten it, Tom."

Aunts and Uncles

Aunts and uncles are important in every family. For someone like me, from a family where the standards were high and the discipline severe, they seemed to provide a buffer. Although aunts and uncles have the same standards as the parents, they deliver the message in a gentler, more nurturing way.

Dad's older brother, Uncle Garland, was an elegant, delightful man, beloved by all who knew him. Dad was proud of his big brother. After Uncle Garland and Aunt Carolyn built their home at La Mota, just before we moved to Colorado, we saw more of them. My earliest memory of

Uncle Garland, when I was five or six years old, is of his coming by our house to see if "old stick-in-the-mud" could go dove hunting. In retrospect, I think he knew I was having a hard time and needed a break, which he provided. Uncle Garland was one of my models for graciousness. I also followed in his footsteps as an aviator, and actually went to

Uncle Garland flies Grandmother Casey home to Albany in the late 1940s. I am standing on the wing.

Mexico, which was one of his dreams. In our last visit before his death in 1997, he told me that my book, *The Lasater Philosophy of Cattle Raising,* was his favorite reference book.

Aunt Carolyn was very dynamic and influenced everything and everyone within her radius of operations. When she was diagnosed as terminally ill, I flew to Falfurrias to spend the night and to pay my respects. I was expecting a somber occasion, but it was a delightful evening, ending with Cousin Edward and me sitting on a bench at the foot of their bed visiting until both aunt and uncle fell asleep.

• • •

I shared a close bond with Mother's uncle, Watt Reynolds Matthews, who was born in 1898, as we were both Princetonians and ranchers. While I was at Princeton in the 1960s, he came twice for the Yale game. Both times, he brought dates and went to my club after the game for the parties, which were on the rowdy side. He said his only regret was that they did not have parties like that when he was a student. He remarked once that from the fall of 1917, he had not seen Princeton lose to Yale.

Uncle Watt lived his entire life at the ranch in a Spartan bachelor cowboy's bunk-room with bed, dresser, desk and chair, just as we had at Princeton. Visits to the Lambshead Ranch at Albany, Texas, which he managed for his family, were special occasions for me as a child. He had

been a mentor to Mother and pals with Dad as fellow Princetonians and lifelong ranchers. A highlight for me was getting to stay with him in his quarters. In my earliest memory, I was worried to the point of sickness about wetting the bed while staying with him.

Uncle Watt, Grandmother Casey and Uncle Joe in 1976.

Mother evidently had alerted him, because he told me it would pass and nobody cared anyway. Such kindness is not soon forgotten.

In 1989, one of the highlights of our family life was flying to Lambshead Ranch for Thanksgiving dinner. Uncle Watt and the ranch are famous for preserving historical buildings and cattle trails. The ranch has restored three historic houses, a one-room schoolhouse and a dugout, as well as the headquarters. That day, he took us on a private two-and-a-half hour tour, showing Isabel and Lorenzo several of his preservation projects for which he was justly famous. When he told Annette and our children that such and such a house was constructed in '76 (meaning 1876), they were witnessing living history. I realized on this tour that it also meant much to him for me, a younger rancher, to bring my family to see his life's work. As often happens, the circle of our friendship rounded out nicely.

• • •

Mother's brother, Watt Matthews Casey, and his wife, Dosia, have been important in my life since early childhood. My first memory of Uncle Palo was his coming home from World War II, in which he served as a paratrooper. I can still see him wearing part of a uniform. Over the years, the age gap has narrowed, and we are now close friends. Throughout our lives, he and Dosia have been like second parents and a vital part of our family and business life. They have been a source of encouragement, knowledge, financing and genetics, all crucial to the success of our business.

During the time my brother Dale and I were in prep school and college, the Caseys operated the Tri-Valley Ranch at Kiowa, Colorado, about 50 miles from the Lasater Ranch. We would go there to have dinner and inevitably stay up all night visiting. Dad usually turned up around

7:00 a.m. the next morning, with the whole ranch crew in tow, to haul the "bodies" home.

Although they were polar opposites in every way, Uncle Palo was Dad's closest friend and business associate—the "first disciple" so to speak.

Aunt Dosia, Uncle Palo and Dad, with me on the truck.

They discussed and debated everything with lots of joking and carrying on, egging each other on in every situation. I remember them sitting in our living room at Matheson in the late 1950s, deciding to switch both herds to fall-calving in order to wean heavier calves in Colorado, and to get better breed-up on the yearling heifers. My favorite business story contrasting Dad and Uncle Palo (nicknamed "Palomino" by Uncle Watt, who called me "Lozo") occurred in 1974 after the great cattle market break. Dad came to San Angelo to visit us for Easter. Annette and I were broke and needed cows. I knew he had not sold his sales cows, so as we drove to the airport, I suggested that he sell them to me and finance them. He flinched, thought a minute, and said that he would look for a cash buyer. That was the end of that. A few days later, I contacted Uncle Palo, who graciously offered to sell me his sales cows and finance them.

My partner in California, Max Watkins, said that Watt Casey defined the term "gentle man" in being kind to all and incapable of a negative word for anyone. Uncle Palo and I had numerous business deals on bulls and females while we lived in Mexico, and we have had numerous other transactions of cattle and frozen genetics since 1974. Their excellent cattle have been invaluable to many of us. In 2000, he and I partnered to purchase stock in Nolan Ryan Beef. Our bull sale on October 4, 1997, was dedicated to Uncle Palo.

From Texas to Colorado

"Young man, you just bought yourself a ranch."
—Mr. Dent

We were a four-generation Texas family, dating from before the Civil War. Dad, at thirty-six years of age, had no intention of leaving Texas when his friend Charlie Dick from Laredo called from the Broadmoor Tavern to tell him there was a good ranch for sale at Matheson, Colorado, 55 miles east of Colorado Springs. Dad was working cattle when the call came into his office in Falfurrias (toll station call: Lasater Ranch, USA). He caught the train at Rivera and got to Colorado Springs several days after everyone had sobered up and gone home. Dad decided to go look at the ranch and stayed at the Simla Hotel, sleeping fully clothed including hat, overcoat and boots to keep from freezing in Colorado's winter. As Dad did research on the ranch's potential, a friend in the Soil Conservation Service told him that the Ogallala aquifer surfaced under the ranch and that pockets of windmill water could be found. Dad's father had been able to buy cheap land and use windmills to water it for cattle in South Texas—a process Dad repeated 50 years later in Eastern Colorado.

"Can you believe that little S.O.B. had that much money?"
—John M. Bennett, Jr.

After Mother and Dad decided to buy the ranch, the negotiations took place in the office of Dad's lawyer and lifetime friend in Colorado Springs, Don Haney. As was customary, Dad had on a suit and tie. Mr. Dent and his lawyer sat across the table. Dad said, "Mr. Dent, I can't pay your price, but am prepared to offer...." Mr. Dent reached across the table to shake hands, and said, "Young man, you just bought yourself a ranch."

In 1948, Dad paid cash for the first 10,000 acres, having sold part of his foundation herd of the Beefmaster breed to his uncle, L.D. Miller (after whom I was named). Dad's friend John Bennett, Jr., framed that check when it came back to the National Bank of Commerce in San Antonio, and showed it to all their mutual friends, saying, "Can you believe that little S.O.B. had that much money?"

Mother and Dad accumulated 28,000 acres in Elbert County, Colorado, which is now the home of the Foundation Herd of the Beefmaster Breed, recognized by the U.S.D.A. in 1954. John Cargile, of San Angelo, told me at the end of Dad's career, that that ranch was closer in environmental purity

to the 1492 standard than any other ranch in the country. My brother Dale and his wife Janine have ably managed the ranch for the family since Dad's retirement. Mother and Dad's success is certainly one of the outstanding ranching business stories of the 20th century. Both of their families had been devastated by the Depression, yet they

Photo by Sally Lasater
Classic winter scene on the Lasater Ranch, looking northwest toward Indian Hill.

raised and educated six children and left the ranch and cattle debt-free.

The ranch at Matheson lies along U.S. Highway 24, fifty-five miles east of Colorado Springs. The defining feature of it is fourteen miles of the Big Sandy Creek that runs through it, providing a sub-irrigated valley and winter protection for the cattle. When Mother and Dad bought the ranch in the midst of the '50s drought, it seemed forlorn, with bare adobe flats and very little grass. But nearly 60 years of dedicated management by Dad and Dale has re-created a paradise of beautiful grasses in the open, rolling high plains.

When Grandfather Edward died in 1930, there was debt against his property and most was lost, except for what was saved with the help of Uncle Laurie Miller and Mr. John M. Bennett, Sr., of San Antonio. Dad withdrew from Princeton in the middle of his sophomore year in 1931, to come home to help, and essentially went to work as foreman at $80 per month on what had been his father's headquarters ranch. Among the assets salvaged were the remnants of Grandfather Edward's upgraded Brahman herd and the remains of his 20,000 purebred Hereford cows. Dad's mother and uncle sold him these cattle on credit. In an interview taped in the 1980s, Dad's friend, John Armstrong of the King Ranch, said that Dad had "paid out" 2,000 cattle by the time he married Mary Casey on December 7, 1940.

The Long Move North

The Tom Lasater family made its first trip to Colorado in the spring of 1949. It was a 1,000-mile trip on two-lane roads in our new Desoto Suburban, with no air conditioning. Besides Mother and Dad, there were four children (Dale, 4; Lane, 1; Sally, a baby; and I, 6) plus a maid and a dog. The two-day trip was broken at Dumas. On all of our trips to Colorado, we stopped at Dumas, and invariably someone was sick.

We arrived at Matheson about May 1, and to our amazement and delight, it snowed the first night we were there. We lived in a modest frame house with only two bedrooms, one bath, kitchen, living room, attic and basement, and Mother cooked on a wood stove. The drought was just getting to Colorado, and the grassless pastures were blowing dust so hard that visibility was minimal. It was a grim beginning.

I remember well the arrival of the first cattle from Texas. Kauffer and Blue Truck Line of Hebbronville, Texas, contracted to haul the herd on 36-foot trailers. They had to search far to find that many trailers, and must have used 30–40 trucks. When the trucks arrived at Matheson in a snowstorm, the Mexican drivers wore only tee-shirts and nearly froze to death.

Our horses, including the "kid" horses, *Flecha* and *Cubana,* also came on the trucks, along with our King Ranch saddles purchased in 1931 for $30. The horses and cattle prospered at the 6,000-foot altitude. Both the older cows and older horses caught their second youth and began growing again. The move was a success. Mother and Dad made up their minds to be successful and never looked back. They were both progressive-minded and politically liberal, and I feel that they subconsciously were seeking new horizons for their cattle as well as for themselves.

I loved Texas and can remember working cattle with Dad in South Texas. I still can smell the horse sweat in the saddle-room on the

Seeligson lease at Premont. I remember the men having Bim, the first great Beefmaster bull, in the chute and the Charbray herd in the house trap prior to shipment to Charlie Dick about 1945. I did not want to leave Texas and never did take root in Colorado.

Looking at the larger picture, I believe that it is not a coincidence that I returned to Texas to pick up the tradition started by Grandfather Edward. I have followed his trail, made a lot of the same mistakes, enjoyed similar successes and feel a strong kinship with him. It is my belief that in every family, half of what is taught is the wisdom of the ages and half is baloney. Maturity comes when we discard the latter.

School Days at Matheson, Colorado

In 1948 we spent the summer in Colorado, and returned in 1949 to live and to start school that fall. We attended the proverbial country school

Dixie, Ruth and Annette Nixon in 1957.

with eight grades in three rooms. I was in third grade and Dale was in first. The school was a Spartan affair. The three teachers, Mrs. McLennan, Mrs. Cain and Mrs. Nixon, ran everything with an iron hand, including discipline, doctoring the wounded and making minor repairs. There were no "aids to education," assistant principals or elaborate playground equipment. We had blackboards, worn textbooks and strict discipline. While one grade had its lesson, the other two studied in silence. To the limit of his abilities, each student learned the lesson every day. If those three ladies were put in charge of elementary education today in the U.S., our education system would be better off.

The school bus, which pulled into the ranch headquarters a quarter mile off Highway 24, picked us up each morning. We waited by the loading chute, having already broken ice for the horses and having fed whatever calves we had on feed.

Our family and the Nixon family became friends immediately. Ruth Nixon, my future mother-in-law, was a pillar of the community, loved and admired by all. Edgar operated a service station and convenience store in town. They had two daughters, Dixie, the older, and Annette, my future wife—two gorgeous girls. Seeing them was a big event in our social life. We learned to drive early, and as the ranch surrounded Matheson on three sides, we children could drive ourselves to the edge of town to go to Sunday school, get the mail, and visit the Nixons or other friends. Our Drivers' Ed vehicle of choice was a 1949 four-wheel-drive Jeep truck.

Before starting the sturdy vehicle, we were taught to check all four tires with a gauge and to check the oil, water and battery. My children now laugh at the fact that I always give an automobile a "walk-around" check, but they did not grow up on the Lasater Ranch. Like all ranchers, Dad was touchy about having his roads torn up. The road to town was a two-lane ranch road, and one day after a rain, he gave me detailed instructions about not driving through the puddles on the way to get the mail. After coming off a little mesa near our house, there was a long, straight stretch of road that had lots of puddles. At each, I stopped, wrapped up the engine, popped the clutch and hit the puddle with tires screaming and blue smoke pouring out of the exhaust. After about three of these puddles, I looked over and saw Dad about a quarter-mile away sitting on his horse on a hill watching the operation. I thought I was in terrible trouble, but the incident was never mentioned. I got the message without a word being spoken.

The Foremen

"Just do whatever Eddie, George or Richard would do."

—Tom Lasater

The foremen who worked on the ranch were nearly as important to us as our aunts and uncles. There was great *esprit de corps* on the ranch due to Mother and Dad's dynamism and the fact that we were all part of a world-changing project. The foremen respected the fact that everyone, including Mother and the children, worked hard and that the children received no favoritism. The men understood that we children lived in a harsh regime, and they did everything they could to ease the passage. We felt great affection for them, a sentiment which was reciprocated.

The first foreman whom I knew well was Norman Brooks, who came to work in 1946, just out of the Marine Corps. Starting in Falfurrias, Norman and his wife, Rena, also made the move to Colorado. Dad and he, both being hard-hitting and energetic people, made a great team. They had figured out how to gentle the cattle with sack corn and to train them to come to a siren, which revolutionized working cattle in the South Texas brush.

Walter Carter and his wife, Virginia, were next. Walter was a Texas A&M graduate, and Dad interviewed them together. At the end of the interview, Dad asked Virginia if she thought her husband could handle the job. She replied, "You just try him!" Walter ended his career as manager of

Photo by Time
Riding with George Evanoika, Eddie Stanko and Dale in the summer of 1955.

the Broseco Ranch in East Texas, a large, famous ranch. While there, he established an outstanding Beefmaster Cross cow herd and instituted a rotational grazing program. He bought bulls from me in San Angelo, which was quite an honor. In 1986, I attended their annual ranch picnic near Omaha, Texas, and had a good visit with Walter and Virginia. As we reminisced, she told me that the Lasater Ranch job was the best they had ever had, but that they had to leave to get a rest.

Eddie Stanko was the main man in helping Mother and Dad develop the ranch in Colorado. As Dad said, "Eddie came to work for six weeks and stayed 28 years." All the children, in succession, worked both on horseback and on foot with him—punching cattle and building fences, pens, and other repairs and maintenance. Eddie was an institution on the ranch, and, along with Mother and Dad, has a memorial plaque on the south face of Flatrock Hill, overlooking the ranch.

Two other men who worked with Eddie were also part of the family. Richard Pazzin and George Evanoika were family favorites. Richard always described himself as "too light for heavy work and too heavy for light work."

Eddie, Jr., George and Richard all attended Dad's funeral in 2001. Afterwards, George told me a great story about Dad. Our family used to camp on the Hammond Ranch, private property on Beaver Creek, in the mountains west of Colorado Springs. One day, Dad asked George to go with him to help make some repairs to our cabin there. On the way through Colorado Springs, they bought a bottle of wine, and when they arrived at La Escondida (The Hideaway), they sat under a tree, visited and drank the wine with no work being accomplished that day. George told me that was how he would remember Dad. When I went East to school, Dad told me that if I were ever in a jam, "Just do whatever Eddie, George or Richard would do and you'll be all right."

In 1956, the U.S. cattle industry was the cover story in an issue of *Time* magazine, which my parents used as their source of information before television, just as Annette and I did while living in Mexico. *Time* sent a photographer from Brooklyn to get pictures for the part of the article on Dad, ("Woe to the Cow that Slips"). This great photograph, taken with a telephoto lens, tells the story of the ranching industry. I was 13 years old and Dale was 11, but we were not boys; we were little men.

The Lasater Philosophy

In a feature business story in its May 7, 1956, edition titled "The Golden Calf," *Time* discusses the improvement in beef quality and quantity due to scientific cattle breeding. The two cattlemen pictured are Bob Kleberg of the King Ranch and Tom Lasater, founder of the Beefmaster Breed. The caption under Dad's picture says, "Woe to the cow that slips," referring to his revolutionary policy of requiring a merchantable calf every year from every female over 24 months of age.

The Lasater Philosophy of Cattle Raising (the title of my book published in 1972) has been the most influential beef production system worldwide since 1960. Dad's concept is based on using natural selection in a large population of cattle for the "Six Essential Characteristics" of beef cattle breeding, which constitute his "Standard of Excellence."

The Six Essentials are Disposition—meaning intelligence and ease of handling; Fertility—meaning reproducing every year without extra assistance or individual attention; Weight—meaning weight per day of age, the ultimate measure of efficiency: Conformation—meaning functionality and red meat production as exemplified by muscling; Hardiness—meaning the ability to thrive under harsh conditions with little assistance; and Milk Production—meaning mothering ability. Any animal lacking any one of these traits cannot be profitable and should be culled, leading to the public view of Dad's program as "ruthless." The use of this program in any herd anywhere will result in the complete elimination of low-profitability cattle.

Visitors and Cattle Buyers

One unique aspect of our childhood was a steady flow of visitors to the ranch from all over the world. Mother and Dad were the first of a large number of Texans to buy ranches in Eastern Colorado. Dad's ideas about raising cattle and working with nature fed his growing worldwide fame as a cattleman. In addition, rather than building a home, Mother and Dad remodeled the ranch barn as a home with the help of architect Carlisle B. Guy. The Texas heritage, the house, the cattle, the six children and Dad's ideas were all topics of interest that led to a number of articles in the Denver and Colorado Springs newspapers. As a culmination of all this interest, the U.S.D.A. recognized the Beefmaster breed in 1954.

Dad was a dynamic teacher, Mother was a great hostess, and all the children played a role in the ongoing public relations campaign. When I was about twelve, I drove visitors on ranch tours. At that time Dad had created a system of number-branding the herd with a code that visitors could not read. One day while I was driving a husband and wife on a tour, I was reading the brands, telling them how many calves each cow had had and which was her calf that year. The husband was bragging on me until the wife finally got mad and said, "Jimmy (their son) can do that." The husband replied, "No he can't."

By the mid-to-late fifties, all the Texas-born siblings could drive, and we looked forward to deliveries when many customers came to pick their bulls. We drew straws to see who got to tour our favorites. Some of them were Weber and Brauchle, Humberto Garza and the Musser Brothers. The Brauchle family, who visited us in Múzquiz, and Garza family are still in the Beefmaster business after more than 50 years.

From the Bernice Musser Collection

Tom, Pat, Bernice and Jack Musser at the Lasater Ranch, circa 1971.

Our many foreign visitors marked the beginning of my focus on international business. Over the years, more than 1,000 Australians have signed the guest book at the Lasater Ranch. Also on the list are many famous animal scientists, including Dr. Jan Bonsma of South Africa, who, along with Dad, revolutionized cattle breeding in the 20th century. I was home from college when Sally Forbes of Wyoming came to the ranch to ask Dad's advice on establishing the Red Angus Registry. I heard him tell her to base the registry on individual animal performance, which they did, and that breed is now the fastest-growing registry in the U.S.

Dr. Dick Clark, a scientist in charge of the U.S.D.A. Miles City Experiment Station where the Line I Herefords were developed, was a regular visitor. He was instrumental in getting the Beefmasters recognized as a breed. I remember Dad and Dr. Clark discussing the relative merits of Limousin and Simmental cattle in the fifties, before any had been brought to North America.

In addition to an extensive array of outstanding animal scientists and cattle people as visitors, we hosted lawyers, writers, artists, architects and celebrities. Although we lived on an isolated ranch with no television and limited phone service, we grew up in the mainstream of the discussions of events and ideas.

As I mentioned, the cocktail hour was sacrosanct at our home. No one (except Mother) was asked to do any work at that time. She would come home from working horseback, put on a long dress, fix Margaritas and cook steaks or Mexican food for the assembled multitude. Dad was a great raconteur. Many times, as he explained something about ranching to an interested guest, I could almost see the light coming on in the visitor's face. Sometimes, when Dad told a joke, he would end up laughing so hard that someone else would have to finish it for him.

Joseph T. Dawson and his wife, Melba, were favorites of everyone. Joe was a flamboyant Texas wildcatter, and Melba, like Annette, was a smart,

Joe and Melba Dawson.

beautiful woman who could make him behave. Joe and I were friends immediately, and although we never were in business together, we always talked business. He had had experience in Mexico before World War II, and when I told him I was going to Mexico, he said, "You're going to learn to suffer, Boy." At the same time, Dad said, "I cannot imagine a man of your personality going to Mexico." They both knew that the patience needed would "try my soul," and they were right.

Melba Dawson was a close friend of my cousin, Peggy Lasater Clark of Corpus Christi. Peggy told me that Joe and Melba, who had two daughters, Diane and Roslyn, considered me the son they never had. Annette and I had a close friendship with them until their deaths. Joe was a war hero, the first man off Omaha Beach on D-Day (leading the Allied breakout). He introduced the President of the United States at the 50th Anniversary celebration at Normandy on June 6, 1994. In September 1997, an elementary school in Corpus Christi was named for him. I had the privilege of attending the dedication of the Joseph T. Dawson Elementary School and enjoyed my last visit with both of them.

Capitalists in the Making

"FCO—Family Cow Outfit"
—Mary Casey Lasater

Everybody on the Lasater Ranch worked hard nearly every day. We were paid a daily salary when working. In addition, a schedule of jobs and wages was posted on the laundry room door: wash cars, wash windows, haul trash, trim horses' hooves, oil saddles, and so on. We also had projects feeding calves for ranch consumption. Dad furnished the calves and feed. We mixed the feed by hand, fed the calves twice daily and, if necessary, broke the ice. We earned good money, and each of us financed our social lives as well as hunting and fishing equipment, athletic equipment, gifts and many other items. Each year, with money in hand, we awaited the new Montgomery Ward catalog with keen anticipation.

An independent bus service ran twice a day from Limon to Colorado Springs. We had a box by the highway where the bus could pick up and drop off items from the city. The bus would also stop if one of us was waiting. Frequently, I would go to Colorado Springs on the early bus, go shopping, deposit money at Columbia Savings, visit a friend or go to the movies and come home on the late bus. My friends in Colorado Springs were in awe of the amounts of money we earned.

Like most ranch families, our lives centered on the work. Dad was a lifelong cowboy and Mother was a fine athlete (swimming and tennis) and horsewoman. She rode a Porter saddle, made by the famed Porter Saddlemakers of Phoenix, which she received from Uncle Watt as a wedding present in 1940. While I was home, the "FCO" (Family Cow Outfit), as Mother called it, consisted of our parents and the four oldest children. Due to the length of the ranch and the fact that we lived near the west end, we did a lot of riding. There was no trailer on the ranch (probably by design), so we rode everywhere and handled all cattle movements on horseback. We kept a night-horse in the corrals, and one of the older siblings wrangled the horses at 6:00 a.m. While Mother cooked breakfast, the older brothers helped Dad get the six horses saddled. Everyone carried a slicker and canteen. Except for hail or lightning, weather was not taken into consideration, and Dad did not tolerate complaints about being cold, hot, wet, thirsty or tired, which took some doing given the age spread of the crew. At that altitude, horses are powerful and we could ride at a slow lope (collected gallop) for long distances. On a really big day, we each would lead a fresh horse to ride home. We rode cavalry style, by twos, and no one was to cross in front of another or crowd them from behind. As we approached a gate, one of the older brothers or one of the two cowboys would

Mother on Ginger.

break ranks and gallop ahead to open it. We did a lot of sorting and cutting out pairs, such as cows with calves, on horseback in the pasture. Dad and the foreman would bring the cuts out while the rest of us held the herd or rode in to help separate the cattle being taken out. We kept the head count, loudly calling the count for each pair.

Everyone in the FCO was taught the classic maneuvers for handling cattle on horseback and on foot. Visitors were at a loss as to what to do. The cattle business was serious business in our home. All of the family was involved in the business and we all carried notebooks and pens to write down instructions, pasture counts, hay bale counts, etc. We had a man from Nebraska who worked a short time, but Dad had to fire him because he talked too much and told too many jokes. We were part of a very successful enterprise, we learned a lot and made money, but we did not do it for fun. Dad once told me, not joking, that we should pay him rather than the reverse, and when I was about thirteen, he and I had a pivotal conversation. At that time he had three men working on the ranch. That day, he told me I could count on the third job if I needed it, but that he did not want any advice or suggestions from me. Some, on hearing this story, think it was harsh. In my mind it was clear communication between two strong personalities. Dad knew I could not work for him, and I did not plan to do so. I left home, went on my own and became his biggest customer. Growing up on the Lasater Ranch was an unforgettable experience that one would not want to repeat or extend. In retrospect, I am thankful for the training I received. After leaving home, I was never anywhere that the standards were as high or the demands as great as on the Lasater Ranch, including Princeton and the U.S. Army. Dad, one of the most famous cattlemen worldwide in the twentieth century, did not exempt himself from the severe standards. I remember distinctly when the first cows were pregnancy-tested in 1945. In 1948, Dad began requiring that all females calve every 365 days, starting at twenty-four months, which is the crux of the program. The adoption of this policy coincided with the onset of the drought of the fifties. By 1954, Dad's cow numbers were way down. One day, Dale and I were helping him, and we had cut out a group of drys and late-calvers in the corner of a pasture. Dad agonized for several minutes over whether or not to turn them back with the herd. Finally he said, "Open the gate." Nobody but Dad would have stayed with such a rigorous program. Thirty years later, Bud Adams of Florida, founder of the Braford breed, told me, "Your dad showed us what a cow is all about."

The Final Phase

Although Dad attended Princeton for a year and a half, the highlight of his educational career was attending Phillips Academy at Andover, Massachusetts, from which he graduated in 1929. Andover, with Exeter and Lawrenceville, were considered the Big Three prep schools just as Princeton, Yale and Harvard were the top colleges.

In 1954 Mother and Dad took me to New York City and to Andover for Dad's 25th reunion, which was one of the greatest experiences of my life. At that time, the Rock Island Rocket ran from Colorado Springs to Chicago, where it connected with the Twentieth Century Limited, the crack train to New York City. Since the ranch ran ten or more miles along the railroad track, the conductor stopped the Rocket at the ranch gate so that we could board. The train trip to Chicago and New York was very exciting, with dinners on white tablecloths and two nights in a sleeper car. Twenty years later, Annette and I rode this same train, which had been sold to Ferrocariles Nacionales, from Saltillo to Mexico City, and as we boarded, I recognized the car named "Spirit of St. Louis" after Lindberg's plane.

After arriving in New York, Mother, Dad and I saw various people, including our second cousins Tom and Dot Brittingham (Mother's family) and my first cousins, Edward and Garland Lasater. Edward and Garland took me out, with their dates, to Eddie Condon's nightclub, which I am sure was a drag for them. But being gracious people and wonderful cousins, they made no complaint. They also took me to Coney Island, where we rode the famous roller coaster, initiating my lifelong love of roller coasters.

We had dinner with Tom and Dot at Luchows, an elegant, renowned restaurant, and the subject of discussion was whether or not scientist J. Robert Oppenheimer was being railroaded by McCarthyites. When our daughter, Isabel, went to Vanderbilt University in Nashville in the 1990s, Annette and I frequently visited Dot (then widowed and living in Nashville) and became close friends.

Knowing how I loved baseball, Dad took me via subway to a Yankees game in the Bronx where we saw Mickey Mantle hit a home run batting left-handed against Detroit. When Mantle died, the national media all ran pictures of him batting left-handed in pinstripes in a home game, just as I had seen him.

After seeing Andover, I counted the minutes until I could leave for prep school. Sometime later that year, Mother and Dad took me to Colorado Springs to Fountain Valley School for a tour and interview with the headmaster, Henry B. Poor. Dad, Mother and I liked Mr. Poor and the school, and I decided to attend FVS. I was accepted to begin ninth grade in September 1955. That summer FVS assigned books to read, book reports to write and also sent a list of clothing requirements. We were to wear dark suits, white shirts, conservative ties, black socks and black shoes to dinner. On Friday nights, sport coats were allowed. The dark suit/blazer formula, followed by all private school graduates for over one hundred years, has served me well.

During the summer, Mother drove me into Denver where we bought the whole wardrobe, including the footlocker we were required to take. Although I had no idea what was ahead, Mother did, and she knew I was going to thrive in my new environment. She also knew that although Dad and I were alike, we were also very different, and that I was leaving for good. She blessed my uniqueness and encouraged me to follow my star. I will always treasure the memory of that day with my mother.

Later, Dad took me to the Exchange National Bank in Colorado Springs and opened a school checking account for my education. When we went down to the vault and cashed U.S. Savings Bonds, bought when I was born, I realized for the first time how much effort Dad had put into being a father and how much he cared for his family. Now that he is gone, I realize how fortunate I am to have had such an experience with him.

Fountain Valley School in Colorado Springs.

CHAPTER 3

FOUNTAIN VALLEY AND LAWRENCEVILLE

On a perfect fall day in 1955, at age thirteen, I enrolled at Fountain Valley School. It was, without question, the greatest day of my life. Mother and Dad drove me into Colorado Springs, and after lunch at the Village Inn we saw *To Catch a Thief* with Cary Grant. About 4:00 p.m., we drove the ten miles to Fountain Valley, a beautiful school with southwestern architecture, set just east of the Front Range of the Rockies.

We checked in at the Hacienda, the school's main dining/gathering place and visited with the headmaster, Henry Poor. After we unloaded my footlocker, Mother and Dad said their goodbyes, and I started my life as an independent agent. I walked outside where I met Larry Matthews from Red Bank, New Jersey, who became my lifelong friend. As we visited, I learned that he had come to FVS a day early on the Rock Island Rocket, and had seen us working cattle as the train came by our ranch.

The next couple of days are a blur, but toward the weekend I was sick, which I later learned was diagnosed as homesickness. By Sunday, I was the only boy in the infirmary and missed the traditional school trip up Pikes Peak. All alone on the campus, being ministered to by Miss Jenkins, I was certain my career was finished. Around noon, Mr. Littell, a math teacher, dropped by to invite me to his home for lunch with his wife and him. The Littells were caring people, and as they assured me that all was not lost, I began to recover.

Academics

Monday we started classes. I had five hard courses with top teachers. Many of the boys, including Larry Matthews, who had attended private day schools, breezed through the classes. Dad's earlier warnings not to come home if I flunked out took on a new reality for me. My most intimidating course was Latin, taught by Mr. Dwight Perry, an old-time schoolmaster and a true scholar who loved to teach. In the beginning, the whole idea of Latin was pretty scary for a ranch boy from Matheson, Colorado. In the end, I loved it, and Mr. Perry seemed pleased to have me as a student.

The dreaded first marking period finally came to an end. A tradition at FVS was that the student body would meet in the Hacienda each night after supper for announcements. That night, Mr. Poor read the honor roll, the merit roll and the top ten students, and much to my surprise, I was number ten academically in the school.

Sports

Monday afternoon was our first "pup" football practice. Our coaches were Jim Hutchinson, our English teacher, and Ralph Quintana, our Spanish teacher. Both were young bachelors and Navy veterans who lived with us in First House. As nearly as I could tell, their mission was to kill us. We suffered greatly on those beautiful Kentucky Bluegrass playing fields. With many talented players, our "pup" football team was undefeated league champion and we were heroes of the school. Everyone came to see us play. We ran a wing "T." I played left end on offense and defense. We had a very successful reverse play in which everyone went right and I went straight down the field. In one home game, we ran the play perfectly, and Larry Matthews threw a beautiful spiral pass to me for a touchdown. In the winter of my freshman year, I took up wrestling, a sport that puts a premium on toughness, which I admire. That spring, I played left field on the "pup" baseball team that was also league champion, with the same talented athletes we had in the fall.

When our class had its twenty-fifth reunion in 1984, Hutchinson and Quintana came back to see us. As I wrote in the Alumni Bulletin regarding housemasters, "They lived with us, they taught us, and they coached us. They loved us and we loved them." There were many wonderful teachers, including these two, who happened to be closely involved in some of my happiest memories. I look forward to being reunited with all my fine teachers, from first grade on, who cared so much about their students.

Social Life

Life in an all-male private school was very Spartan, but lots of fun. Although smoking was prohibited for freshmen and sophomores, I believe that 25 in our class of 29 smoked. The smokers lived in fear of expulsion, and the faculty tried very hard not to catch anyone in order not to have to report them. It was always a sad night when the headmaster announced that "so and so" had gone home and would not be back.

We had town-permission on Tuesday afternoons. One of our favorite hangouts was the M&M Cigar Store in downtown Colorado Springs, which had pinball machines and girlie magazines in the back. One Tuesday, a group of us were hanging out at M&M, smoking up a storm, when Professor Dwight Perry passed by on the sidewalk. He was holding up his overcoat collar, covering the left side of his face so that he could not see us, but letting us know that he knew we were there.

It is easy to describe the love life of a freshman at Fountain Valley in 1959; there wasn't one! We did not leave campus often and were not permitted to attend the one dance a term, except as waiters. The highlight of my social life that year was going home for the one or two weekends off each term, always accompanied by five or six friends. My parents were great hosts, and we had lots of fun on the ranch. Sometimes we invited girls from Matheson and Simla to the house for a party. One weekend, when Mother came to get us, she encountered some forlorn waif in the hallway and informed the housemaster on duty that she was taking him also.

Sophomore year things improved socially. I had a romance with my then-roommate's sister, Jill Matthews, a beautiful girl. Jill attended Castle Rock High School near Denver, Colorado, and that year Fountain Valley wrestled at Castle Rock High. I was on the FVS wrestling team and pinned my man that evening in the leadoff match. My friend Steve Cochran followed with another pin on his man. In addition to Jill, my parents and her parents were there, so that was an exciting event and a high point in my athletic career.

• • •

Junior year we took the College Board exams for practice, and my scores were only fair. Soon after, Dad ran into Ralph Quintana in the Antlers Bar in Colorado Springs and was bemoaning my being such a failure. Mr. Quintana read Dad the riot act to such an extent that he came home and apologized to me for having said anything negative.

In the spring of 1958, my junior year, Henry Poor was fired as headmaster in a typical small-school shakeup. My parents were concerned that the upheaval would affect my college admission, so arrangements were made for me to transfer to Lawrenceville School at Lawrenceville, New Jersey. The headmaster was Allan V. Heely, one of Dad's teachers at Andover, and he accepted me on Mr. Poor's recommendation. It was difficult to leave Fountain Valley after three wonderful years, and I will always wonder how things would have turned out had I finished there.

My First Travels

While at Fountain Valley, I began my career as a trans-continental bus traveler. The summer after my sophomore year, I traveled from Colorado Spring to Santa Fe to visit my FVS classmate, Jay Simms, son of the governor of New Mexico. As I recall, the round-trip ticket cost me fifteen dollars. My visit occurred during Santa Fe's Fiesta. Just to add to the excitement, Jay was involved in some type of war with a gang called the *Pachucos*. We would go downtown and throw rocks at the *Chukes*, who would chase us back to the front gate of the governor's mansion.

The summer after my junior year, I rode the bus from Colorado Springs to Los Angeles, going out by the northern route through Nevada and coming back the southern route through Needles and Albuquerque. This was my first in-depth look at the Western U.S. I went to visit another FVS friend, Grant B. Schley, whose family had a ranch in the Santa Ynez Valley (where President Reagan's ranch is located). Even in 1957, the valley was a high-dollar neighborhood. Grant was older and more sophisticated than I, and drove a convertible. We had a rollicking good time swimming in their pool, hunting doves, riding in his flashy car, and chasing girls.

Lawrenceville

In the fall of 1958, I left Limon, Colorado, by bus, headed for Ohio and New Jersey. From Limon to the Port Authority Terminal in New York City, the trip was 48–56 hours depending on connections. As each of us went East to school, Dad proposed to buy us plane tickets, but added that if we wanted to ride the bus, we could keep the difference in cash, a substantial amount. To get the cash, my brothers and I made many long bus trips.

My first stop was Dennison University in Ohio, where I interviewed and stayed with my cousin, Ardon Judd, in his fraternity house. I had a good time and decided Dennison would be great. There is nothing like older cousins! From there, I traveled to New York City, where I met former FVS headmaster Henry Poor and his wife, Tink, who took me to Amherst for an interview, and then to Lawrenceville School for my senior year.

Lawrenceville Friends and Classmates

At Lawrenceville, I lived at Belknap House, where my cousin, Ed Lasater, had lived four years earlier with the same housemaster, Mr. Ed Herrick. When Mr. Herrick met me, he said, "I've seen that face before." "Big Ed" had broken ground for me, and the housemaster knew he was in for another exciting year.

Belknap was an off-campus house with sixteen residents. We developed great *esprit de corps* from the first day taking on all comers in touch football. The common room, where we could smoke, joined my room and was our gathering place. The first week, Steve Turner from Evanston, Illinois, instituted the practice of buying a carton of community cigarettes (Marlboros) for all to enjoy. We had great fun telling jokes and generally tormenting Mr. Herrick.

My roommate and good friend, Henley Webb, from Montclair, N.J., was taking a postgraduate year to get into Yale. He was a little older than most of us and more serious, which was fortunate for me. I also became friends with Ralph Warner of Larchmont, New York. We roomed together for two years at Princeton and spent a lot of time together, both at his home and at mine in Colorado.

Social Life

"Under the clock at The Biltmore."
—F. Scott Fitzgerald

On the social front, things brightened in a hurry. Early that fall someone lined up five blind dates for a mixer. We drew straws for our dates and I was lucky to draw the blonde. When I met Jean Allen at the train station in Trenton, I saw that she was a pretty girl; we liked each other and dated for a period of time. Later, she dated Ralph, and they married our senior year at Princeton.

My social life consisted of going home with Ralph. Sometimes we would go out in New York City, where I became familiar with many famous nightspots such as the Village Gate, Upstairs-Downstairs, the Starlight Room and The Café Pierre, among many others. The meeting place in New York (per Scott Fitzgerald) was "under the clock at The Biltmore." Sometimes we would go to roadhouses in the Hudson Valley where there was live music. Of all the places I have been, those roadhouses were my favorites—loud rock and roll music and cheap whiskey all night long. Everywhere I have been in my life, I have enjoyed tremendous hospitality, and nowhere more so than during my five years on the East Coast.

Academics

"Oh that Lasater, he's not too smart but he's
got peasant cunning."

—*Norval F. Bacon*

The five courses I took were appropriately challenging, except trigonometry, where I met my academic waterloo. It was taught by Mr. Wallace, a Princetonian (nicknamed Pontiac Bob). Although I could not do one problem after the first week, he gave me a 60 the first marking period. I sat in the back with a fellow classmate named Barbour. After each demonstration at the board, Mr. Wallace would turn and say, through clenched teeth, "Is everybody on the bench? Barbour? Lasater?" Oh, how we dreaded that moment.

After that first marking period, in which I had all honors grades except in Trig, Mr. Wallace called me into his office and said, "Mr. Lasater, you are a nice young man, and we have to get you out of this class so that you can go to college." He arranged for me to repeat Algebra I. Later, I saw him occasionally on Princeton University campus. I think he liked having saved my academic life.

The highlight of my academic year was American history, taught by Professor Norval Bacon, who had been a year ahead of Dad at Andover. None of us in that class had taken American history, so we had to do two years' work in one. Mr. Bacon was a Harvard man and a Northeasterner with black hair slicked back, horn-rimmed glasses, herringbone jacket and a rope for a belt. One day he was trying to get our class to come out with some concept, and I got lucky with the right answer. He rocked back on his heels with a huge grin, hooked his thumbs in his belt, and said, "Oh, that Lasater, he's not too smart, but he's got peasant cunning." The second marking period, without trigonometry, I made *Cum Laude* and found my bearings academically. Several years ago, I wrote Mr. Bacon on his retirement and received a wonderful letter saying that our class was the best he ever had. In his reply, he remembered and listed each student by name with his grade. He wrote that I had been second behind Bill Marsden, an English exchange student taking a postgraduate year.

• • •

> "Withdraw all applications. You're going to Princeton."
>
> —Dean Rufus Hyatt

The Lawrenceville director of college admissions, Rufus Hyatt, and his wife held a salon several evenings a week so seniors could drop by for coffee and cookies to visit and to discuss their college plans. Ralph Warner and I went regularly and became great friends with the Hyatts. I remember one evening, holding my coffee and cookie, trying to explain delicately to Mrs. Hyatt the procedure for pregnancy-testing a cow. Although I knew Mr. Hyatt personally, he told me in my official college interview with him that I was probably not socially or academically suited for Princeton, and to plan on Dennison.

In the fall of 1959, I interviewed with Dean Edwards, director of admissions at Princeton, and uncle of my future Princeton classmate and friend, Selden Edwards. I had the interview of a lifetime, helped by the fact that cousins Garland and Edward Lasater rowed on the crew at Princeton and Ed was captain. After the interview, Dean Edwards told Dean Hyatt that I could go back to Princeton with him that afternoon or enroll the next fall. Mr. Hyatt called me into his office and told me, "Withdraw all applications, you have been given early admission to Princeton." After just twelve weeks in New Jersey, my prep school career was finished. Throughout my life, things have often come together very quickly, and I am thankful for that. I was not at Lawrenceville very long, but I made many friends there. Thirty of us went to Princeton, including my freshman-year roommate, Dick Banyard, the son of the Episcopal Bishop of New Jersey.

One winter night, the uproar from our Belknap common room became too much for Mr. Herrick to bear. He came in, red-faced and shaking his finger at me, "You common-room cowboy, you're in college and the rest of these boys aren't going to get to go." Happily, everyone did get into college, and we gave Mr. Herrick a television set as a going away present in gratitude for a fun year.

Sports

Wrestling is a big sport at Lawrenceville, and the first match of the winter season was with the Princeton freshmen at Princeton, a big step for a boy just off the bus from Colorado. I was in the 130-pound class with two highly-regarded veterans. We had to "wrestle off" every week. By some fluke I won the starting slot for the first match. The starting lineup was printed at the top of the front page of the Lawrenceville paper, and served as my debut in the school.

Highlights

Another highlight that year occurred when Fidel Castro, accompanied by Che Guevara, came to the school to speak to the student body. Our anticipation was rewarded when the whole entourage marched in and took over the chapel, wearing their fatigues and boots and carrying pistols. Fidel's soldiers sat among the students, and without a microphone, he spoke to us in broken, but very powerful, English. Everyone there was ready to go to Cuba. In retrospect, it seems unfortunate that our government refused to cooperate with him. It might have saved our country a lot of headaches and expenses over 46 years.

CHAPTER 4

PRINCETON

"Is there a Lasater here?"

—*Head Proctor*

After four years of prep school, it was a thrill to go to Princeton, where we had tremendous freedom and were on our own to set academic, social and athletic priorities. I was seventeen when school started in the fall of 1959. The fact that thirty of us came from Lawrenceville, combined with being accustomed to rigorous academics, made the shock of entry less for us than for the half of our class who were public school graduates.

Dick Barnyard and I roomed in Pyne Hall. We had a little room with bunk beds, two desks, two dressers and a refrigerator. There were no easy chairs and the bathroom was down the hall. The first Saturday night in our dorm, things got rowdy, and there was some damage to university property. The proctors (campus police) came, and seventeen of us were summoned on Monday to Head Proctor Mike Kopliner's office, a tiny basement room. With all of us standing crammed in front of his desk, he asked, "Is there a Lasater here?" I glumly raised my hand. "Your cousin Garland was in here this morning and said to go easy on you fellows." Evidently there also had been a party in Garland's dorm, 1879 Hall, on Saturday night. Mr. Kopliner said, "You guys get out of here, and I do not want to see you again."

Freshman year is a blur of getting oriented, meeting people, and getting into the swing of things. Around the middle of the year, I met Bill Jarman, who became a lifelong friend. I was impressed that he could set me up with a charge account at Cousins Liquor Store, which had a delivery service to our rooms.

Academics

The academic life at Princeton was very rich, and that richness was magnified by the brilliance of the faculty and student body. My most amazing experience in that regard was being in a small discussion group in a politics course with Russ Carpenter, who was number two academically in our class of 800. In class, Russ sat quietly while everyone else, including the professor, talked. Then he would modestly and perfectly summarize everything that had been said and give his conclusion, thus terminating the discussion. When Russ was finished the discussion was finished. The professor would clear his throat and raise the next question.

The highlights of my academic career at Princeton were the distribution courses required of freshmen and sophomores, which were taught by the most distinguished professors there. Mine were history, Spanish, economics, accounting and European literature in translation. Each was a revelation of breath-taking intellectual horizons of which we had never dreamed. I will never forget the day Professor Ira O. Wade, a world-renowned specialist on Voltaire, came as a guest lecturer to our freshman course in European literature. In one hour, he sketched for us the intellectual underpinnings of western European (and American) civilization. I took every course he taught at Princeton, and our class of 1963 made Professor Wade an honorary member. The academic workload was very rigorous. We read a book a week in five hard courses and wrote approximately ten long papers each term, culminating in a 20,000-word thesis senior year.

Exams were of the three-hour essay variety administered on the honor system. We could go to our rooms, the library or anywhere else during the three-hour test. The exams were turned in with a hand-written pledge, which each student signed, stating, "I pledge my honor as a gentleman that, during this examination, I have neither given nor received assistance." There was no cheating.

In my junior year, I majored in the Special Program in Latin American Civilization, an intense course of study of the language, culture, politics, history and economics of the region. I didn't imagine that going to Princeton and majoring in Latin American Civilization would be the ideal preparation for a long career in the cattle business. Thirty years after graduation, I sold a million-dollar herd of cattle to a South American. The transaction took place partly because I could speak Spanish. When you have taken the trouble to learn someone's language, it creates a bond of trust. I wrote my junior paper on Land Tenure in Mexico. That research was the basis for our purchase of a 22,000-acre ranch in Mexico in 1966, to which we added another 10,000 acres later. Now, at 65, I am studying harder and learning faster than I ever did in college. My education has proven very valuable, and I will always be thankful for being born into a family that aimed high in everything, including education.

Athletics

I played 150-pound football. Sophomore year I made the traveling team to play Navy. Although I did not play, it was a thrill to be in the stadium at Annapolis with all the great naval and marine battles listed around the stadium ring (Midway, Iwo Jima, Chosin Reservoir). That night, dinner in the mess hall was exciting as the cadets held a pep rally before Navy's first football game with Air Force.

My athletic career came to an end the middle of my sophomore year at Princeton when it became increasingly difficult to train and to make weight for wrestling. It was pretty grim to walk back to the dorm in the dark after a hard practice and have an ice cube for supper (no food and very little water). That year, Princeton was weak at 123 pounds, so the coach asked me to go down to that weight. It was too drastic a move. I became sick in the process and had to quit. My hat is off to those mentally and physically tough enough to stand the strain. After quitting wrestling, I took a part-time job, working until graduation at the Tax Institute, a company that published newsletters on changes in tax laws for subscribers. It was a worthwhile job, and I enjoyed the people there. The Institute was approximately a mile from campus. Since Princeton did not allow students to have cars, I walked the mile to and from work.

Social Life

The social life at Princeton, like the academics, was intense, and revolved around dorm life and membership in an eating club. Dorm life was enjoyable. We roomed in large groups of friends who were compatible and enjoyed the camaraderie typical of all-male institutions. Our romantic life revolved around football games and party weekends, when our girlfriends came on the train to Princeton Junction. We were allowed to drink in our rooms, and the girls could stay until midnight, so it was very festive. Our dates stayed with families in town who hosted them for a modest fee.

Football weekends are a wonderful tradition for students and alumni. Since Princeton and Rutgers had played the first college football game in U.S. history some 130 years earlier, Princeton's first football game each year was always scheduled with Rutgers. It is a much-anticipated fall weekend, and in my sophomore year, Annette came from Colorado for the game. Having a serious girlfriend and exciting weekends added great quality to the all-male environment. I was fortunate to have several girlfriends who were a great part of my life while at Princeton.

Princeton dormitories were divided vertically into "entries." Upper classmen were assigned rooms by seniority in a lottery, and they could set up any combination of people and rooms on any number of floors. Sophomore and junior years, six of us, including Ralph Warner, Ralph Smith, Forrest Pragoff, Jack Tower and Thrus Pettus, had a whole floor in one entry of Lockhart—three sleeping rooms, two living rooms and a bar. The rooms were assigned unfurnished, with no light bulbs, and the tradition of buying furnishings each year from graduating seniors or the local Army/Navy store made for a variety of decorating schemes. Housekeeping arrangements were unique to nonexistent as there was no janitorial or maid service.

In the middle of the sophomore year, students can go through a selection process for the eating clubs, Princeton's equivalent to fraternities. I was fortunate to be bid to several, and ultimately followed my friend Bill Jarman into Tiger Inn. Belonging to a club upgraded our lives tremendously. Aside from three good meals a day in elegant surroundings, we had a very attractive place to take dates on weekends as well as the everyday bull-sessions and a poker game, which I enjoyed, that ran nearly non-stop.

I pitched on Tiger Inn's intramural softball team, an activity I dearly loved. On that team, I became acquainted with Dick Springs. Dick was an outstanding athlete, who appreciated my playing to win. We became friends, and he later visited us in Mexico, invested in our ranch, went into the Beefmaster business in Oregon and served a term as president of the Beefmaster association.

Senior year I lived in 1879 Hall, so named because it was a gift from the class of 1879, with Al Barrett and Scott Marsh, both members of Tiger Inn. At that time, 1879 was probably Princeton's most prestigious address for seniors, situated halfway between the clubs and the main classroom buildings; living there was a delight. My roommate, Al, became a prep-school headmaster, and Scott, who was excellent in economics, became a highly successful money manager on Wall Street. Scott and I have remained friends, and he has been an important business partner.

The Chapel

Assistant Dean of the Chapel, Carl Reimers, was married to Jane, the widow of a relative of ours, Watty Reynolds. They came to Princeton in the fall of 1959, the same year as our class. I was a regular visitor there. Jane had two little boys, Watt and Tom, and they had their own son, Carl, Jr., so in addition to enjoying their gracious hospitality, I did some babysitting with their boys. I enjoyed my times with them, including many delicious meals accompanied by memorable philosophical discussions on all subjects.

Through my friendship with Jane and Carl, I became a deacon of the chapel and became acquainted with Dean Ernest Gordon, a survivor of the Japanese prison camp on the River Kwai, and author of the book *Through the Valley of the Kwai*. As a deacon, I was invited to the Gordon home for dinners with fine wine and great fellowship. Many of my ideas on the Christian faith were influenced in conversations with Deans Reimers and Gordon and their wives. I thank them for adding so much pleasure and enrichment to my life.

The Princeton Chapel is a beautiful Gothic cathedral. In addition to church services, the deacon's duty was to usher other events in the church, and we were fortunate to hear world leaders speak there. I was at my post at the side door, less than fifty feet from the pulpit, when General Eisenhower, Martin Luther King, Jr., and the Archbishop of Canterbury spoke. Being a deacon was a life experience that becomes more important with the passage of time.

The Summer of 1960

"Come on down to Mexico, Boy."
—Roger Sanford

The summer after my freshman year at Princeton was a turning point in my life. I accepted Bill Jarman's invitation to visit his family's ranch in Nuevo Leon, north of Monterrey. Mother and Dad loaned me a car for a month with the understanding that I would write a postcard every day. I

Bill Jarman and I in Nuevo Leon, Mexico, in 1960.

left Matheson, and on the first day drove to Rankin, Texas, where I stayed in the Rankin Hotel in a room with three double beds for $1.50. The next morning I was on my way well before daylight. As I drove toward Eagle Pass, and saw the great Southwest Texas terrain for the first time, I said to myself, "This is where I'm going to live."

I met Bill at the Hotel Chulavista in Monclova, Coahuila, and we drove to his family's El Sauz Ranch at Bustamante, Nuevo Leon. We had a great time, highlighted by riding horseback some forty miles to Espinazo, Coahuila, a very small, dusty, desert pueblo, to receive some Angus bulls, which arrived by train from Kerr-McGee in Oklahoma. We drove the bulls back to the ranch in 110-degree heat, enduring a very hard two-day trip each way. The Jarmans had relatives visiting at the ranch at that time and several of the men also had driven over to receive the bulls. The train station at Espinazo was a Spartan affair with only one water hydrant sticking out of a wall. As soon as I dismounted, I took a big drink and one of the men followed suit, then asked me if the water was safe. I replied that I did not know, and I could see him getting sick before my eyes. What I had not told him was that I was taking Entero-Vioform, a medicine that kills everything below the Adam's apple. When we arrived back at the ranch with the bulls, he was at death's door with *turista* (dysentery).

After I left El Sauz Ranch, I drove to Sabinas, Coahuila, where I met several family friends: the Phillips family, the Sanfords, the Finans and the Roberto Spences. My first stop was the home of Bob Spence. The moment I met Bob and Elizabeth, they treated me like a long-lost relative, beginning a wonderful friendship. Next I went to the home of Ruth and Duke Phillips. Duke, operating in partnership with Killam and Hurd of Laredo, Texas, was leasing the Bocatoche Ranch, west of Monclova. At that time, Ruth and Duke had three small children and a fourth on the way. They had been in Venezuela and were just getting established in Mexico, so it was natural that everything they were doing was of great interest to me. They made me welcome in their home for the first of several hundred nights I would spend with them over the next fourteen years.

As Bob Spence drove me to Hacienda Cloete to meet Roger and Violet Sanford, we met Mr. Sanford on the highway, coming to Sabinas to meet me. Mr. Sanford owned, and was famous for, a fleet of ancient, luxury Pontiacs, which he drove in relays, abandoning one when mechanical problems developed and calling his chauffer, Vicente, to bring another. Just as we met him on the highway, his car quit and he rolled it into the ditch, stepped out of the still-moving vehicle to get in with us—pretty spry for a 65-year-old veteran of World War I. We returned to the Spence's house where I became acquainted with two of the great personalities of Northern Mexico. Bob had partnered with Dolph Briscoe, Sr., on the Margaritas Ranch. Mr. Sanford had also partnered with Mr. Briscoe in buying Dad's first Beefmaster bull calf crop in 1941, the year I was born. Mr. Spence spoke very slowly and used extensive hand gestures before, during and after saying anything. Mr. Sanford was very dynamic and to the point. That day they got into a discussion about some past ranch deal. To clarify a point, Mr. Spence got out his map and unrolled it on the concrete floor in front of Mr. Sanford, who planted his shoes on the map, whipped out his ball-point pen and began making slashing motions as he drew lines on the map. Mr. Spence was so aghast that although his hands were moving, he was unable to speak.

The next morning, Bill Finan flew to Sabinas to take me to visit his Valle Colombia Ranch. Like all the people I met there, Bill and his wife Nelly were interested in my plans and supportive of my desire to ranch in

Mexico. Bill's ranch, one of the great ranches, is stocked with some of the best purebred Herefords. Bill moved there in 1939, at nineteen years of age, and has devoted his life to the ranch and cattle. One of the highlights for me was eating breakfast at 5:30 a.m. while watching the sun rise over the Valle Colombia.

Later, I visited the Sanfords at their beautiful home, Hacienda Cloete, which was surrounded by a nine-hole golf course that Mr. Sanford had built. He was a Cornell graduate and an old-time cattle entrepreneur, having moved to Mexico in 1926. Mr. and and Mrs. Sanford were a devoted couple who graciously called each other "Love" and "Lover" after nearly fifty years of marriage. During that visit and cocktails, overlooking a garden with tropical plants, Mr. Sanford made the mistake of saying, "Come on down to Mexico, Boy. I'll loan you $50,000 anytime." He said that to the wrong "Boy."

Duke Phillips, Bob Spence and I drove down to the Bocatoche Ranch for a day, a great experience for me, as both men were self-made and had partnered as a means of acquiring capital and management help. The final chapter of my first visit to Sabinas was a several-day trip to Bob and Elizabeth Spence's beautiful Margaritas Ranch. I also became a friend of their children, my contemporaries, Chavela and Bobby, both of whom still ranch in that area.

I wrote a postcard, which Mother saved, from the Margaritas Ranch. From the day I left Rankin, Texas, at sunrise, I knew where I wanted to live. Since that trip, our horizons have expanded greatly, and we now do business all over Latin America, but it all started in the summer of 1960.

The End of the University Trail

The main event at Princeton for every graduate is the senior thesis, with Princeton being the only university requiring a thesis for a Bachelor of Arts degree. I decided to start early on mine and do a good job to atone for the many academic opportunities I had missed. I had a straight "A" departmental average, but unfortunately, I did not get along with my thesis advisor. Although he knew I was working for an A, he told me that regardless of my efforts he would only give me a B+. It is ironic that one of my few academic setbacks occurred in my main endeavor. I learned a valuable life lesson, however, in that you cannot work on important matters with someone with whom you do not get along.

Each spring, with theses turned in, classes ending and graduation near, Princeton seniors are in a celebratory mood their final days there. While celebrating, I unfortunately had a serious car accident with my friends Philip Cannon, Bill Conner and Dexter Peacock as passengers. Philip, Dexter and I were not hurt, but Bill was seriously injured. As he nearly died of a ruptured spleen, he could not take final exams and had to repeat

the last semester. Having only a broken hand, I was able to take finals orally, but the discipline committee met after exams, suspending me for a year for driving under the influence, and I did not receive my diploma until 1964. My graduation would have coincided with Dad's 30th reunion, so all those important events were cancelled to my parents' great disappointment. I will always regret causing them such heartbreak.

I have stayed in touch with Philip, Bill and Dexter over the years, and all three

Spring 1963.

have visited us on various ranches and invested in Isa Cattle Co., Inc. We have had a lot of laughs in looking back; however, I always have been aware of how fortunate we all were and how my life would have been very different had Bill not survived.

With my company at Fort Leonard Wood. I am standing in the third row, on the right end.

CHAPTER 5

LAREDO AND
FORT LEONARD WOOD

I left Princeton, glad to be finished with school and thrilled by the prospect of being in charge of my own destiny. Mother and Dad wanted me to go to graduate school; however, I was determined to get started in the cattle business as soon as possible. To placate them, I took a battery of tests at the University of Denver and scored high in aptitude for law or for being a humanities professor, careers far from ranching. The only obstacle to my going into the cattle business was the military draft. In June of 1963, I was eighteenth on the draft list in Elbert County, Colorado, which had drafted only one man per year since World War II.

Life in Laredo

"El Presidente Kennedy está muerto."
—*news broadcast*

After several weeks at Matheson, I left for Laredo, Texas, to partner with Bill Jarman in buying cattle in Nuevo Leon and Tamaulipas, Mexico. I drove to Laredo in a white Ford Galaxy with a $5,000 stake. Having completed his military service in the Marine Corps Reserves, Bill had moved to Laredo and rented an apartment on Victoria Street. We lived the fine bachelor life, spending time working on ranches in Texas and Mexico. Our headquarters was the Hamilton Hotel in Laredo, where the cattle traders congregated. During those months, we spent a lot of time in Mexico on his family ranch in Nuevo Leon. I also visited Coahuila, making further plans to settle there. We could buy only one group of cattle at a time to bring to the border and dip for fever ticks, a process taking three weeks. The slow processing of a small number of cattle turned out to be fortunate for us as the cattle industry was headed into one of its bad cattle market drops. Most of the big buyers, who were our competition, went broke.

In late November 1963, we were driving north from Monterrey to Laredo, listening to *ranchera* music on the radio in Bill's pickup, when the program was interrupted, giving reports of the almost inconceivable events in Dallas. Suddenly, a voice came on and said in Spanish, *"El Presidente Kennedy está muerto."* The station then played the National Anthem. I think all Americans remember where they were and what they were doing that day, and I am no exception. On that same day, Roger Sanford was visiting Dad in Colorado to look at some Lasater Beefmaster bulls on feed at Monfort Feed Yards of Greeley, Colorado. He told Dad the bulls were perfect for Mexico and that he would help import and sell them. My career as a bull-seller was born the day John F. Kennedy was assassinated.

The Draft

"We'll have you in ninety days."
—*medic administering physical exam*

Several days after the President's death, I received a telegram from Dad stating that I was first on the list for the military draft in Elbert County and had better come home. Some of my contemporaries in Eastern Colorado avoided military service by having their fathers write a letter saying they were needed on the farm or ranch; however, Dad did not offer to do that and I did not ask him. I drove directly to Matheson where I received notice for a pre-induction physical. Five of us reported to the sheriff's office in Kiowa, and a deputy drove us to Denver for the physical. When we walked into the pre-induction center, one of the medics signing us in took one look at me and said, "You're just what we want. We'll have you in ninety days." He must have known something I didn't because I was the only one of the five who passed. After my physical, I checked into all the reserve programs and joined the National Guard.

The day of the physical was comical with all the instances of bad knees, high blood pressure and a hundred other pretexts to avoid the draft. The Army's fix for nearly every ailment involved a six-inch needle. My favorite was the cure for deafness. While I was taking my hearing test, I saw a would-be "goldbricker" get the treatment. The medics put him in a chamber, closed a soundproof door (with a wheel similar to one on a submarine's hatch) and turned the wheel. We could not hear the siren or whatever noise was turned on, but we could see the "testee" frantically pounding to be let out of the chamber.

Interlude at Nichols Tillage Tools

I had approximately three months before reporting for basic training, during which time I worked at Nichols Tillage Tools in Simla, Colorado. Nichols was the only industrial employer in our area. It was a successful family-owned foundry that manufactured sweeps and chisels for use on farm implements. The company bought raw steel, and then cut, heated, shaped, tempered and painted the finished tool.

Mr. Nichols gave me the opportunity of working in every department and learning the business, including pulling a furnace. He offered me various opportunities to help market his products. He was one of my many mentors, and he and Mrs. Nichols visited Annette and me in Múzquiz, where he gave me a small handmade anvil, his trademark.

Fort Leonard Wood, Missouri

"Get those duffel bags off those trucks."
—*Drill Sergeant*

In April of 1964, I reported to a National Guard Center in Denver, where a group of us were flown to Fort Leonard Wood for basic training. It is the general belief that Fort Polk and Fort Leonard Wood are the two worst posts in the Army. Fort Leonard Wood is hot and humid in summer and bitter cold in winter. Since everything is coal-fired, it is impossible to keep anything clean.

At a processing center we were issued uniforms, inoculated, had our heads shaved and surrendered our civilian clothes, which were mailed home. After our processing, we mainly spent the time lying around the barracks and playing poker, where my Princeton education came in handy. Instructions to the several thousand men in the processing area came over a loudspeaker. One day our company was directed to report with duffel bags to a loading area where trucks waited to haul us to our training company. Everything changed in a hurry when we arrived at Company B-3-2. Most of the cadre, as well as the company commander, a first lieutenant, were veterans of the Korean War. They awaited us standing at parade rest with their black helmets gleaming in the bright sunshine. The seriousness of the situation was impressed on us well before we dismounted as they hollered, "You girls (he used another word) get those duffel bags off those trucks."

Basic training was a good experience. The Army knows how to train men for combat and does it well. The people in charge can take a group of young men who do not want to cooperate, clean them up, teach them how to behave, and make soldiers out of them in thirteen weeks. As the lieutenant told us, "Our job is to take nice young men and make killers out of you." Sleep deprivation the first few weeks was an effective way to break down any resistance. We were paid eleven cents an hour for a 24-hour day. Since we were paid for the whole day and night, the Army felt free to use us for any or all of the time. Our $2.64 per day just covered our beer and Pall Mall cigarette expenses, so life was simple.

Nearly everyone who has been in the Army has a KP story. In my case, we reported at 3:30 a.m. and were informed by the mess sergeant that he was "getting short" (20 days left) and had nothing to do but harass us, which he succeeded in doing. I stayed inside the number-two grease trap until 9:30 p.m. Since truck drivers were exempt from KP, I became one the next day.

The Army was hard on those who did not fit the norms. We marched constantly, always with two "dumbells" carrying the stop signs at the front and rear of the company. At each hour came the order, "take five," at which point we laid down flat on the ground and smoked a cigarette. "Take five" was immediately followed by "fat girls fall out" for the soldiers they deemed overweight. They ran laps while we rested, and in thirteen weeks, they never sat down.

During our time at Fort Leonard Wood, we got two weekend passes, and both were memorable for different reasons. On the first, several friends and I went to what is now Branson, Missouri, which in 1964 was just a few fishing cabins and family-style weekend hotels. Although we were cold sober, dressed in starched uniforms with ties, we were refused admission to all hotels because we were soldiers. This was my first unforgettable taste of discrimination. Our second weekend leave in St. Louis, Missouri, was much better. Several friends and I were guests of Mr. and Mrs. Edgar Idol, parents of a close friend, Janie, who treated us like royalty.

• • •

The arched sign over the rifle range at Fort Leonard Wood says, "Through These Portals Pass the World's Finest Riflemen." The Army's rifle program is very impressive. We used the M-14 (U.S. Rifle M-14, 7.62 mm), which is an excellent weapon with tremendous range, hitting anything the shooter could see. In our case, they trained 110 men, many of whom had never fired a rifle, to be competent riflemen in just a few days. I was able to make "Expert" on the range.

I especially remember one afternoon that seemed surrealistic as we were returning to the company area from a long, hot march with rifle and pack. About a half-mile out, the sun went behind a cloud, a little breeze sprang up, and we could feel the electricity as the cadence picked up. We marched in with flags flying and everyone, including the cadre, feeling proud of what we had accomplished. I left Fort Leonard Wood with a good impression of the Army, as well as of the average citizen-soldier.

While in training in Missouri, I was thrilled to receive a classic letter from Roger Sanford (as mentioned earlier, he was a veteran of World War I) congratulating me on the training I was receiving and stating that he had a place for my cows that fall at Múzquiz. The place turned out to be La Lajita Ranch, a 3,100-acre ranch with four pastures, a trap and good pens, which lies in a beautiful valley next to the Santa Rosa Mountains west of Múzquiz, Coahuila.

ROGER SANFORD

CLOETE, COAHUILA

June 2, 1964

Pvt. Laurence M. Lasater
NG-26250066
B-3-2
Fort Leonard Wood, Mo. 65475

My dear Laurie:

I am happy to state that in the past
30 days we have had some rains in this country
and out at the Lajitas I have had about 7" and
in that I have disposed of all of my crossbred cattle, you can ship those cows on down
and we will work out something that will be
mutually satisfactory.

I envy you your youth and training that
you are now getting and you will look back on
it with both pleasure and satisfaction.

Sincerely yours,

R. A. SANFORD

CHAPTER 6

FORT CARSON AND MEXICO

When I finished basic training, in the best physical condition of my life, the Army put us on a bus to Colorado. My parents met me at the bus station in Limon. After several weeks' leave, I reported for advanced training at Fort Carson, Colorado, just south of Colorado Springs, headquarters of The Fifth Infantry Division-Mechanized. The Fifth Division was a precursor to today's rapid deployment combat units.

At Fort Leonard Wood, we had taken our army placement tests to determine our assignment (MOS). I had scored the maximum in several areas and could have had my pick of specialties, but against the advice of the placement office, I had previously chosen maintenance mechanics thinking it might be useful in ranching. On the contrary, I had condemned myself to three months' wasted time and mind-numbing boredom. Educationally, Fort Carson was as much a failure as Fort Leonard Wood was a success.

The good news was that Annette Nixon and I finally got together romantically after having been "friends" since 1949. I always knew that Annette did not want to marry a Lasater, go into agriculture or go to a foreign country, so of all the great sales I have made, this was my greatest, and I thank her mother, Ruth, and her sister, Dixie, for being on my team all the way. During this phase, I had most weekends off and was able to see her. Some weekends I took Army friends to the ranch, which everyone enjoyed so much, and as always, Mother and Dad were terrific hosts.

Going to Mexico

"You're going to learn to suffer, Boy."

—Joe Dawson

I was released from the Army on September 16, 1964, Mexican Independence Day, and it was a great day for me. I invited Annette to go to Mexico to see the region and to meet my friends. With her mother's blessing, she accepted my invitation. After finishing with the Army, we left Colorado Springs in my Ford Galaxy. I will never forget the thrill of driving through Raton, New Mexico, with the girl I had always wanted, heading for a career I had been yearning to enter for many years.

We drove through Texas in beautiful fall conditions. Fortunately, it was cool or Annette might have changed her mind. South of San Antonio, there is a sign that says "Eagle Pass 98 miles," and as we passed the sign, it was raining and extraordinarily beautiful. That sign marks where the big, wild country starts, and I still get goose bumps remembering the thrill.

The Border

Arriving in Eagle Pass, Texas, we stopped at the historic Hotel Eagle, headquarters for the ranchers in Coahuila. Legend has it that more cattle were traded at the Hamilton Hotel in Laredo, the Del Norte in El Paso and Hotel Eagle in Eagle Pass, than anywhere else in the United States. Since 1950, Mexico has exported 1,000,000 calves per year to the United States. Most of them crossed at those ports, and a lot of cattle changed owners in the coffee shops of these hotels. When I first visited the Hotel Eagle in 1960, I came in the back door from the parking lot and saw a man standing in the lobby with his spurs on. I said to myself, "This is where I'm going to live." I later learned that he was a local cowboy lobbying for a bit part in a western being filmed at nearby Brackettville, Texas.

Hotel Eagle stories are part of the local legend in that area. Our favorite first-hand experience involved Stewart Bagby, a big buyer of Mexican cattle. One night, Annette and I were in the room adjoining his and the phone rang literally all night long. The walls were thin, and Stewart had a resonant, deep voice so we could hear his conversations in Spanish, buying cattle, and then in English, selling them. We finally went to sleep when Stewart left about 3:30 a.m. the next morning. About 10:00 p.m. that night, we were asleep, as was he, when his phone rang. We could hear him answer the phone and a long silence. Then, we could hear, "Oh Honey, I'm so sorry" and a long pause, then "Oh Honey," followed by more silence. It seems he had forgotten his wife's birthday, and she gave him a "working-over" to end all "working-overs."

On our first night in Eagle Pass, I took Annette across the river to the elegant El Moderno Restaurant, which belongs to the de los Santos family. It was there that I introduced Annette to nachos and tequila sours, which sealed the deal. She loved the border and El Moderno.

In 2004, Jack Grafa, a friend from San Angelo, and I had lunch there again with Nelly and Bill Finan and their daughter, Patti, now married to Rodolfo "Yopo" de los Santos. The restaurant was just as elegant then as it was forty years earlier and even more renowned, as the following story illustrates. Its current owner, Yopo, was flying from Piedras Negras to Saratoga, Wyoming, in his pressurized Cessna 210. He had planned to buy an aviation map in Amarillo, but none was available, so he flew on to the Denver Terminal Control Area without a map. The Denver controller, hearing his Mexican airplane numbers, asked where he was from. Yopo replied, "south of San Antonio." "Where south of San Antonio?" "Piedras Negras." "Do you know El Moderno Restaurant?" "I own it." The controller and his wife had become engaged there. He vectored Yopo directly to Saratoga and insisted that Yopo call him at home on the return flight so that he could go to the airport to vector him safely back through the control area.

Sabinas, Coahuila

Our next stop was Sabinas. It is a relatively small city located on the Sabinas River south of Eagle Pass/Piedras Negras. The town sits in a hot, brushy, desert setting. It has wide streets and is more modern in architecture than other towns in the area. It is, however, distinctly Mexican.

On September 28, 1964, we crossed the border and drove southward through Coahuila's desert. As we came into the city, we passed a dusty Chevrolet pickup and a wild-looking man with a mustache, dark sunglasses, a Bowie knife in hand. The man leaned out the window, not five feet from Annette, raised the knife and yelled a savage *grito* (shout). It was Bob Spence, Jr., welcoming her to Mexico.

We stayed at the Gran Hotel Sabinas, which had a tiled lobby with a grand, curving staircase, for $4.00 a night. Annette's stark room had the standard tile bathroom, bare ceiling light bulbs, no rug, and no shower curtain. During our two-day stay, she saw the region, met the Sanfords, Ruth and Duke Phillips, the Spences and the McKellars, and had her first taste of the exciting world of which I was so eager to be a part.

While I had high hopes that the girl I loved would be my companion and partner for the rest of my life, I did not dream that we would have an exciting international career in the cattle business, would associate with the most interesting people in the world, and be blessed with outstanding children, children-in-law, and grandchildren. On a different level, I did not know that I, a person who values originality and creativity, was going to create a job for myself in a very traditional, declining industry that punishes originality and creativity. One of my goals was to live in a gracious manner in a beautiful home. Little could I imagine then the serene and gracious homes and offices Annette would design for us. They enabled me to create the thousands of letters, deals, books, proposals, speeches and articles that are a key and unique part of our business success. I am not an artist, but I work in an attractive office, see fine cattle and come home to a lovely and comfortable home, all of which are basic to my creative process.

Setting Up Housekeeping

I took Annette back to Eagle Pass for her bus trip and flight to Colorado. She had a lot to think about on the long trip back home. As we planned to be married at the Colorado College Chapel in Colorado Springs at Christmas, I began making arrangements with Roger Sanford to ship our cattle to Mexico. Mother and Dad were giving us thirty-five Lasater Beefmaster cows and two herd bulls as a wedding present. Due to a new government Brucellosis requirement, the shipment was delayed until November 1.

In the meantime, I lived at the Hotel Monterrey and stayed busy finding a house to rent and setting up housekeeping. I rented a new half-duplex on Calle Ocampo 540. I bought a bed and hot water heater and leased a refrigerator. All our friends gave us much-appreciated help, advice and items, and in short order we had a comfortable, first home. Ruth and Duke Phillips gave us important essentials, such as a gas range and a fan, and Elizabeth and Robert Spence gave us a table with chairs. Roger Sanford gave us a beautiful hand-turned lamp he had made from two antique wagon axles. Having seen my room with used furniture at Princeton, I think Annette was pleasantly surprised.

Annette came to Laredo in November to finish locating furniture and household items and we ordered her wedding ring at Aladar Deutsch, a famous jewelry store in Nuevo Laredo. While there we had a reunion with Bill Jarman and his wife, Lydia, at their ranch home— an attractive, simple rock house with no electricity and lighted by butane lamps. It was cold when we arrived, and the big fireplace, smelling of mesquite, made it very cozy. When we returned to Monterrey, we bought my ring. During this trip, I decided that trying to marry in Colorado was complicated and that we should get married in Laredo the following week, called our parents with the news, and they began making plans to fly to Laredo.

Annette as a young woman.

Our Cattle Arrive in Mexico

"These cows are way too good for these boys."
—Roger Sanford

I had made arrangements to import our cattle in early November. Gaddy Truck Line hauled them from Matheson to the U.S. export pens at Eagle Pass, then owned by my friend J.D. Cage. I was waiting in the Hotel Eagle Coffee Shop when I was paged that a trucker was calling me. I met the truck and escorted it to the cattle pens, where the cattle were unloaded in good order. There is nothing more exciting than to hear trucks rev their engines to back into position to load or unload cattle. This was the first of many loads of registered Beefmaster cattle that Gaddy hauled from Colorado for me. The 35 cows and two bulls spent the night in Eagle Pass while Tom González, the Customs broker, did all the export paperwork for crossing. Since then I have made many shipments to

Mexico, and the procedure is identical. While the cattle were in Eagle Pass, Bob Cage and Bill Finan went to see them. Bill advised me that I should have left one cow in Colorado. I still remember the cow distinctly, as she turned out not to be a good cow. Because of our coming and going

The Foundation herd of the Beefmaster breed in Mexico arrives at La Lajita.

at Eagle Pass and Hotel Eagle, we formed a friendship with Bob Cage, a boyhood friend of Dad's, who took an interest in our family and business.

Early the next morning, the cattle crossed the river on two trailers and were unloaded in the Mexican Customs pens, where they were inspected and then reloaded onto three bobtail trucks. I drove the 120 miles with the trucks to Múzquiz, and then rode on one of the trucks to guide them to La Lajita. It was a pretty fall day, and as we drove west of town, in this spectacular scenery, with all three truck radios blaring Mexican music, I nearly had to pinch myself to believe it was happening. It had rained the night before, and although we had no means of communicating, my foreman, Eugenio de la Rosa, was waiting at the turnoff with a saddled horse as he knew the trucks could not drive down the muddy road. The trucks backed up to the lane's ridge to jump the cattle off, and Eugenio and I trailed them on horseback the three miles to their new home.

The ranch is brushy, but close to the mountains west of Múzquiz, so is very fertile and productive with good, reliable rainfall. It belonged to Cuca Riddle, a widow of one of Mr. Sanford's friends, and is one of the best of the 65 ranches I have operated. Mr. Sanford offered me one year's pasturage for my cattle. He came out several days later and looked them over carefully. After a long pull on his Chesterfield, he said, "Laurie, these cows are way too good for these boys."

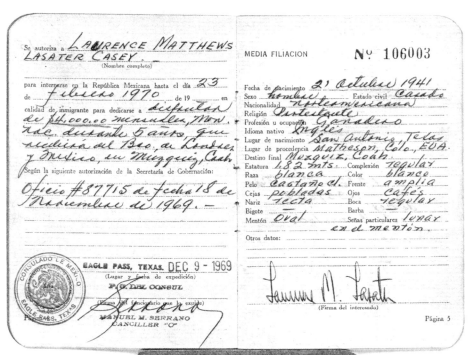

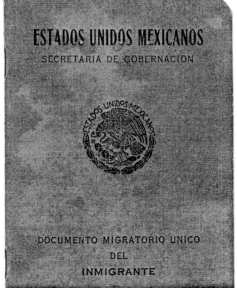

My residence passport.

DA025

D CZA038 CGN PD=CORPUS CHRISTI TEX 21 1014A CST=
MR AND MRS LAURENCE LASATER, DLR 330PM=
    HAMILTON HOTEL LAREDO TEX=

THINKING OF YOU ON THIS VERY SPECIAL DAY. SEND LOVE
IN ABUNDANCE, HOPE YOU WILL COME TO SEE US AT EARLIEST
POSSIBLE DATE=
    MELBA AND JOE DAWSON=

B Y   W E S T E R N   U N I O N

DA026

D FWA090 CGN DL PD=FORT WORTH TEX 21 1010A CST=
LAWRENCE LASATER AND MISS ANNETTE NIXON=
    HAMILTON HOTEL LAREDO TEX=

MY ARMS ARE AROUND YOU IN MUCH LOVE AND GREAT GOOD
WISHES MAY THIS DAY BE THE BEGINNING OF A LIFE OF REAL
AND ABIDING HAPPINESS TOGETHER HOPING TO MEET MY NEW
NIECE SOON AND AGAIN MY LOVE=
    AUNT LUCILLE=

B Y   W E S T E R N   U N I O N

CHAPTER 7

TWO TO MEXICO

Annette and I decided that we would marry in Laredo, Texas, on November 21, 1964. We made arrangements to be married by the Reverend Robert Hinkelman at the First Methodist Church (a beautiful Spanish-style church) with Bill and Lydia Jarman as our attendants. As soon as our parents arrived, they met the minister and saw the church. Our mothers were a major part of our wedding planning. Ruth had made Annette's wedding gown, Mother helped Annette select her veil, and both mothers put together a reception at the Hamilton Hotel.

Uncle Palo drove Grandmother from Albany, Texas, for the ceremony. Everyone stayed at the Hamilton Hotel, visited the famed Cadillac Bar and had dinner at an outdoor restaurant in Nuevo Laredo. Méjico Típico had a large mariachi band, which kept playing for the evening with Dad and Bill laying a steady stream of U.S. dollars on the table. The days before were exciting, thanks to the great company and happy occasion. Both the wedding and reception were a fun, intimate time for all. After the reception, we left for Mexico, with Mother's gift of two engraved silver cups to toast each other on our wedding night.

The Honeymoon

I thought I was handling everything very well until I bumped the car in front of me on the bridge to Nuevo Laredo. We both got out of our cars and the other driver, an American, was getting ready to take a swing when he saw my boutonniere and realized I was not in possession of my faculties. He saw there was no damage, mumbled an expletive, returned to his car and drove off. Customs and Immigration waved the *novios* (newlyweds) through, and we drove to the Motel Rio, Nuevo Laredo's finest, for our wedding night.

The next day we drove to Monterrey and stayed at the Gran Hotel Ancira, a favorite in that city. We spent the day shopping and ordering hand-crafted wicker chairs/tables for our living room. The following day we drove to Hotel Arízpe-Sáinz in Saltillo, a beautiful old colonial-style hotel built around a traditional patio with fountain. (Coincidentally, my parents had stayed there on their honeymoon.) When we returned to our house, Duke Phillips flew us to Sierra Hermosa to spend Thanksgiving, the final stop on our honeymoon. No man ever was more thrilled to be married and in business than I was.

At Christmas, we drove to Colorado to see our families and to load our gifts and possessions. While there, we traded Annette's new vintage Mustang and my Galaxy for a used Ford pickup and cash to boot. We started home to begin our new life in Mexico on New Year's Eve. I may not have known it then, but on January 1, 1965, I was in as fine a position as I have ever been—new wife, new home, and new herd of cattle. Our cows started calving on January 10, and like that first calf, everything that year was brand new and exciting. One of our thirty-five cows produced a bull calf, later known as *El Gallo,* still famous in Múzquiz for the number of cows he bred. He was the first of the great bulls we have raised over the succeeding forty years.

Our First Year Together

"Laurie, these girls can see things you and I can't see."

—Roger Sanford

Annette and I were fortunate to be Mr. Sanford's last "project," to use one of his favorite words. In retrospect, I realize that he (while being a close friend of my parents) took on a heavy responsibility in helping us get started in a foreign country. With no experience and very little capital, I planned to live and buy a ranch in Mexico. My parents gave us Beefmaster cows valued at $400, and Dad had co-signed a $10,000 note at the Colorado Springs National Bank. Although we had a used pickup and only a small amount of cash, I was surprised when Dad told me several years later that he had been sure we could not last six months.

Roger and Violet Sanford were important mentors and models of how we wanted our marriage to be. In addition to helping us get started in business, they took a great interest in our personal lives. We enjoyed many meals and visits in their beautiful Spanish-style home. As soon as our modest little home on Ocampo Street was established, they came to dinner, staying late before they left to drive two hours to Eagle Pass en route to Mr. Sanford's 50th reunion at Cornell. Roger came by our house frequently to visit and to monitor our progress, and Annette always fixed hot tea for him. We had many wonderful times with him and received much valuable wisdom. One day he dropped by as I was refinishing a piece of furniture. I was complaining bitterly, and after a sip of tea, he said, "Laurie, these girls can see things you and I can't see. Just go ahead and do what she tells you."

Mr. Sanford was involved in several major undertakings with me. He leased me La Lajita Ranch and sold me his excellent Charbray cows on credit. (They were out of well-known herds, Hudgins cows and a Michaelis bull.) One of these cows, bred to a Lasater Beefmaster bull, raised a 900-pound calf with no feed, an example of how good the cattle and the ranch were.

One day, Annette was there while we were working Mr. Sanford's cattle at La Lajita. Because the Brahman cows were wild, she was standing on the platform above the cutting chute for safety. The chute collapsed, she fell into the lead-up pen, and was run over by the cows that were coming down the alley. She was unhurt, but Mr. Sanford told her, "You'd better quit cavorting around with that boy."

Discovering the Neighborhood

With no children and only a few cattle, we had time to explore the neighborhood ranches, including Roger Sanford's Encantada, as well as the Margaritas, Sierra Hermosa and Valle Colombia. We became acquainted with Manuel Padilla, a rancher, businessman and partner of Bill Finan. We also met Guillermo Osuna, another friend and business associate.

At that time, our friend Charlie Jackson was the U.S.D.A. employee in charge of monitoring the screwworm eradication program and outbreaks in Coahuila (every ranch collected samples and marked a big lime "X," visible from the air, so sterile flies could be dropped). Each Monday, Charlie left Del Rio in his U.S.D.A. pickup and made a five-day circle calling on ranches. He was a great personality—his nickname was Charlie Mosca (Fly)—and he knew everyone, including all the kindest people and the best places to spend the night. I made the circle with him several times, and through him learned the area. Like me, Charlie was looking for a ranch, so Annette and I enjoyed his company. Later he bought part of the Encantada Ranch from Mr. Sanford, and became successful in the oil business in Midland.

Birthdays are a big event in Mexico. Bob Spence's birthday in 1965 was a mid-day stag event held at the Gacha Ranch. I will never forget meeting Jesús "Chui" Santos there. He walked up to me, introduced himself, and told me he had a ranch in Ocampo County where I was welcome to move my cows anytime. He knew who I was and offered his friendship the moment we shook hands. Forty years later, we are still close friends.

1965

When the first blast of the summer inferno hit our little house facing the sun on Ocampo Street, we turned on our new Sears window air-conditioning unit, the biggest one sold. The lights of Sabinas immediately dimmed as the city's electrical power could not carry it. Our unit's motor could not turn over a revolution, so we were forced to abandon it and to sleep on cots in the patio courtyard, using wet towels to try to stay cool enough to sleep.

We knew we had to move and decided to move nearer the ranch. In discussing rental possibilities in Múzquiz, Chui Santos told me he had an unoccupied house called Rodríguez, on the only highway into town, that we could rent. I made an appointment to meet him, and was met by a delightful lady who treated me like a long-lost brother. I finally figured out that she was Esther, Chui's wife, and that he had been detained. While waiting, we sat in the dairy, enjoying a light breeze, and had the first of several hundred delightful visits. When Chui arrived, we all went to look at the house. It had been built around the time of the Mexican Revolution and consisted of two-foot-thick rock walls, fourteen-foot ceilings and a screened porch on three sides of the house. A nice yard, trees and a perfect location completed the picture. Having been neglected for years, all that the house needed was some tender loving care. We rented it for the princely sum of 500 pesos ($40 per month).

Starting the next morning, Annette and I would get up early, haul a load of our possessions to Rodríguez, and paint all day. We painted each room and the screened porch, Annette the bottom half and I the top. In short order, Annette transformed this neglected landmark into a comfortable home. The fact that we did the painting created a stir in the community. A steady stream of visitors came by to see our work and to encourage us. Renovating the house and moving there integrated us into Múzquiz society, which we enjoyed greatly. During this time, Annette was teaching herself Spanish. She was determined not to miss anything due to the language barrier, and all our friends were very helpful and supportive.

• • •

That spring, we had our first brush with the dreaded cattle tick fever (Piroplasmosis). La Lajita was in the fever tick zone, so we dipped every 21 days to minimize the infestation. Nevertheless, our best bull died because I was not ready with medicine on hand when he fevered. As a result, we immunized all the imported cattle by injecting them with blood from cattle born in the zone. The new vaccinates had to be watched carefully and doctored with Ganaseg and Steclin for Piroplasmosis and Anaplasmosis, a tick-born blood disease, when they fevered. We were moving large numbers of very good quality, mature "high-line" cattle into the fever tick zone in order to be able to sell registered cattle born in the zone but immune to tick fever. To the best of my knowledge no one has done this before or since. We had some death loss, but our most costly losses were fertility problems due to Anaplasmosis, which was eventually stopped with the availability of Anaplaz vaccine.

• • •

During that same year, Roger Sanford located a ranch that he thought would work for us. He suggested that we buy Maderas del Carmen, a piece of undeveloped land across the Rio Grande, adjacent to Texas' Big Bend Park. His plan was that we partner with his friend Humberto Siller, the mayor of Sabinas, which would take care of the political/ownership problem.

Looking at Maderas del Carmen was an interesting adventure. When I arrived, it was terribly cold, maybe 20 degrees, and windy. It was open range, and a family that kept goats lived there in a camp just as shepherds have since Biblical times. Someone gave me a letter of introduction to the head of the family. I introduced myself, and one of the sons was designated to take me around on horseback. Their shelters were made of woven stalks and were more shade than shelter. We stayed in bed until the sun was well up, built a fire, and had beans, tortillas and coffee before riding all day. We returned home at dark for the second meal of beans, tortillas and coffee, then went to bed for warmth. I spent several days on horseback looking over the property. At one point, from the top of a ridge, I could look down into the Santo Domingo, a 1,000,000-acre ranch belonging to George Meiers, a well-known rancher and legend. It is an experience I will never forget.

> *"He is a nice young man with a lot of good*
> *ideas and no money."*
>
> —*John Maher*

I needed $20,000 for my half of the deal, so I wrote my Uncle John Maher in Houston regarding a possible loan. He replied that I could have my financing and that he would send his plane to Eagle Pass to fly us to Houston to get the check. Annette and I enjoyed visiting Aunt Lois (Dad's sister) and Uncle John in their home on Lazy Lane. While there, Uncle John, who can be described as "bigger than life," with a booming voice, took me downtown to meet some of his business friends. His standard introduction was, "This is my nephew, Laurie. He is a nice young man with a lot of good ideas and no money." On a visit to one of his farms, riding in his Rolls Royce, he told me he preferred to go to the country when the temperature was between 60 and 80 degrees, with no wind.

The paperwork and negotiations to buy the ranch dragged on for months, and at one point, I told Mr. Sanford that I was afraid of missing out on buying another ranch. After a long pause, he told me, "Laurie, you'll run out of money way before they run out of land and cattle." Much to Uncle John's and my disappointment, we never could get the title cleared, so the deal didn't happen. Forty years later, a big cement company purchased the property as a national park for Mexico.

• • •

Duke Phillips was the only person in the neighborhood who knew how to pregnancy-test cows in 1965, having tested many thousands while working for the Rockefeller family in Venezuela. Since there was no one to test our cattle, and with Annette's encouragement, I rode the bus to Garnett, Kansas, to attend the Graham School to learn pregnancy-testing and artificial insemination. Not only did I test all of our cattle, but Duke and I tested many cattle in the area. I made the first sale of pregnancy-tested cows in the Múzquiz area, some 200 Hereford cows bred to Beefmaster bulls. The cows were springing with fall calves and were a sight to behold. My crew and I drove them on horseback halfway to town, where we met and delivered them to the buyer and his crew. He and I counted the herd between our horses, and he wrote me a check on the spot. Over the years, I bought a lot of cattle. I would pregnancy-test them, buy the breds or opens, and either haul by truck or drive on horseback to our ranch.

That fall, Gaddy Truck Lines brought down our second set of cattle as well as fifty Lasater Ranch export bulls for resale. All these cattle came to La Lajita and were immunized against tick fever. That same fall, we weaned our first calves. After hard bargaining, I sold the best 15 bull calves (minus *El Gallo*) to Arturo Siller, Pedro Aguirre and Dr. Garza-Dávila for 5,000 pesos ($400 U.S.), the same value that Dad had placed on their mothers.

Our Visitors

My mother-in-law, Ruth, visited us regularly and was a big part of our lives. I still miss her. She was a pioneer herself, interested in everything we were doing and loved the cattle, as did Annette. My parents and all of our siblings also visited. When Mother and Dad came for the first time, Roger Sanford sent his driver, Vicente, to get them in Eagle Pass, and hosted a dinner at Hacienda Cloete that night. The next day, Bob and Elizabeth Spence came to see my parents and to have lunch at Rodríguez. When Elizabeth asked Annette if we planned to have children, she replied, "It's on the drawing board." I took Dad to see the cattle at La Lajita. Chui joined us and drove Dad in his pickup. On the way, there was an *arroyo* (creek) with water in it. I crossed with no problem, but they drowned out. Dad said to Chui in Spanish, "Lorenzo will be back in a minute to pull us out." Chui replied, "Don Tomás, you don't know your son; he has already forgotten us." I went on to the ranch and about twenty minutes later they arrived.

De sierra a sierra (from mountaintop to mountaintop).

CHAPTER 8

HACIENDA SANTA CRUZ, LTD.

In 1966 we realized the necessity of expanding our business. We had sold two groups of fifty Lasater Ranch bulls at a profit and had weaned and sold our first crop of Beefmaster bull calves. It was evident that there was a lot of interest in our Beefmaster cattle, one of Mr. Sanford's reasons for helping us.

Bill Jarman, who then lived in Odessa, Texas, told me he had met various independent oilmen from Midland who would be a good source of venture capital and introduced me to Pomeroy Smith. Pom had been the youngest man in Patton's army and was one of the many Princetonians who came to Midland in the 1950s. On one of our return trips to Mexico, Annette and I stopped in Midland so that I could visit with Pom about his possible interest in Mexico. At that time, he had a modest office with Searle McGrath, another Princetonian, in the Vaughn Building in downtown Midland. Pom was interested in the Mexico venture, and while we were talking, he asked about my wife. I told him Annette was waiting in our pickup. He looked out his window and saw our loaded, un-air conditioned Ford pickup parked on the street below. Annette was patiently waiting, reading a book with both windows open.

Like many ranchers, I was fascinated by the feedlot industry. Unlike ranching, feedlots have a fast turnover and the manager can control the volume of production. Our house at Rodríguez was surrounded by Chui's rich farmlands and a feedlot built by his father. Múzquiz is an area famed for production of large numbers of quality calves. We were perfectly situated to buy calves and grow them on very simple silage and cottonseed meal rations.

Pom and his partners, George Conly and Boyd Laughlin, flew to Múzquiz in George's Mooney to see the feedlot. Over lunch with us, they agreed to finance the venture. I worked for many months to work out an arrangement with Chui, but could not get it off the ground. I will never forget calling Pom from the public telephone office in Sabinas to tell him the plan was not going to work. I did not realize it then, but avoiding a sure loss made my reputation with the Midland group.

We shifted our emphasis to looking for a ranch. After I looked at several, Roger Sanford came into the picture again. He had told me of a ranch belonging to the Padilla family where he had bought calves after World War I. Mr. Sanford said there was a shallow, hand-dug well at the

North view of the valley on Rancho Santa Cruz.

foot of a mountain that could pump water to the top of the mountain and water the whole ranch by gravity. One day, he and I were sitting in Manuel Padilla's office in Múzquiz, and Mr. Sanford told him, "You don't need that ranch. Sell it to this boy and finance him." The next day Manuel flew me to the ranch, and then I returned to ride it on horseback with Alberto Gaitán, a cowboy on the ranch, as my guide. Rancho Santa Cruz, an old ranch, is located in very rough, very beautiful country with the centrally-located well. It is situated in a wide valley in the Santa Rosa Mountains, 100 miles southwest of Del Rio, Texas (210 degrees on compass). Those mountains are the southern extension of the Rockies, running north and south. None of the canyons had been opened, and only part of the central valley had been fenced and used for grazing.

Manuel and his brother, Praxedis, agreed to sell us the ranch and cattle for $140,800 with 29% down and 6% on the balance, payable in five years. They would hold the ranch and cattle (300 Hereford cows) in their name until we had children born in Mexico, who would be able to take title as Mexican citizens. Pom Smith and the Midland group agreed to finance the venture, provided a certain amount of capital was raised and committed. Annette and I were to be general partners owning 40% of the venture, plus house, pickup and $500-per-month salary.

By coincidence, the capital was raised on my twenty-fifth birthday, October 21, 1966, when my friend Dick Springs committed to invest by telegram. We attended a party in Múzquiz that night with friends including Chui and Esther Santos and the Padillas. At the party, the completion of the sale was announced. Our gracious friends were pleased that we had settled there and had brought the famous *Ganado Bifmaster* (Beefmaster cattle) with us. We bought an additional 150 crossbred cows from Dr. Garza-Dávila to stock the ranch. As nearly as I can recall, we paid 150 pesos per hectare ($4.80 U.S. per acre) for the land and about 1,250 pesos ($100 U.S.) for the cows. Starting April 1, 1967, we exposed the cows to Lasater Ranch bulls.

Hacienda Santa Cruz, Ltd., was set up as a tax shelter for investors. Pom had a wealth of business experience, having sold drilling programs in the East, and was the first of the small independents to go public. Pom, along with his accountant, George Conly, who handled the financial aspect of the public offering, and his lawyer, Boyd Laughlin, who drew up our limited partnership, were the three who represented the investors. These gentlemen were among the most sophisticated business people in the United States. I could never repay them for the high-level business training they gave me. Annette and I invested our little herd and owned forty percent of the business from the outset. Our new partners wired us the money to get started before seeing the ranch or drawing up the documents. Dad could not believe it.

Shortly thereafter, the three partners came to the ranch in a chartered plane to view their investment. Evidently, the pilot had not had experience landing on short ranch strips before. When he finally stopped the airplane only yards from the fence at the end of the runway, sweat was running out of his shirt. Annette served lunch, and they seemed to enjoy the ranch, the adventure, and the day. Upon leaving, they said that if we had not "borrowed" the ranch for the day, everything looked good. In retrospect, the Midland people, who were riskers themselves, were fascinated by what we were doing.

This partnership, combined with what I had learned from Duke Phillips about deal structuring, has served as the basis of all my subsequent ventures. In 2003, using the Phillips' model, Lorenzo and I bought part of the Vista Beefmaster herd in California with financing from Bill Richey, a friend and business associate from Florida.

We became close friends with Betty and Pom Smith. They visited us at the ranch, and although they are retired in Florida, we are still in touch forty years later. We made periodic visits to Midland and stayed with them in their home. On some of the visits, there were dinner parties, and we were able to meet their friends. Pom gave me a lot of valuable, succinct, personal and business advice. One memorable bit of advice happened one day as we were driving to La Lajita when Annette was expecting our first baby. I was discussing the drawbacks to a baby being named "junior." He said, "You have a nice name, use it." On another occasion, I had some Midland oil stock that had increased dramatically in value. I asked him what he would do. He said, "Would you buy at this price?" I said, "Heck no." Then he said, "Maybe you should sell it." Before Pom's company went public as Coquina Oil Corporation, he allowed us to buy stock out of the safe in their office. This generous offer allowed us to invest a small amount of money, which turned into a valuable asset for us.

CHAPTER 9

OUR FIRST DROUGHT

"You're finished! You have to get these cattle out of here."

—Bill Finan

On January 1, 1967, Annette and I moved to Rancho Santa Cruz. It was bitterly cold, and although there was a new hunters' cabin. It had no heat, and we were dependent on the fireplace for warmth. At times it was so cold that the butane line to the kitchen stove froze. There was no electricity, only Aladdin lamps for light, and there was no hot water, so we took a cold shower each day. One cold morning in February, huddled in the kitchen drinking coffee by a kerosene lantern, waiting for sunrise, I noticed that Annette was weepy. I asked what was wrong, and she replied, "Do you know what day it is?" "No." "It's Valentine's Day." Realizing I needed to solve the problem somehow, I made a list in a notebook of the holidays she felt were important to observe. From that day forward, I have carried a calendar in my wallet with the five "mandatory" holidays noted: Valentine's Day, Mother's Day, birthday, anniversary and Christmas.

I was the youngest man and the least-experienced on the ranch. Each morning at 6:00 a.m., as I drove to the camp to start my crew of six cowboys, I had to steel myself by saying, "This is my ranch." In typical young-man's thinking, I stocked the ranch to make the payments and hauled water to the cattle while we built the water system. When Uncle Palo visited the first time, he commented that only a Lasater would buy the cattle, then build the water system.

Essential ranch supplies were not available in Mexico, so in Northern Mexico, ranch equipment was customarily smuggled in from the West

Texas oilfields at very reasonable prices. In order to install a ranch-wide water system, I needed to cross the plastic pipe. After making arrangements with a Mexican Customs official at Boquillas, a neighbor and I crossed eight truckloads comprised of sixteen miles of plastic pipe as well as electric light plants, pump jacks, engines, refrigerators, a washing machine and myriad

cables, tools and other implements needed in the winter of 1967.

When we bought Santa Cruz, there was a house, a camp house, two wells and two sets of pens on 22,000 acres, with two pastures, two traps and a good airstrip. Water from the centrally-located, shallow well was pumped by two yoked mules, walking in a

Left downwind for landing on our airstrip, flying north over Rancho Santa Cruz.

circle, just as in biblical times. In a few months, we had created a ranch with seven pastures and fifteen waterings. After two years of being without electricity, we had our Witte Diesel electric light plant installed and running 24 hours a day. We hired the *maestro* who had originally built the house to build an addition and to help Annette remodel the house, adding electrical wiring, putting in large windows in the dining room and living room, taking out the artificial ceiling and staining the beams, putting Saltillo tile on the floors, and rocking the fireplace. All of the walls were constructed from crushed rock and the fireplace wall was chiseled by the crew from rocks on the ranch. It was an attractive, though modest, home. After Lorenzo was born, we had the same *maestro* and his crew build two *casitas* (little houses). One was a guesthouse and one was for the maids.

When I first looked at Santa Cruz in the summer of 1966, it was very dry and had been for some time. By the spring of 1967, we were in a real crisis, having received less than two inches of rain in over a year. Not only were we short of grass, but our famous well pumped down so low that we ran short of water for 450 cows in 100-degree heat. Our neighbor to the south, Vidal González, allowed us to load water into our truck at night after his stock had watered and his reservoir had refilled. In effect, he gave us his surplus water at no charge. He told me several years later that a neighbor, a Tex-Mex, had suggested that he cut me off water so that they could divide the ranch. Don Vidal, a gentleman, refused.

As the spring progressed, we were in desperate straits trying to keep our cattle alive, hauling water and burning pear (cactus) around the clock. We had no money to move the cattle, and there was no market for thin cattle in Mexico. There were no government programs to bail out people caught off base. Just like the old-timers, we had two choices—let all of the cattle die and walk off carrying our suitcases or stand and fight.

Our more experienced neighbors were very concerned. Ruth or Duke Phillips dropped by several times a week to check on us, to bring parts or other needed items or to fly us to Sierra Hermosa for an overnight break. One day Bill and Nelly Finan flew in for lunch, and when I showed Bill our main well, producing about one gallon per minute, he became so upset that he shouted, "You're finished. You've got to get these cattle out of here." He was trying to get me to take action, but all we could do was hang on. Several weeks later, while pulling the deep well at our house for repair, we dropped the pumping barrel down the well, 700 feet deep. Bill loaned me a fishing tool, and somehow we managed to extract the pumping barrel, which was no small feat.

Our deep well had 35 twenty-foot joints of three-inch pipe in the hole. Due to a steel crisis, we could not buy new pipe, so ours had to be re-threaded. We tried to do each joint by hand, but it was too difficult. Joe Finley, a friend of Dad's, and his son, Joe, Jr., who operated the Carrizalejo Ranch, two valleys west, offered to help us. They sent their truck, a six or seven-hour trip, loaded our pipe to take to their ranch shop, rethreaded it on their pipe-threading machine, made a nipple the exact length of the cut-off threads, and returned the like-new pipe to us. The pipe fit perfectly—to the inch. These are only the most dramatic stories. As I write this, forty years later, I am deeply moved at the memory of a hundred kindnesses received and how everyone in the neighborhood was pulling for us.

In the spring in 1967, it became hotter and drier. Even though we had crews working long hours every day opening the mountain canyons, laying water pipelines, and burning pear for the cattle to graze, the situation worsened each hour. As the cows calved, we had to sort off the weak ones, move the cattle to better pear and dip for fever ticks. There were many long herd drives to our dipping vat, with weak cows struggling to walk. Annette hauled the new baby calves in our pickup. During this drought we became acquainted with the geography and capabilities of the ranch, learned a lot about the cattle business, and got command of a nucleus of good men who stayed with us. Although she was not raised on a ranch, Annette pitched in from day one and loved the business as much as I.

> *"I underestimated lo terco y trabajador."*
> —*a ranch neighbor*

During the worst of the drought, we kept the weaker cows in a water lot by the public road that went through our ranch so that we could hand

The 50,000-gallon reservoir we built on top of a small mountain.

feed them chopped pear and meal. Although this saved our cows from any death loss, anyone traveling on the road saw only thin cows. Each time one neighbor who traveled through our ranch to his saw those weak cows and just knew we could not survive. After the rains came, this same neighbor stopped by one day to buy a

bull. In discussing the drought over coffee, he said to Annette and me, "I underestimated *lo terco y trabajador* (your stubbornness and willingness to work). Through this crisis, Chui Santos kept us abreast of the local gossip in town. When it looked as if we might not make it, the saying was *Como Padilla fregó el gringo.* (Padilla really thrashed the *gringo.*) After the rains came, it was *Que suerte tiene el gringo.* (The *gringo* is really lucky.) The truth is we were too young to appreciate how desperate our circumstances were and too dumb to quit. The Good Lord had to send 35 inches of rain to wash away our sins.

We built a 50,000-gallon steel reservoir on top of the small mountain behind the original well. Except for the caterpillar, which built the rugged, barely passable road up the mountain, we used no modern equipment. We had a 1948 Chevrolet truck with which the men hauled the sand, gravel, concrete, reinforcing iron and bolted steel reservoir. The concrete floor was mixed and poured by hand in one 20-hour day. One day a *cuarterón* (quarter black) from the village of Nacimiento who worked for us was driving the truck down the mountain when the brakes failed and he lunged out of control off the road, yet he and the truck survived somehow. Our foreman, Federico Arias, reported that the driver was as "white as a sheet."

• • •

Our ranch was naturally fenced on the east and west by the Santa Rosa Mountain Range. The deed read *de sierra a sierra* (from mountaintop to mountaintop.) Our east line was the first big mountain range rising above Mexico's desert floor, so clouds coming from the Gulf of Mexico collected there, condensed and rained in our valley. Around the Fourth of July 1967 while my sister Sally was visiting, I stepped onto the porch after lunch and could not believe my eyes as I saw long ribbons of rain marching down the mountainside and across the valley toward our house. It was hard to envision that the "ribbons" were rain streams. I called to Annette and Sally to come and see. I will never forget when that rain hit our house; it sounded like fifty people were throwing five-gallon buckets of water on the roof. Over the next several months, it rained 35 inches. We had springs running out of the hillsides, and for many months our main well was a river of water flowing ten feet wide.

Between my twenty-fifth and twenty-sixth birthdays, we had remodeled and expanded our house, laid sixteen miles of pipeline, built a reservoir on top of a mountain, divided the ranch into seven pastures, exported 200 steers, sold our third crop of registered Beefmaster bulls and survived a very serious business crisis. We grew up in a hurry and gained a lot of self-confidence in our ability to survive, cope, and improvise in any situation.

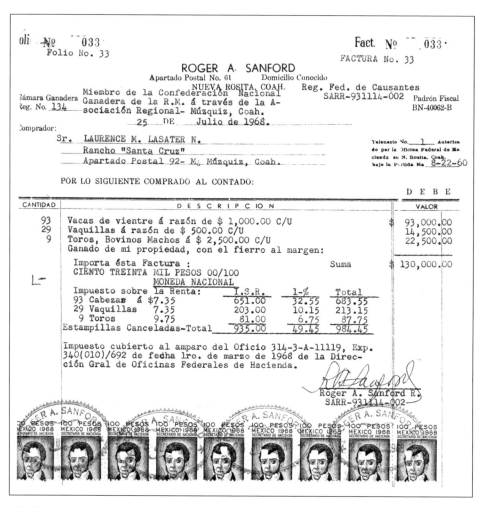

oli No 033
Folio No. 33

Fact. No 033.
FACTURA No. 33

ROGER A. SANFORD

Apartado Postal No. 61   Domicilio Conocido
NUEVA ROSITA, COAH.   Reg. Fed. de Causantes
Miembro de la Confederación Nacional   SARR-931114-002   Padrón Fiscal
Ganadera de la R.M. á través de la A-   BN-40062-B
Cámara Ganadera
Reg. No. 134   sociación Regional- Múzquiz, Coah.

25 DE Julio de 1968.

Comprador:

Sr. LAURENCE M. LASATER N.
     Rancho "Santa Cruz"
     Apartado Postal 92- M; Múzquiz, Coah.

Talonario No. 1   Autoriza
do por la Oficina Federal de Ha
cienda en N. Rosita, Coah.
bajo la Partida No 8-22-60

POR LO SIGUIENTE COMPRADO AL CONTADO:

D E B E

CANTIDAD	DESCRIPCION	VALOR
93	Vacas de vientre á razón de $ 1,000.00 C/U	$ 93,000.00
29	Vaquillas á razón de $ 500.00 C/U	14,500.00
9	Toros, Bovinos Machos á $ 2,500.00 C/U	22,500.00
	Ganado de mi propiedad, con el fierro al margen:	
	Importa ésta Factura : Suma	$ 130,000.00
	CIENTO TREINTA MIL PESOS 00/100	
	MONEDA NACIONAL	

Impuesto sobre la Renta: I.S.R.   1-%   Total
93 Cabezas   á $7.35   651.00   32.55   683.55
29 Vaquillas   7.35   203.00   10.15   213.15
 9 Toros   9.75   81.00   6.75   87.75
Estampillas Canceladas-Total 935.00   49.45   984.45

Impuesto cubierto al amparo del Oficio 314-3-A-11119, Exp.
340(010)/692 de fecha 1ro. de marzo de 1968 de la Direc-
ción Gral de Oficinas Federales de Hacienda.

Roger A. Sanford R.
SARR-931114-002

Bill of sale transferring our Beefmaster herd to Lorenzo, who was almost two months old.

CHAPTER 10

THE BIRTH OF OUR CHILDREN

"¡Nació Beefmaster!" (It's a boy!)
—Norberto de Luna

Each couple has different feelings and experiences while awaiting the arrival of their children. In our case, everything was magnified by the fact that we were living in a foreign country and counting on having two Mexican citizens to own our ranches. The whole subject of family size was much discussed on our ranch. We were trying to get our cowboys to have fewer children, and they were trying to get us to have more "because you are very rich." I provided birth control pills for every wife on the ranch, but they never understood to take them while in town on vacation, or the men would forget for several days to ask me for a refill. In 1967, every wife on the ranch, including Annette, was pregnant—so much for population control.

Our doctor, Norberto de Luna in Piedras Negras, delivered a whole generation of ranchers' children in Coahuila and Southwest Texas. Norberto had interned at Doctors' Hospital in Washington, D.C. and was a rancher. Due to medical terms being spoken in Spanish, Annette asked that I go with her to appointments. While discussing the baby's progress, Norberto and I also talked about the cattle business.

Norberto advised us that labor could not happen earlier than two weeks before the arrival date. Since Lorenzo was due in mid-June, 1968, we planned to go to town on June 1, and would have time to shop for baby items and have everything in order.

Norberto had assured us it would be a boy, so we decided to name him after me.

About five in the morning on May 31, Annette told me labor might be starting. I had not laid out work for the crew, and told her that before we left I needed to stake out a set of pens with our foreman. We left the ranch about 7:30 a.m. and drove the two hours to Múzquiz. Between our ranch and town, there were numerous large ranch gates to open, each wide enough for trucks, and Annette opened them all. At that time, we had a four-wheel-drive Jeep Commando and the trip from the ranch to Piedras Negras took four hours. We stopped in Múzquiz, got the mail and called Norberto before starting the remaining two-hour drive to his office.

About halfway to Piedras Negras, our Jeep broke down. We happened to be near La Questa, the only restaurant for many miles, in the middle of nowhere. I parked the Jeep beside the black bear the owners kept chained by the front door. Inside, I asked the two men who were having lunch to take us to Allende, the next town, where we could get a cab. Annette was sure her symptoms were a false alarm, so when we arrived in Piedras Negras, we went to Norberto's second-floor office instead of the hospital. He took one look at her and told us to go straight to the hospital. La Policlínica México, an old hospital, was absolutely first class with delicious food and superb medical attention.

Annette went directly to the delivery room and LAURENCE M. LASATER, JR., was born minutes later. The doctor came out of the delivery room, shook my hand, and said, "¡Nació Beefmaster!" (It's a Beefmaster!), meaning it's a boy. What a thrill, and he has been such a terrific son! A few minutes after the birth, the nurses brought our baby boy and Annette back to the room. In Mexico, the babies could stay in the mother's room and the parents brought all their own supplies to the hospital. Of course, we barely made it to the hospital, so instead of having two weeks to shop, we had brought nothing. We had to borrow from other mothers in the hospital.

There was a motel near the hospital where I was going to stay. The rooms were 100 pesos ($8.00 U.S.) a night. I asked the motel clerk what their weekly rate was. The clerk nodded, went behind the desk to the old-time adding machine with a handle on the side and punched in 100, cranked it seven times and told me the weekly rate was 700 pesos.

• • •

Shortly after Lorenzo's birth, I went to Múzquiz to register him at the county clerk's office. When a baby is registered in Mexico, the registration follows Roman law instead of English statute law. In some cases, including birth certificates, the Roman system is far superior. The parents are clearly identified by their complete names, including the mother's maiden name, as well as their address, occupation and status as to taxes. I am Laurence Matthews Lasater Casey. Lorenzo is Laurence Matthews Lasater Nixon, which defines him and differentiates him from me. There are also two witnesses, both likewise identified. In this case, it was Jesús Santos and Manuel Padilla.

In Mexico, I am known as Lorenzo, and our son is known as Lorencito or Lorencín. In our family and everywhere else, our son is known as Lorenzo. After his birth on May 31, a series of steps were taken. After his birth was recorded, the Padillas deeded the Santa Rosa Ranch, where our home was located on the ranch, to Lorenzo—probably in June 1968. At the same time, they issued a bill of sale for the cattle corresponding to that *fracción* (a piece of property reduced in size to comply with the land reform laws from the Mexican Revolution). The *factura* (bill of sale) had the income tax stamps affixed and noted the brand registered to our son. With this factura, Ed C. Lasater's brand, the L Bar, was registered to his great grandson in Múzquiz, Coahuila.

In July 1968, at two months of age, Lorenzo joined the Múzquiz Cattlemen's Association, and Chui's cousin, Jesús Santos Landois, signed his application. Joining was mandatory for obtaining export permits. In this same month, Roger Sanford issued a bill of sale, with the tax stamps affixed, to Lorenzo for our Beefmaster herd. The herd was valued at $10,400 and the taxes thereon were $79. Also, we obtained Lorenzo's tax identification number, still valid, which was necessary for him to conduct business in Mexico. Someone advised us that we needed to register his birth at the American Consulate in Monterrey, which we did in December of 1968. As you can see, Lorenzo was a busy little man during the first seven months of his life. It is complicated to maintain two citizenships and do business in two countries.

June 29, 1971

"¡Mujer!" (woman!)

—the attending nurse

When Annette learned that she was expecting our second baby in mid-1971, and Dr. de Luna assured us that it would be a boy, we thought we knew what to expect. Were we ever in for a surprise! Since Lorenzo's arrival had been so close, the doctor advised us to fly to Eagle Pass to stay well before the baby was due. Lorenzo was three, and Annette's mother had come to help with him. Life in motel rooms is very boring and very close, so we changed towns and motels from time to time. After about ten days, we moved to the Holiday Inn in Del Rio. When we had had enough of Del Rio, we moved back to the Holly Inn in Eagle Pass. We were in touch with Norberto by phone on a daily basis. The timing of delivery was complicated by his going to Mexico City to a funeral.

It was pouring rain on the evening of June 28, 1971, as Beulah, one of the greatest hurricanes, hit Southwest Texas and Northern Mexico. Norberto called earlier in the evening to say he had returned and for us to meet him at 7:30 a.m. the next morning at the hospital to induce labor. About midnight, Annette awakened me and said that labor had started. We crossed the international bridge to Piedras Negras and drove to La Clínica Especialistas.

As we registered, the new hospital was very quiet except for a family gathered around their dying mother in another part of the hospital. We were the only ones in the maternity ward. In Mexico, women in labor are more dramatic than in the U.S. Because Annette was quiet, the nurses were not overly concerned that labor was advanced. I was timing the contractions frequently and reporting to the nurses. Finally, when I adamantly told them to call the doctor, one of the nurses decided to check on Annette herself and shouted to the others, *"¡Ya! ¡Ya!"* (Now! now!) Norberto was summoned immediately from his home. When he arrived, he invited me into the delivery room, but I declined. I was sitting on a bench in the hallway by the nurse's station when a nurse came out of the delivery room carrying a newly-born baby. At that same moment, a gurney bearing the mother who had just died came by my bench, followed by her grieving relatives. I tried to be respectful of the deceased lady while jubilant over the birth of our child. A poet could have written of the new life and the just-ended life crossing simultaneously in front of me. As the nurse put the baby on the scale and started cleaning it, I asked, "What is it?" "*¡Mujer!*" (Woman!) For a moment I could not believe it. We had not even selected a girl's name. On the spot I named her ANNETTE ISABEL LASATER. At 4:00 a.m., on June 29, 1971, with the rain still pouring down, Annette had given birth to a healthy baby girl who has brought us joy ever since.

On July 5, 1971, we flew home in our own plane with two babies and Annette's mother aboard. We returned to an unfamiliar landscape as 25 inches of rain had created havoc in that mountainous country while we were gone. All fences, roads, pipelines and many landmarks were gone, and we were without a road to Múzquiz for nearly a year. Upon landing, we learned that the water had risen around the headquarters,

Lorenzo, Isabel and Annette.

located between two small creeks, forcing the men to get on the roof of the cowboy camp house.

We went through all the same legal procedures for Isabel as we had for Lorenzo. I registered her in Piedras Negras in the early days of July with Dr. de Luna and Dr. Barboza as witnesses. In 1972, we finished paying off the Padilla brothers; Rancho Santa Cruz, where our main water well was located, was transferred to Isabel on October 3. In January of 1973, Chui Santos registered her brand, the Open A Bar. On December 23, 1972, at six months of age, she received her tax identification number. We were fortunate, living in such isolated circumstances, to have two perfectly healthy children with no problems whatsoever.

The cover of *La Hacienda* magazine, featuring our replacement heifers at watering on Rancho Santa Cruz.

CHAPTER 11

THE SAN LORENZO PASTURE

"¡Es una maravilla!"

—the cowboy crew

J oining Rancho Santa Cruz on the north was a 3,500 hectare (8,750 acres) scenic piece of virgin country, unfenced and very wild, with no improvements and no permanent water. It was a natural addition to our ranch, as this piece of land could be added legally to Lorenzo's tract, Santa Rosa. The ranch belonged to a family named Hausman from Corpus Christi. We saw the brothers regularly at the Hotel Eagle in Eagle Pass, and they used our airstrip the few times they came to that ranch. Since they had no reason to own the property, the subject of our buying it came up early. I told them we could only buy it with complete owner financing. It would have to be put in Lorenzo's name for land tenure reasons, and since they had no legal status in Mexico, they could not take a lien on the property. The brothers asked if Dad would co-sign the note. I assured them he would not. It was all I could do to keep from laughing at the anguish caused by these negotiations, which went on for several months. In the end, they deeded the ranch to us and took an unsecured note, which we paid off on schedule. From these negotiations, I learned a valuable lesson about using owner financing to buy something someone wants or needs to sell. I have operated on the principle of using 100% owner financing during the ensuing forty years. That concept has enabled us to run significant numbers of cattle with very little capital.

Since the new pasture had no improvements, we had to figure out how to fence and water it at very little cost to be able to utilize it. In order to stock the San Lorenzo pasture, we had to build three or four miles of drift fence over rough terrain. In today's dollars, that fence would cost $40,000, which was much more than we paid for the ranch. I spent a lot of time studying the terrain on horseback and realized that it was possible to build a crooked fence running from flat rock to flat rock. I had angle iron posts made in town with notches for two barbed wires. The posts were driven into holes drilled by hand every 75–100 feet. The posts and wire had to be packed in on mules. We built a perfectly adequate, maintenance-free fence, using our ranch cowboys, at a cost for materials of around $2,000.

We needed a strong, durable truck to get over such rough terrain, so Duke put me in touch with a large Army surplus dealer in San Antonio where I bought a 6 x 6, two-and-a-half ton truck. I hired a man in Piedras Negras to drive it from San Antonio to Santa Cruz. When I asked if he could get it across the border, he assured me he could cross anything that fit the width of the international bridge. He crossed the truck in style, and said that in every town he passed through, people turned out *en masse* to see it. When he arrived at our house, he told Annette and me how much he enjoyed driving it. Everybody on the ranch loved the truck, which was equipped with a removable jet-engine container for hauling water. It was a sight to behold. Our airstrip ran in front of our house, and in the evening when the men came into camp from work, they drove up the strip with the truck running wide open and with everyone *gritando* (shouting) at the top of their lungs.

Since this virgin land was in the mountain foothills, another challenge was how to water the property and what class of cattle to run. Before buying it, I had decided to winter our weaned heifers there as they could travel farther and would consume fewer gallons of water. I had a picture that Dad had sent me of a rain trap built by the U.S. Department of Interior for elk on B.L.M. land. I expanded this concept to fit Coahuila standards, using a rolled steel roof over a 50,000-gallon steel reservoir. Somewhere I found a formula for calculating how many inches of rain generate how many gallons of water off so many square feet of surface. I figured our annual rainfall and "guesstimated" the water consumption over the winter for 180 heifer calves. As I recall, the design called for a 2,500-square-foot roof feeding into the reservoir. The roof would also shade the reservoir against evaporation and prevent any buildup of moss.

Riding horseback, our foreman, Federico Arias, and I found a perfect place for the rain trap right in the center of this unutilized country where two canyons came together in a fork. We had to get a bulldozer to build a road in order to haul the steel and concrete to the site, which, following the canyon terrain, was eight or nine miles from our headquarters.

I tried to explain to the crew why we were building a water reservoir in such an isolated upper canyon. But it wasn't until we had the road built and started hauling steel, concrete, metal roof and pipe for the frame to the site that the men realized this was serious. Although we had built various ranch improvements together, my guess is that they thought I had finally "gone over the edge." While building the rain trap, we moved our whole crew there. They camped with a chuckwagon until the

The rain trap we built in an upper canyon.

project was finished—digging a hole for the reservoir floor, laying reinforcing iron, pouring the concrete floor by hand, bolting the wall panels, building the pipe frame and bolting on the roof.

The men had been camped out for several weeks when one evening, just before dark, the truck came roaring up to the house with everyone *gritando*. We stepped outside to see what was happening, and the men excitedly reported *"¡Es una maravilla!"* (It's a miracle!). They said that just as they had bolted the last sheet of steel on the roof, it had started raining and beautiful, clean water cascaded into the reservoir, which was never empty again. The plan worked perfectly! We wintered our heifers there on meal and salt and bred them as yearlings, bringing them back to the main ranch around July 1 to allow the pasture to recover for the next group. The total improvements needed for the San Lorenzo pasture cost about a dollar an acre. It is rare that a really difficult challenge can be solved so successfully. This concept has been used, greatly expanded and improved upon by other neighbors in Coahuila. Of the many projects I have been part of, this is the one of which I am proudest.

Photo by Watt M. Casey, Jr.

Clemente Barrera—cowboy, camp cook, gardener and much loved by our family. He was a member of a large family, of which some six members worked for us.

CHAPTER 12

LA GENTE
(THE PEOPLE)

O ne person who enriched our lives was Mario Cortez, a skilled carpenter whom we met through Ruth Phillips. Mario was a talented man whose workshop was an abandoned garage with walls on three sides only. Our home today and those of our children, are full of beautiful mahogany furniture made by Mario.

Like anyone who has worked with large numbers of people, we had lots of varied experiences, some humorous and some not. In the environment where we operated, there was no social security or Medicaid, so we doctored the sick, buried the dead and ran errands for them in Mexico and the U.S. The men wore Levis, Lee Storm Rider winter jackets and Justin boots and carried Case knives.

Once we developed a nucleus of good people, they worked hard and were reliable. They enjoyed working for us because of the good cattle, interesting visitors, and varied routine. The employees would technically be called semi-literate; however, we did not pay any attention to that. When we were gone, I left detailed written instructions, and they gave me written reports of what they had done and kept the cattle inventory perfectly. I taught our *caporal* (foreman), Federico Arias, how to do artificial insemination (by taking reproductive tracts from the U.S. for him to practice on) and checked behind him when we started breeding heifers. After a day or two, he was better than I was. These were competent, hard-working people, trapped in a system where they could not significantly increase their productivity or earning power. One of the keys to the ranching business anywhere is having a *caporal* who is smart and a leader, working in concert with a dynamic boss who is entrepreneurial. During my 40-year career, I have been fortunate in having seven foremen who fit this description.

One of the main concerns and problems we had was providing medical care for the extended families. In Mexico, everything is difficult as it requires personal attention. If someone is sick or injured, the individual

Lorenzo on *Centavo* (the Penny), riding his brand-new saddle made by Adán Valdés.

has to be taken to town. To lessen this problem, we had an arrangement with Dr. Jesús Pader in Múzquiz to take care of any employee's family members who needed his attention and to bill us for it. I would then deduct the cost from the worker's check. He helped me solve the problem of "gold-bricking" by putting anyone not actually sick on a series of vitamin-B shots every two hours. The shots were painful, so most of the "patients" were "cured" within four hours.

The scourge of all ranchers was the local radio station XEPQ, known as "PQ" (pronounced peh-coo). Periodically throughout the day, the station would send messages to the various ranches, i.e., "Calling Rancho Santa Cruz to advise Manuel Arias that Aunt So-and-So is sick and your presence is needed in Múzquiz." At this point, everyone related to "auntie" would stop work and head to town. It was useless to explain that what she needed was for her menfolk to keep working to pay for her treatment. Of course, the trip provided a wonderful opportunity to get drunk and to visit the local houses of ill repute. We learned in a hurry to take these medical "bulletins" with a grain of salt.

In the beginning, we had constant problems with family members living on the ranch "needing" to go to town until we figured out the ultimate solution was to move all the women to town. Over time, we evolved to having a bachelor camp of five or six men at Santa Rosa, where we lived. Roberto Barrera and his wife, Verónica, lived at Santa Cruz, where our main well was located and where the *Camino Real* (Kings Highway or public road) passed. The cowboys in camp went to town for a

LA GENTE (THE PEOPLE)

week every two months. The men were happy with this program. Only once did we have a bad instance, when the whole crew quit in the middle of dipping several hundred cows.

The Death of Cruz Martinez

"Cruz está un poco malo."

—*Rosendo*

It is hard to believe that during the ten years we operated in Mexico, we had no injuries more serious than broken legs, in spite of tough horses, rough country, working with butane tanks, dynamite and old, worn-out equipment. One man, Cruz Martinez, died in bed at our camp, probably of a heart attack.

When Cruz died, I knew it was vital to get the coroner to the ranch before moving him. The roads were washed out, so I flew to town in our airplane, taking a friend of his named Rosendo to help me tell his wife. We landed at the Múzquiz airport and took a cab to Cruz's house. We both had on clean, white shirts, and as soon as we arrived at the door, the widow became hysterical. Since I did not know her, I thought Rosendo was going to tell her. Although his friend had been dead for several hours, his opening gambit was, *Cruz está un poco malo* (Cruz is a little sick). I realized he was unable to tell her, so I put my arms around her and told her. She started shrieking and screaming, bringing out the whole neighborhood. Rosendo and I beat a hasty retreat downtown in the cab to purchase a coffin to be delivered to the airport. We picked up the coroner at the courthouse and flew back to the ranch. After the coroner signed a certificate of natural death, we loaded Cruz into the plane. I needed our foreman to help me load him into the back seat and unload him at the airport. Since our airplane was a four-seater, Federico had to ride in the baggage compartment (which was open to the main cabin) and the coroner and I rode in front.

When we landed again at Múzquiz, the hearse with the new coffin was waiting at the airstrip, as were several taxicabs with numerous friends and relatives. Federico and I put Cruz in the coffin, closed the lid, slid the coffin into the hearse, then flew back to the ranch. Although Cruz seemed old to me at that time, he was probably only 50–55 years old, and his death was very unfortunate.

Federico Rábago and Clemente Barrera

"Las granizadas en seco."

—*Federico Rábago*

Two of our favorites of the many men we employed during our ten years in Mexico were older men, Federico Rábago and Clemente Barrera. They were probably 55–60 years old when they came to work for us. Both had worked for Bill Finan at the Valle Colombia, Clemente for many years.

At the time Federico Rábago asked me for a job on the street in Múzquiz, I did not need anyone, but liked him so much that I hired him

Vaccinating cattle with Federico Arias.

anyway. He told me that he preferred not to ride young horses, a comment I took to mean that he preferred to work on foot. Federico became a mainstay on the ranch. One day, while the crew was working on the San Lorenzo fence, I asked him why he had left the Valle Colombia. He told me it was the *granizadas en seco* (hailstorms out of a clear sky) when Bill Finan suddenly appeared on the scene. Needless to say, that statement became a byword around our house.

Little did I realize that day in Múzquiz that I was hiring a real, old-school cowboy. One day, we were cutting some three-year-old colts that had never been touched. They were kicking up clouds of dust as they ran in circles. Lorenzo, who was about three years old, was sitting on the cutting chute for safety, watching the spectacle as the colts raced around the pen. Without a word, Federico rolled out a loop, fore-footed a colt and had the horse down as slick as you could want. I asked him where he had learned that, and he said that he had ridden broncs every day for many years for Mr. George Meiers. During one of our visits, Federico told me that he liked working at Santa Cruz because the days passed quickly and the men never knew what the new day would bring. We maintained contact by letters until Federico died in 1996. The last year, in November, he wrote that he was visiting his daughter in Glen Rose, Texas, for Christmas just in case we were sending his annual Christmas check.

Although he was a good cowboy, Clemente Barrera worked for us as camp cook. He also helped Annette with the yard, took Lorenzo horseback riding and taught him all the cowboy ways. He was a much-loved part of our lives until his death in the late nineties. Each Christmas, we sent Clemente and Federico $100. Bill Finan told me that after Mexico devalued the peso, those checks turned into serious money for the men. They each would have someone write us beautifully-worded thank you letters. No one ever received more gracious letters than we did for those small checks.

In 1995, twenty-one years after we left Mexico, my friend James Sammons pulled into a service station in Múzquiz to buy gasoline. An elderly gentleman sweeping the floor saw James' Texas license plate and asked him if he knew Lorenzo (meaning me) and James replied, "Of course, we are good friends and live in the same neighborhood." I guess Clemente assumed that any nice-looking American cattleman was bound to know me. It is a small world. During our ten years in Mexico, I estimate that we employed more than 100 men. After we sold the ranch, I paid off the six remaining cowboys, who all thanked me for what I had taught them. It broke my heart to know that these deserving men would never again get jobs as good as the jobs they had had with us.

Photo by Watt M. Casey, Jr.

Duke Phillips was a fighter pilot during World War II and my aviation mentor.

CHAPTER 13

AVIATION

I have always loved flying and admired people who were pilots. Uncle Garland was a lifelong pilot, trained in the military, as is Garland, Jr., an outstanding marine and civilian pilot. Like most people, I thought airplanes were for rich people, not realizing that they are for people who need them. One of the many blessings of going to Mexico was becoming a pilot. In 1964, I did not dream I would fly 3,000 hours over nearly thirty years.

I have been privileged to fly with many excellent pilots. Bill Finan and Guillermo Osuna are exceptional pilots, who to their credit have flown for many years with no injuries. I made long trips with both of them. I also made long trips with J.D. Cage, who has an airline transport rating. On trips to Florida and Colorado, we flew through rain, snow, ice and fog in his pressurized Cessna 210. John Cargile of San Angelo, Texas, started late but became an excellent instrument-rated pilot. Annette and I flew with Ruth Phillips, who trained during World War II as a WASP at Avenger Field in Sweetwater, Texas. Duke Phillips was my mentor in aviation, and the finest pilot I have known, having been a fighter pilot in the China-Burma-India Theater in World War II as well as a flight instructor. From 1960, until we bought a plane in 1969, Annette and I flew many trips with Ruth or Duke in several different planes. I never had any illusions of being the caliber of pilot Duke was, but I credit his example and expertise for the safe and successful career I had.

• • •

"Mejor esperamos."

—Duke Phillips

In the winter of 1963–64, I had a great experience when I flew to Mexico City with Ruth and Duke in their Cessna Skylane. It was a momentous trip in my life for several reasons. We were going to meet with the lawyer who had obtained their immigrant passports, whom I also planned to use. Both during the flight and in Mexico City, we enjoyed the varied restaurants and nightlife and spent a lot of time conversing. During one conversation, Duke told me that I would surpass anything he had accomplished. It was a watershed moment in my life—that a man whose briefcase I could not carry would say such a thing is something I will never forget. The return trip from Mexico City to their Sierra Hermosa Ranch was eventful. South of Saltillo, we ran into a cold front, and because of icing, had to land on the highway. We could not get into the airport and did not have enough fuel to turn back. After pulling the plane off the road, Duke hired someone to guard it. As we stood by the roadside it was blowing sleet; Ruth was wearing a silk dress and Duke and I had on only city clothes. A cab, headed toward the city, stopped and the driver rolled down his window. Duke asked, "How much to Saltillo?" The cabbie quoted some outrageous figure, and Duke replied, "Mejor esperamos" (We'll wait). The cab driver, incredulous, drove off. Five minutes later a pickup stopped for us and delivered us to the Hotel Arizpe-Sáinz. When the weather lifted a day or two later, we took a cab back to their airplane with a five-gallon can of gasoline and completed our trip in good order.

• • •

"I'll never get in a plane with that crazy gringo."
—La Rana

One afternoon in early 1969, Duke dropped by our ranch and told us that now that we had a baby, we needed an airplane. He said that there was a Piper Cherokee 235 demonstrator for sale in San Antonio, and that Mr. Joe Finley, owner of the Carrizalejo Ranch, would finance it through a company he owned, Upper Valley Aviation in McAllen. Trusting Duke's advice and airplane knowledge, we became owners of N9336W in short order. Duke flew us to San Antonio where we took a test flight over the city. Annette and I would both get our pilot's licenses and would fly in it for ten years, selling it for the same price we paid, $16,000.

We had no hangar and had to build a barbed-wire pen beside our house to keep the horses from eating the plane. The day the plane was delivered to Santa Cruz is unforgettable. Two planes from McAllen circled for landing on our ranch airstrip, and after we signed the papers, the second plane left with both pilots. To buy a powerful airplane without ever having flown it is unorthodox to say the least. To take that plane to Mexico and hire a pilot to teach us to fly at the ranch was also unconventional. But that is how we did everything. On February 1, 1969, Gene Lux of McMichael Aviation in Del Rio came to stay with us at the ranch to teach us both to fly. I had my first lesson that day, and I will never forget the engine quitting while we were practicing basic maneuvers. Gene had forgotten to switch from the left- to the right-wing gas tank. The 235 is a powerful, complex plane with a constant-speed prop and approximately 130-knot cruising speed. It is unusual for a student to learn to fly in such a powerful plane rather than a trainer, much less on a very short, high-altitude strip. Since we could not use the plane unless we could fly from our ranch, it was the only feasible way. On February 20, I soloed, and the instructor signed me off to fly student solos from our ranch to Múzquiz and to Del Rio, Texas. Annette was learning at the same time, and she soloed in Del Rio sometime later. Lorenzo was a baby, so while one of us flew, the other took care of him. We flew continuously and studied the ground school material when not flying.

Since our cowboy crew had never seen flight school up close, there was very little work done at Santa Cruz while we were learning to fly. After I soloed, I practiced touch and goes, which were very ragged, on our strip. Annette was still flying with the instructor, shooting letter-perfect "touch and goes." During these same days, we had an electrician from Múzquiz, a man nicknamed *La Rana* (the toad), working on our light plant, who told everyone in town, "I'll fly with *la señora* anytime, but I'll never get in a plane with that crazy *gringo.*"

After a couple of months, I felt ready to take the written test. Our instructor suggested I take it in San Antonio in order to get my solo cross-country out of the way as well. I left Santa Cruz at daylight to fly student solo to Del Rio, where Gene signed me off for a solo cross-country and gave me detailed directions on how to go into San Antonio International

Airport. When I called San Antonio Approach, however, I was given a different set of instructions, and I got completely lost. Fortunately, the tower realized I was a student pilot, and talked me down from Randolph Air Force Base.

After the test, I flew home to Del Rio and Santa Cruz, where Annette and Lorenzo waited. Since we had no telephone or way to communicate at the ranch, it was important that I return home before dark. Only a young couple could have withstood this much stress. To top it off, I failed the test and had to repeat the process, passing on the second try. On July 12, 1969, I took my flight test at Uvalde and became a licensed pilot. When Annette followed suit several months later, the FAA examiner told me she was an excellent pilot.

New Pilots

We built a hangar near our house to replace the wire pen. Hangars are difficult and expensive to build. The structure has to be strong and wide enough to accommodate a plane's wingspan. One day while we were gone, the first one we built collapsed when struck by a violent windstorm. Its replacement also collapsed in another windstorm with the plane in it, but by a miracle, the hangar roof came to rest on the pitot tube, (which sticks up vertically out of the plane's cabin), doing no further damage to the plane. Rebuilding the hangar a third time was a charm, as there was no damage to the reconstructed building.

There is a saying in aviation that a new pilot with 100 hours thinks he knows how to fly, but has not yet been tested. This adage was especially true for us, as we were flying from our ranch to towns and other ranches where we had no navigational aids and no weather reports. The weather behind us could also change and close in minutes. When we left our ranch, whether going east or west, we had to cross mountains and fly into a different weather system.

Annette and I traded off flying solos to Múzquiz. When the fuel got low, we would radio Manuel Padilla's office for a pickup with a barrel of gasoline to come to the airstrip, where the gas, after being strained through a chamois cloth, would be pumped into the plane. The plane carried about five hours of fuel, enough to travel some 650 miles. The trip to Múzquiz was 30–40 minutes round-trip. One day, when fuel was getting low, I told Annette I would fill up on my flight to save her having to do so. When I arrived at the airport some thirty minutes later, a cloud front had moved in; I could not land and had to return to our ranch on empty tanks. I flew home, changing from gas tank to gas tank, and traveling from airstrip to airstrip, in case my fuel ran out. Fortunately, I made it with no problem. Before landing, I radioed Manuel's office to send a barrel of aviation fuel to Santa Cruz.

• • •

Cold Air Turbulence (CAT) is a common occurrence in the Santa Rosa Mountains. We had several encounters, always terrifying. On the first occasion, we had just taken off from our strip on a beautiful winter afternoon and were about five hundred feet off the ground when the plane seemed to go berserk. The CAT currents were so strong that the gyros were spinning and the airplane's controls would not respond. We were petrified. Finally, by flying straight and level in our valley, I was able to stabilize the airplane to bank a slow, wide right turn, and we landed safely. It was so fearsome that neither of us spoke a word. We put the plane in the hangar and went to bed exhausted.

Our ranch was due southwest of Del Rio. The mountains that constituted our east fence rose to 6,500 feet just northeast of our house. In flying to Del Rio, we always made a right turn, paralleling the mountains to climb to altitude before crossing them. One clear morning we took off with Lorenzo and Isabel, a tiny baby, strapped in the back seat. We had climbed to 7,500 feet and turned to a heading of 30 degrees to cross over when a tremendous CAT current hit our plane so hard it popped open the baggage door and threw our suitcases into the abyss. We flew all the way to Del Rio with the door flapping in the gale. In hindsight, this was a dangerous situation, as it could have ripped off and destabilized the plane.

• • •

Everyone's favorite story from Annette's book, *Two to Mexico,* recounts her retirement from aviation. The normal route to Sierra Hermosa from Santa Cruz was through the Alameda Canyon, which connected the valley of the Phillips' ranch with our valley. Many times there would be cloud cover in the canyon, and a pilot would have to try to find a route above or below the clouds to fly through the mountains and/or turn back. One afternoon as we were heading to the Phillips' ranch for a visit, Annette was flying, and I was holding Lorenzo. There was a cloud bank in the canyon, but plenty of daylight underneath, or so it seemed to me. After a few minutes flying around the south end of our valley, looking for an opening, with me "encouraging" her to fly through, Annette got mad, undid her seat belt, climbed from the pilot's seat into the back, leaving me to stabilize the plane while climbing into the pilot's seat. Needless to say, between the electrician's town-wide declarations that I was a crazy *gringo* pilot and that he would not fly with me, and the tales of this incident, my reputation has never recovered.

Our Long Cross-Country Trips

Our family made many long trips in our planes, including trips to Colorado Springs, Puerto Vallarta and Santa Barbara, California. Our first big trip was a vacation to Colorado Springs from Santa Cruz in May of 1970, ten months after I got my license. The first leg of the trip was from Santa Cruz to Del Rio where we cleared United States Customs. Pilots coming from Mexico always had to call 30–40 minutes out so an official could be at the airport. Planes were not cleared to land until the agent raised the Customs flag. In good weather, the flight to Colorado Springs was pleasant, with pretty, open country. All told, it was a four-hour trip, which we made many times.

Our second big trip, from our ranch to Puerto Vallarta in July of 1970, was more eventful. We left Santa Cruz with Annette, her mother, Ruth, Lorenzo and me on board. We had planned to make our stop in Torreón, Coahuila. It was broiling hot, and the *capitán* in charge of the airport decided to check our papers and "work us over." After the family had reboarded, he informed me that our papers were not in order and that we could not continue our flight. With the family being "fried" in the heat in the plane, he and I negotiated for two hours. He walked me through the cost and inconvenience of our returning to Piedras Negras to correct the "problem," establishing what this was going to cost me. I didn't say anything or show how angry I was. Finally, after failing to get me to do or say anything regrettable, he said, "You know, it is a shame that your family's vacation would be ruined. I am going to resolve the situation here." I replied, "Thank you, how much do I owe you?" Of course, the unspoken question was how much payoff I was expected to pay. "Not a thing," he replied, "it is just part of my job." We left Torreón, two to three hours late, vowing to never return. Our friend and bull customer, Bill George, Jr., who was a pilot also and lived in Torreón, told me that the *capitán* thought I was a fine fellow and that he hoped I would be back soon; we never returned. After the ordeal, we flew through the very rugged Sierra Madre Mountains and down the Pacific Coast to Puerto Vallarta, where we met Dixie and her family for a great time at the Posada Vallarta. The trip home also was very difficult, taking us through Guadalajara and Zacatecas, where the plane struggled to take off with a heavy load at such a high altitude.

Flying on Business

Although the family, numerous friends and relatives flew with me over the years, the majority of my flying was done solo on hundreds of business trips, something I thoroughly enjoyed. It was a great way to see the country as well as to get a fresh perspective while enjoying God's creation. There was satisfaction in planning and executing a successful trip as well as in what could be accomplished with such striking power. Flying is also a good time for thinking, and I made many important decisions during my more than 350 working days flying in planes.

There were 65-plus ranches we leased, owned or pastured cattle on in many locations around Texas and Mexico. We also had cattle on feed in the Texas Panhandle and Oklahoma, and managed cattle in Florida and California. Except for those places close to San Angelo, I flew to most of those sites over 200 miles away. I logged every flight, and those flight logs reveal an interesting history. Having a plane enabled me to make deals that otherwise I would not have made. Where one might hesitate to drive 200 miles to look at pasture or cattle, I could do it in a half-day. Each year that I owned a plane, I made at least one deal that paid the plane's annual cost. Shortly after getting my license in 1969, Eve Avery, Bill Finan's sister, asked me to help her with the management of her ranch, La Gorriona, which was just over the mountains to the west of Santa Cruz. The ranch was one of the best in which I have been involved, and this opportunity is typical of the chances that arise if one has mobility. The Beefmaster breed of cattle really got its momentum during the first thirty years of my career. As the principal market-maker for the breed, the opportunities for me were unlimited, and having a plane allowed me to take full advantage of them.

• • •

In 1974, while flying to Pecos, Texas, to visit the Anderson Ranch, I ran into bad weather. Before takeoff, I had called the weather bureau, and the report was 8,000-foot ceiling and 15 miles visibility. Flying west into desert country, one does not expect to encounter bad weather; however, the farther I went, the worse it became. In the meantime, Mike Harrison, owner of the Anderson Ranch, called Annette to tell her the weather was really bad in hopes of reaching me in time to turn back, but I could not be reached. By the time I got to Pyote, I was flying right down the Interstate, just above the cars, in ice, snow and fog. I had enough gas to fly to Arizona, if necessary, and I remember telling myself, "I am not going to die here." Upon arriving at Pecos, I circled the Holiday Inn pool and called the Unicom, asking where the airport was. The lady gave me the exact heading. I never saw the airport, but I dropped the plane on the first concrete I saw below the plane, which turned out to be an airport ramp. A Gulfstream on instruments behind me aborted landing and flew to California. After I had landed, I called the weather again and heard the same report I had received earlier. I learned never to trust a weather briefing, good or bad. My policy, thereafter, was to call someone at my destination to get an actual, real-life report, preferably from someone who understood aviation.

One of a Kind Flights

In 1982, Annette and I took Lorenzo to Colorado Springs to enroll at Fountain Valley School. It seemed as if 1955, when I had enrolled as a freshman, was only yesterday.

In March of 1985, Lorenzo and I flew to Falfurrias to celebrate Carolyn and Garland Lasater's Fiftieth Anniversary and the publication of Dale's book, *Falfurrias,* a biography of Ed C. Lasater, which won the Texas

State Historical Association award for the best book of the year. This was a great occasion and a chance for Lorenzo to catch up on 100 years of family history.

• • •

When my mother-in-law was diagnosed with terminal cancer, she had been in Tucson for chemotherapy treatments, but concluded there was nothing more medically that could be done. We always told her that when she felt ready, she was welcome to come be with us and that I would fly there to bring her to San Angelo. She called to ask me to come get her, and on Thursday, October 31, 1985, I picked her up in Tucson. We ran into bad weather at El Paso and had to spend the night, which turned out to be a bonus for both of us, as we had a nice dinner and a wonderful visit together.

• • •

In March 1993, I was invited to the King Ranch to advise them on the ranch's new Santa Cruz breed. I flew there and spent two interesting days with John Armstrong, Tío Kleberg, Tommy Haegelin, Scott Wright and other managers, traveling over roads and pastures that my father and grandfather had known. At one point, sitting behind John Armstrong, I wondered aloud how many times these same conversations had taken place on these same roads, and John said he was thinking the same thing.

• • •

An enjoyable flying experience occurred in July 1995 when Harry Holzer, head of the Israeli Government's Cattle Department, visited San Angelo. He was the guest of Angelo State's Department of Animal Science and was specifically interested in Beefmasters. After leaving San Angelo, he was to travel by car to College Station, a long trip, so I offered to show him some of our cattle and to fly him to Texas A&M. He was delighted, and after seeing a few cattle, we went to Mathis Field for our flight. It was a beautiful day, and Central Texas had never been prettier. After we leveled out for the two-hour flight, I invited Dr. Holzer to put his feet on the pedals and to hold his yoke to get the feel of flying. I have never seen anyone enjoy anything so much. When we landed at College Station, I did not have the heart to tell him to ease off on the controls. We managed to shoot a perfect landing with him "helping," and in spite of his 200-pound suitcase, which I had mistakenly loaded in the baggage compartment instead of the back seat. He told me at the terminal that it was the greatest day of his life, which made it all worthwhile for me.

• • •

"I'm going down."

—Laurie Lasater

On November 2, 1997, returning from Tom and Carol Cooper's Camaleche Ranch, north of El Paso, I had the experience every pilot dreads—an engine-out forced landing. About twenty-five miles west of San Angelo, I had let down to check on Ray Clark's ranch where we were pasturing cattle, when the engine threw a rod and the cabin filled with black, greasy smoke. The plane kept flying but the noise was terrible, and I was having trouble breathing. My main concern was fire. As student pilots learn, I set up a glide, but there was no place to land. I was following a farm-to-market road that went right over a small mountain. When I cranked the engine, it fired so I was able to clear the pass, flying under an electric line which crossed the highway, and shot a perfect landing on Farm to Market Highway 2469, just north of Mertzon. When the trouble started, I radioed San Angelo control tower to get me on radar. They asked if I wanted to declare an emergency, but I did not answer. I later found out that if you do, you pay all the expenses—fire department, sheriff's office, etc. My next transmission was, "I'm going down." Everyone at Mathis Field (my home field) could hear the whole episode. After I landed on the ground, I could not talk to the tower, but a passing plane relayed my message that I was fine and to please call Annette to get me. A pickup came by, and the driver helped me pull the plane off the highway and park it. In less than ten minutes, a deputy sheriff arrived and drove me into Mertzon, where we waited for Annette at an intersection. Since there was no damage, the FAA accepted my telephone report and issued no citations. The insurance paid $5,000 to retrieve the plane, but did not pay to rebuild the engine, due to its having 2,000 hours. If I had totaled the plane, however, they would have paid $76,000. The next day, John Cargile and I were going to Mertzon to look at a bull, Lasater 2516. He was shocked to see Frank Hinds loading my plane, with the wings removed, onto a trailer. For the first time, I realized how dangerous the terrain really was. Frank recommended that we rebuild the engine, which took over two months and cost $20,000. During that time, I had to decide whether or not to sell the plane. My uncle, Palo Casey, helped me make the decision when he said, "You have had a great career and maybe you should sell it." On February 2, 1998, I made my first flight since the forced landing. We decided to sell it, and for fun, I flew several times a week until it sold.

The Sale of N2235C

"A tailwind both ways."

—*Charles Probandt*

After I decided to sell the airplane, I invited our nephew, Colin Lasater, an airplane enthusiast, for an aviation week. I purchased his first log book and had an instructor check him out on the ground. Afterwards, he had several lessons and we enjoyed flying several trips together with Colin handling all the radio work and navigation.

In July, I listed the plane with a new Internet service. We received dozens of faxes of interest from the U.S. and abroad, and on July 16 sold it to Bob Strate, a restaurateur from East Texas, having had it on the market for less than two weeks. Bob came over with a pilot in a rented plane. It was love at first sight, and he was going to return home to bring his brother, an aircraft mechanic. I told him he could leave a down payment and take the plane home. Bob e-mailed me five or six years later to say that the plane had lived up to all expectations and that he would never need another one.

Owning and flying the Piper Dakota that Charles Probandt and I purchased in 1979—a sleek (140 knot) airplane—was one of the great events in my life. Its I.D. was N2335C. On our first trip, Charles coined the Isa Cattle Co. slogan—"a tailwind both ways." The joy of sharing a week of flying with Colin and the fun of selling the plane to an enthusiastic pilot took the sting out of ending one of the happiest chapters of my life.

Christmas 1971 at Rancho Santa Cruz.

CHAPTER 14

LIVING WITH
THE SYSTEM

Annette and I went to Mexico in 1964 with the idea of settling permanently, learning the language and getting permanent resident/investor papers. Like most people who settle outside their country of birth, we did not realize that we would always be foreigners, and that we would never become accustomed to some of our adopted country's ways, even though we found other aspects of life, such as friendship, loyalty and hospitality, more rewarding there. Annette believes that the Mexicans need the Americans for commercial reasons, and the Americans need the Mexicans to help preserve family values, and personal loyalty and friendships.

The first step in moving to another country is the passport to live there. In 1963, I had my first taste of "officialdom" when I got my first "Buyers Card" permitting me to buy steers in Mexico for export. From my perspective, this document, which involved several days' effort and a lot of paperwork, did not amount to much or give me any rights. In all cases involving the Mexican legal system, the cost and inconvenience far outweigh the value of the document in question. It took me many years to learn not to evaluate legal matters from a U.S. perspective.

Following what we had learned from Duke Phillips, we planned to get *Inmigrante* passports allowing us to invest in ranching in Mexico, and to own land after five years. As it turned out, in 1964 this type of passport was not being granted at all, and we did not make any headway until we were put in touch with a corporate law firm, Basham, Ringe, Correa, in Mexico City. They obtained resident/investor papers for us with no problem and little cost. Our bank in Eagle Pass mailed our checks to Múzquiz each month to meet the country's *Inmigrante* requirements. The only legal business status available to us was through having children born as Mexican citizens; parents and guardians of a Mexican citizen have legal rights to live there. In retrospect, if I were ever going to a foreign country to do business, I would partner only with a native, and make no effort to legalize myself. My ownership would be through Bearer Shares or notes payable in dollars in the U.S. Regardless of legal arrangements, a foreigner is always an outsider. We are a nation of laws and very few, if any, Third World countries are. Our broiling two-hour episode on the tarmac in Torreón epitomized the truly offensive aspect of the Mexican legal system.

Other aspects of the lifestyle there were very positive and we enjoyed them. Múzquiz, in 1964, was one step removed from the pioneer era of ranching and mining. Like the wool houses in West Texas, the general stores served as suppliers, lenders of operating expenses, and depositories for cash and valuables. Manuel Padilla's family operated Casa Padilla for many years, and the family was justly esteemed in the neighborhood. We bought our feed, mineral, aviation gas and vet supplies there. Manuel's daughter, Sandra, handled our bill-of-sale books, got our vehicle licenses, driver's licenses and did many other chores for a monthly stipend. We bought all our ranch groceries from Almacenes Múzquiz. They were shipped monthly on a cattle truck, along with feed, mineral, gasoline and diesel in barrels, barbed wire, posts, etc. We had a bulk butane tank on the ranch, which was refilled by a tank truck from town; gradually, we converted all vehicles and pumps to burn butane. When we started dealing with Almacenes, an old-time wholesale grocer-selling groceries and supplies in bulk—we had a big camp of men working and were buying a lot of supplies. For many months, we did not receive a bill. I finally asked, and was given a foot-tall stack of receipts. When I asked why we had not been billed earlier, I was told, in essence, that it was bad manners to submit a bill to someone who might not be ready to pay. They were accustomed to waiting for payment of their bill until the customers' calves were sold.

Politics can also be funny. One day while I was running errands, Manuel Padilla was driving me around town so that we could visit. We went to the hardware store, Ferretería Hernández, where we each made various purchases and were standing at the counter when the owner, our mutual friend Guillermo Hernández, gave me my bill marked "with your discount," and gave Manuel his bill without. Manuel, a lifelong resident and at that time mayor, asked why he did not get a discount. Guillermo replied, "You never asked."

Politics Mexico Style

"Ganamos en votos."
—*Manuel Padilla*

At that time, Mexico was a one-party country, with the PRI being the official party. Manuel Padilla served one term as *presidente municipal* (mayor) of the county of Múzquiz. The day after the election, I was in his office while he was taking congratulatory phone calls. He told one caller, *"Ganamos en votos"* (We won on votes). Although the outcome was a foregone conclusion, he had actually received the votes to win as opposed to just winning. It was an interesting civics lesson for a U.S. citizen.

In certain cases, politics were taken very seriously. Shortly after Manuel became *presidente,* he took off in his airplane from the Múzquiz airport, and just as he became airborne, his engine failed and he crashed at the end of the runway. When the engine was being repaired, they found that it failed because sugar had been added to the fuel tank. When the mystery of who put sugar in the tank was solved, we learned that another candidate for mayor had done so after losing the election.

Los Bancos

I could write a book about my banking experiences in Mexico. At that time, it was not legal to own gold in the U.S., but it was readily available in Mexico at $35 an ounce. I knew it was under-priced and could have bought some each trip to town, leaving it in the bank vault. For some reason, thinking that I could not take it to the U.S. prevented me from buying, even though I could have stored it permanently in the bank vault. As I look back, I realize that was a financial mistake.

As hard as it is to believe now, the peso was a hard currency in 1964, along with the dollar and the German mark. The exchange rate was 12½:1, making the peso worth eight U.S. cents. We had a bank account in Eagle Pass and moved money back and forth. Peso checks on Mexican banks were accepted anywhere in Texas, no questions asked. Because the banks in Mexico did not want to credit deposits at the full legal exchange, our account at the bank could not balance. We battled with the bank over that as well as their taking money out of our accounts without authorization. The Banco de Londres did not have computers at that time and could not balance our monthly statements. The bank finally gave up, told us to figure our own balances and take the figures to them. When I went to town, one of my stops was at that bank to give them the correct balance and to bum a cigarette off Antonio Zertuche, the bank manager.

My first bank loan was 300,000 pesos ($24,000 U.S.) for operating expenses. The interest was one percent per month with the interest deducted in advance. I gave Mr. Zertuche my financial statement, showing the ranch at cost. He said that I did not have enough net worth for the loan. I asked him to let me have the loan application back, returned to the ranch, and Annette typed a new one showing fair market value on the land. After glancing at it, he said that was fine and made the loan. I learned a valuable lesson about banking that day, namely, that as long as one is performing, the banks will accept one's values.

With Guillermo Osuna's help, we obtained a large operating loan at the Banco de Comercio. When we sold the ranch, that loan was paid off, leaving a small bank balance of approximately $320.00 U.S. Each month, after receiving the bank statement, I would write a check to close the account. But the check would bounce, due to recent charges the bank had made to our account, i.e., service charges, phone calls, etc. After several months, I asked Sandra Padilla to go to the bank to get the rest of the money. She phoned back that the money was gone and that my account had been closed.

• • •

Every year around Christmas was a favorite time for shakedowns by *Los Federales* (federal officials). One year they came to Múzquiz to catch a known smuggler in our area who flew the same type of plane as ours. I normally did not go to town within two weeks of the holidays, but for some reason, I broke my rule that year and the officials grabbed me, claiming my papers were not in order. It was late afternoon, and I convinced them that Annette, who had no telephone at the ranch, would be very worried if I did not return home by dark. They let me go with the understanding that I would be back at nine the next morning. The next day Annette, Lorenzo and I landed right on time. They wanted 50,000 pesos ($4,000 U.S.) to correct my "problem." I refused. They impounded the plane and loaded me into their van. After I left, Annette and Lorenzo took a cab to the Santos' home, where Annette phoned our Mexico City lawyers who began applying pressure from there. I was taken to a back room behind the 130-kilometer Customs checkpoint at Rosita, where I was informed that I would be taken to jail in Monterrey. I was in no mood to negotiate, and told them that suited me fine. In the meantime, Chui negotiated a deal with them and borrowed 4,000 pesos ($320 U.S.) at a meat market in a nearby town to bail me out. In the ensuing hours, the agents received instructions from Mexico City to turn me loose immediately. Thanks to the Santos' help and hospitality, everything ended well—the officials accepted the 4,000 pesos and released me.

On a lighter note, during another Christmas season, a group of Customs officials drove to our house at the ranch. I invited them in, and over coffee, they asked if the Jensen jack on our main well was legal. I replied, "Of course not. As you well know, everything here was smuggled in through your port on your shift. Is Christmas coming?" They grinned sheepishly, and I gave them a small check and sent them on their way.

• • •

Our one encounter with big-time corruption came in relation to our land ownership. The Mexican Constitution, written after their Revolution, provides for land reform. Fifty years later, it was evident that the land distribution rhetoric needed to be reversed in the interest of economic stability. New laws were passed, whereby *Pequeñas Propiedades* (legally owned properties) were not subject to expropriation and would receive *Certificados de Inafectabilidad* (Certificates of Inaffectability). In reality, these certificates were authorized by the government in power whose officials sold them rather than issuing them. A friend introduced me to the government "bag-man" in Eagle Pass, and I wrote him a check for 150,000 pesos on two ranches totaling 12,500 *hectares* ($12,000 U.S. on 31,500 acres). In due course, Rancho Santa Rosa, belonging to

Laurence Matthews Lasater Nixon, and Rancho Santa Cruz, belonging to Annette Isabel Lasater Nixon, were announced on the front page of Mexico's official register as being exempt from expropriation, which ultimately enabled us to sell the ranches.

The consequence of corruption on this scale is tragic for Mexico's poor. Those hundreds of millions of dollars were taken out of the national capital and have not been available for job creation. No taxes were paid on this money, and those who participated in this corruption lived in mansions and owned homes in the world's favorite watering holes. Now, thirty-five years later, after discovering some of the world's richest oil and gas reserves, Mexico is worse off economically than it was in 1970, with its problems now compounded by the growing menace of the drug cartels. In retrospect, I would have enjoyed Mexico more had I not battled against the minor irritants that could not be changed. Now, when a buyer from Mexico calls, I mentally shift gears. They are delightful, honest people whom we enjoy immensely. When they ask for something extra, I just say, *"No hay problema"* (Not a problem).

CHAPTER 15

THE KICKAPOO WARS

*"That gringo at Santa Cruz is very dangerous.
He's ready to die."*

—the Kickapoo Indians

The Kickapoo Indians (Kickapu) were given land and Mexican citizenship in the nineteenth century by President Benito Juárez in return for their fighting the Apaches, who were marauding in the Coahuila area at that time. As dual citizens, the Kickapoo were allowed to come and go freely across the border and to take weapons into Mexico. No one else was allowed to enter Mexico with weapons.

During our years at Santa Cruz, we had a running battle with the Kickapoo. Some, including the chief's son, asked permission to hunt or cut *garrochas* (yucca stalks) for their houses, but some did not. I operated under the American idea that trespassers should be confronted. We had numerous encounters over the years. One of the most interesting occurred in the high virgin country west of our house where I had a crew building a fence. I was there on foot when I saw a horseman flash by in the brush. I ran up and intercepted three Indians with pack horses heading for the backcountry for some serious deer hunting. Their horses were wearing moccasins on their hooves so as not to leave hoof prints. They gathered around me in a semi-circle and tried to stare me down. Knowing they would not shoot an unarmed man, I stood my ground. Finally, the leader said in part Kickapoo and part Spanish, "We have come a long way, and our horses are tired. When the sun is there (gesturing to an imaginary 3:00 p.m.), we will leave." I said that would be fine, knowing they had probably left their Rancherías village at 3:00 a.m., had traveled the public road while everyone was asleep and had not planned on meeting *gringos* in the high country.

Various ranches had experienced problems with the Indians over the years. Max Michaelis had had run-ins with them, and several years earlier Max had confronted the chief on his ranch and told him that they could not cut fences or hunt, and that if they did touch the fence, he would have to shoot them. At that challenge, the chief smiled, reached out and grabbed the wire. Duke Phillips had had local police arrive at his ranch to arrest several trespassing Indians; the police asked to be driven to where they thought the Indians were hunting. When they arrived, no one could be seen, but the leader, hidden behind the brush, called out for the policemen to drop their guns and strip naked and for Duke to sit to the side as he was not part of the standoff. After the police dropped their guns and stripped, Duke was told to drive back to his ranch headquarters and the policemen were left to walk.

• • •

> "Tu comoquiera vas a morir."
> —Laurie Lasater

In 1969 there was a big change in the tribe. The chief, Papikuano, died and the entire Kickapoo nation assembled for the coronation of a new chief. Their religion is based on deer for ceremonial sacrifices, so they were running wild, hunting over the whole territory. Although the Indians never hurt anyone, many of the Mexicans were terrified of them.

Our next encounter with the Kickapoo happened one foggy, drizzly, spring morning in 1969, when I stepped out of the house to get some wood for the fireplace and heard semi-automatic rifles firing in the pasture. I had a horse saddled behind the house, so I rode to camp and told the men to take the 6 x 6 truck to go one way and I would go another. I could tell by the looks on their faces that they were not going to do much. From the house I made a circle to the west and south, and found the Indians' two pickups. I dismounted and pulled the distributor from one pickup, and was ready to disarm the second when the Indians arrived, yelling and pointing their rifles at me. I remounted, told them to get off the ranch, and headed back through the brush to the house. They followed by the road in the second pickup.

I rode to the house, tied my horse, went inside to get my sixteen-gauge, double-barreled shotgun, and went out the front door just as they arrived. Annette, holding Lorenzo, stood right behind me on the porch. The pickup stopped at the end of the walk to our house with rifles sticking out of all windows and the camper on back. I said in Spanish, *"No se bajan."* (Don't get out.) To challenge me, one Indian opened the right front door and stuck out a foot. I fired one barrel in

Photo by Watt M. Casey, Jr.
The Kickapoo Indian Reservation near Santa Cruz.

front of him, a sensational effect at close range. They all bailed out and faced us in a semi-circle, armed with M-1s and 30-30s. The leader was right in front of me. I had my shotgun aimed at his belt buckle and said, *"Tu comoquiera vas a morir"* (You're going to die, regardless). After a long pause, he said in effect, "Just show us where you threw the distributor and we'll be on our way." I replied, "You get away from the house and I will go back to show you where it is."

They pulled forward about one hundred yards. I remounted, and they followed me back to where we first met. I retrieved the distributor cap and wires in the brush and told them to get off the ranch. Of course, they screamed, hollered and pointed their rifles as they tried to surround me, but I knew this incident was finished. I returned to the house, and we flew into town in below-minimum flying weather to report the incident. The authorities arrested eleven of them. I never saw the cowboys again that day.

We thought the matter was over, but that was just the first chapter. The Indians went back to their village and shot a hole with a rifle in the fender of the pickup. Pictures came out in the newspapers in Monterrey and Mexico City showing a Kickapoo pointing at the hole in his pickup inflicted by a *"gringo* landlord" who had attacked them on a public road.

• • •

"Señor, I can't—your wife has the keys."

—the driver

Several weeks later, I went to Del Rio, Texas, and when I returned to the ranch and taxied into the hangar, a pickup pulled alongside the plane. It was a U.S. pickup with two civilians and one quasi-policeman, wearing part of a uniform and carrying a pistol, who said he had a warrant for my arrest. I asked who had signed it, and the policeman named someone. I said, "He's a friend of mine and would not have signed it," at which point, they grabbed me and threw me into the pickup. The main man (local cop) had me sitting on top of him with his arms locked around me. I was terrified as I thought I was being kidnapped. In my fear and rage, I was like a wild animal in strength. I kicked off a stereo tape deck which was mounted under the dash, ripped the liner from the cab's ceiling, and jerked the steering wheel, bending it to the right. I convinced them to drive to Annette, who with Lorenzo and the maid, was watching beside our house, so that I could tell her I was leaving. As the pickup rolled to a stop to speak to Annette, she opened the door, reached in and pulled the keys out of the ignition before the driver could grasp what had happened. At the same time, I hit the main man in the eye as hard as I could with my elbow, incapacitating him, and as the pickup slowed, the two "picnickers" along for the ride, bailed out, leaving me with the cop. I was still so mad that I was shaking and picked up two big rocks, intending to bash their brains and then decided just to break the windows. It never occurred to me that the *jefe* could pull his gun. As I was screaming at them to get off the ranch, the driver said, *"Señor,* I can't—your wife has the keys." I finally calmed down, Annette gave them the keys and they left, limping their way to town. If they had not slowed the pickup for me to speak to Annette, they would have driven me to Múzuiz to arrest me.

I was concerned about the legal ramifications from this altercation, so we flew to Sabinas and went to the Spence home. Bob and Elizabeth got a big kick out of our story and called a local judge, Edmundo Faz Felán, to come to their house. I told the judge our story, and he assured me that the only crime committed was the police letting me get away. The judge made arrangements for me to give a deposition. The next morning we drove to the *Presidencía Municipal* (county courthouse) in Múzquiz and received a hero's welcome. The damaged pickup was parked in front of the courthouse, and the officer I had elbowed, his whole head swollen and a bandage over his eye, was waiting to shake hands. He asked me to help pay to repair the pickup, which I agreed to do. I gave my deposition, and we returned to the ranch.

I received interesting feedback from the incident. Mr. Bridges, an old-time manager of one of the local ranches, told me that the Indians had said I was very dangerous because I was "ready to die." They loved the fact that I was not afraid to confront them. Chui told me that my new nickname in town was *Búfalo Bill* (Buffalo Bill). He advised me that the next time the Kickapoo came to get under the bed and stay there until they left.

• • •

Again, we thought the matter was over. We did not know that it had moved into the political realm and that they now had something to play with. Our house, camp and airport were in a fenced pasture trap, with a private road coming in the south end and going out the north. After the original incident, we locked both gates so that no one could drive to our house uninvited. Several weeks later, while we were sitting in our living room in the late afternoon, we saw three men walking up the airstrip. They came to the house ostensibly on official business and took our Mexican passports, but actually for the purpose of harassing us and extorting a little money. One of the men made the mistake of forgetting his camera, so this gave our friend Chui something to bargain with; he retrieved our papers the next day.

The next week, I went to town to run errands. There was a parade, and I made the mistake of going to the *Presidencía* to get the mail. The state police chief was there for the festivities and, upon seeing me, summoned me to appear at his office in Saltillo for questioning. He told someone that I would be like a "deerskin glove" when he finished with me. This was disturbing, so I asked Guillermo Osuna for help. He made an appointment with the state attorney general and rallied the ranching community to call on our behalf. Duke Phillips was also being "fined" for not fighting fires started by lightning on top of the mountains at Sierra Hermosa. Duke flew Guillermo, Chui and me to Saltillo where we met with the attorney general, a friend of Mr. Sanford. Thanks to Guillermo and other friends, the state police chief and all officials down the line were ordered to cease and desist. We spent the night in Saltillo, and I ended up having a good trip. Annette and I learned from this experience that we could never feel secure, even in our own home, and that we would always be dependent on our friends in times of crises. That is true of everyone in Mexico, not just foreigners, and helps to explain the importance the Mexicans place on friendship and loyalty.

Some of the Kickapoo thought of us as friends, and a representative of the tribe came to our house to give Annette and me moccasins they had made for us. We were invited to attend their private ceremonies, but we were afraid to go by ourselves at night. We were very fortunate that nothing bad happened. I had had military training, as had several of the younger Indians, so we all could handle weapons. Luckily, they respected the fact that I was not afraid of them, and I give them credit for recognizing that the situation at our house had escalated out of hand. For my part, I never carry a gun. I learned then, that in certain circumstances, I would gladly shoot someone. I will always admire Annette for keeping her cool throughout all these very difficult incidents. In recent years, the tribe has opened a casino at Eagle Pass, Texas, and hopefully, after many years of terrible poverty, they are prospering. Like most Indians, they are admirable people whose dealings with the "white man" have been disastrous.

CHAPTER 16

VISITORS
TO THE RANCH

"It has been the greatest week of my life."
—Tom Lasater

I n addition to the interesting and varied social life we enjoyed in the Múzquiz area, numerous visitors to the ranch added greatly to our lives. Many people are fascinated by the ranching business, and ranching in Mexico is a great drawing card. Dick Springs was a frequent visitor and an investor in the ranch. Because he also tutored the Phillips' children in the Calvert School correspondence curriculum, he spent a good amount of time in Coahuila. My brother Dale tutored there one summer, so spent time with us on our ranch.

Lorenzo in front of our house at Santa Cruz.

In addition to our parents, we had frequent reunions in Mexico and Texas with Annette's sister Dixie and nieces Holly, Laura and Nola. They followed our ranching career from day one. It was my privilege to teach the three girls to dive, ride and drive. Everyone should be as fortunate as I was to enjoy such adoring nieces. As far as horseback riding, our modus operandi was to leave the house with one niece and me on horseback and everyone else following in the pickup. When niece number one had had enough, niece number two mounted up, and so on. As to driving, I remember teaching Holly, my first student. We had a one-ton Ford pickup with a standard

transmission, and once I got her checked out, she was turned loose on the ranch airstrip in front of our house to drive to her heart's content.

In addition to Dick Springs, other Princeton friends were visitors in Mexico: Bill Conner, Philip and Maurie Cannon, and Tom and Jan Newsome. Tom and Jan visited the ranch before the light plant was running, and although

With Grandmother Casey, Isabel, Annette and Lorenzo.

the guest room was wired for electricity, there was none. They reported that it was not until the second night that they learned to take the Aladdin lamp with them to the bathroom at night. After their visit and seeing how we lived, they wrote that when their family was in a crisis, they asked themselves, "What would the Lasaters do?" All of these friends became stockholders of Isa Cattle Co., Inc.

When Bill Conner came with his nieces, we were re-modeling the house and the walls were knocked out. It was extremely hot with no electricity for fans or air-conditioning. Annette kept the doors to our two butane refrigerators taped shut so that they could make enough trays of ice every twenty-four hours. Bill suffered terribly with the heat. One night, Dixie, who also was visiting with her daughters, heard a noise in the kitchen, and upon investigating, found Bill untaping the refrigerator door trying to get an ice cube. Everyone enjoyed these visits and the visitors seemed to relish the adventure.

One day I had sent the pickup to town, and by an incredible coincidence, a friend from Fountain Valley School who was on his honeymoon was looking for me in Múzquiz, when someone pointed out our pickup to him. He and his new bride caught a ride back to the ranch. It was dark when I saw the pickup returning in misting rain, and as I came out our front door, I heard the unforgettable voice of my school friend, Rich Cross, a rancher from Douglas, Wyoming.

In the beginning years, we headquartered in Eagle Pass and had the opportunity of becoming close friends with Julie and J.D. Cage. Julie and J.D. flew to Santa Cruz to visit us one weekend, and J.D. was interested to see that, as general partner in a limited partnership, I was boss and that it was in effect my ranch. As a result of seeing those possibilities, they bought, with investor capital, a ranch in Costa Rica where they lived for several years.

Grandmother Casey, to celebrate her 85th birthday in 1971, chartered a plane from Del Rio and came to Santa Cruz with Uncle Palo for lunch and the day, and to see her great-grandson, Lorenzo, and her newly-born great-granddaughter, Isabel. From there, they went to Sierra Hermosa to spend the night with the Phillips family. Grandmother and that adventure will always stand in my mind as a hallmark of the pioneer spirit.

In November 1970, Annette, Lorenzo and I met Dad at San Antonio International Airport and flew him in our plane to Santa Cruz. He made the trip, which must have been hard for him, without complaint. We had invited him because we wanted him to see everything while the conditions at Santa Cruz were ideal—perfect fall weather, our cattle in good shape, a beautiful home and a wonderful grandson. During his trip we visited on consecutive days the

Annette and Dad during his visit to Santa Cruz.

Phillips, Finan and Osuna ranches, each unique in its own way. I will never forget Dad standing looking out our picture windows at the breath-taking panorama, holding his scotch and water, with tears in his eyes. No words were needed. When I took him back to San Antonio, Dad said that it had been the greatest week of his life.

We treasure the memory of the dozens of visitors who enriched our lives. All seemed to enjoy being there as much as we enjoyed having them, and all were generous in their compliments on our home, ranch and cattle.

CHAPTER 17

COSTA RICA

We became acquainted with and enjoyed Costa Rica while Annette's sister, Dixie, and family lived in the capital, San José, from 1967 to 1974. Our first holiday trip to Costa Rica was exciting. We enjoyed the holidays with Dixie's family before meeting my family in Mexico City for Dale and Janine's wedding on December 30, 1967. All went well until we returned to Múzquiz. In our mailbox was a notice that I was being mobilized for active military duty and was to report the next day to the draft board in Uvalde, Texas. We left the ranch early the next morning to drive in misting rain. Since it is a ranching community, the board understood the complications and responsibility of my having just made a down payment on a ranch and ruled that I was exempt from being activated.

In 1968, we were to spend Christmas holidays in Costa Rica, and looked forward to showing off Lorenzo, then six months old. We drove to Saltillo and caught the train to Mexico City to spend a day before flying to San José. When we left the ranch, we could not have imagined the immigration nightmare we were to face—something out of a suspense movie in which the authorities "find a defect" in the paperwork that cannot be resolved without divine intervention, just to detain the traveler. The morning we were to fly to Costa Rica, we arrived early at Mexico City International Airport to proceed through the international departure lounge. We realized there was a problem as one official conferred with another, then went to another room to confer with others. Lorenzo was both a Mexican citizen and a U.S. citizen by birth, and although we were living legally in Mexico and were traveling from our home there, we had decided for reasons of expediency to have Lorenzo travel on his mother's passport as a U.S. citizen. When we presented our U.S. passports, however,

Annette's stated that the baby had been born in Mexico. As far as the officials were concerned, Lorenzo was a citizen of Mexico and could not travel out of the country without a Mexican passport—or Annette had to have a special permit to carry him in her arms. To quote Shakespeare, we were "hoist on our own petard." Since Lorenzo was a Mexican citizen and landowner, the officials refused to let us leave Mexico, and we missed our flight. We were devastated as there was not another flight until the next day. Because of the holidays, we also learned that all the trains were full, so we could not leave Mexico City. When we called our hotel, it was already fully booked for the night. We somehow convinced the manager to give us a room.

As soon as we could, we contacted our law firm, Basham, Ringe & Correa. They sent one of their lawyers to take us in a taxi to the federal office buildings to try to get the permit "to carry Lorenzo." This was precarious as all the government offices were closing that afternoon until January 6, so we had very little time. We taxied from one building to another, to another, to convince some official to issue a permit. At each office we were told that that government branch did not do them there, but another office (in another building) did. After hours and several different offices later, the law firm was able to get a signed permit in hand. The Basham, Ringe and Correa firm is probably the only reason we are not still in that city.

• • •

Since Costa Rica is a great market for Beefmasters, and since my then brother-in-law was ranching and well-acquainted in the cattle business there, he and I made various interesting trips to see cattle and ranches. He had decided to buy fifty Lasater Beefmaster yearling bulls in September 1968, delivered to Tapachula, Guatemala. These bulls were on the road seventeen days, crossing eight countries on trucks of three nationalities. Only Beefmasters could have survived such a trip and only a man in his twenties could have tolerated such risks. There were no cell phones, faxes or e-mails, and since we had no phone at the ranch, we could be reached only by letter or telegram to our postal box.

The credit for the success of the shipment has to go to the truckers. Gaddy Truck Line hauled the bulls from Matheson, Colorado, to Eagle

Pass, Texas. Tom González, the customs broker, made the arrangements for the bulls to traverse Mexico "in bond." Ricardo Enríquez used three bobtail trucks to haul thirty bulls, plus we used Bill Finan's tractor-trailer to haul twenty head. The Mexican trucks met the Costa Rican trucks at Tapachula on the Guatemalan border, where they actually backed up to each other to transfer the bulls. Even now it is hard to conceive the coordinating and timing on that shipment and transfer without communications. Since it is nearly 3,000 miles from Matheson to Tapachula, the bulls and the drivers had to be inspected at road stops throughout Mexico and had to stop to rest several times.

• • •

In 1970, I made a contract with my brother-in-law to ship some 36 registered Beefmaster cows and four bulls from the Miller Ranch at Falfurrias, Texas. This shipment was made by air, and turned out to be an even bigger adventure than the shipments by land across Mexico. In this case, I was dealing with two of the most unusual personalities I have encountered in business—Laurie Miller (L.D. Miller, Jr., the breeder) and the customs broker in Houston, whom I will call Mr. Guerra. Laurie Miller would have loved e-mail. Since we had no communications, he used to send me two or three business letters per day, each consisting of one line such as "10 bales of hay @ $2.00," or "the vet says we will have to T.B. test the cows." Each time I went to the post office in Múquiz, there would be ten or fifteen letters on the Miller Ranch stationery waiting for me.

In Mr. Guerra's case, I would phone him from the Santos home in Múzquiz, and he would give me a long list of shipping requirements, none of which I had any way of fulfilling. My stock answer was, "just forge the papers" or "just pay somebody off," to which he would reply with a hysterical shriek, "Mr. Lasater ..." Each time we talked, the level of hysteria rose to a higher pitch. I heard that he had a nervous breakdown some time later. I hope it was not due to this shipment.

All the comedy with Laurie Miller and Mr. Guerra was just a prelude to the shipment itself. When the cattle were loaded onto the airplane, they were evidently misloaded as to weight and balance. On takeoff, the plane barely got off the ground at Houston, then fell back onto the runway—tail first—damaging the plane and injuring some of the cattle.

The damages were covered by insurance, and some of the cattle finally made it to Costa Rica, although I cannot imagine how.

While ranching in Costa Rice from 1968 until 1977, J.D. Cage shipped a large number of Beefmaster bulls, many of Uncle Palo's breeding, to his ranch at Liberia, Guanacaste, using Ricardo Enríquez' bobtail trucks and Bill Finan's tractor-trailer. To make sure the shipment went smoothly, Ricardo went with the trucks. J.D.'s ranch was east of Liberia in the mountains. It was a very beautiful and productive ranch, which I visited. After he sold out, it was made into a national park.

• • •

Thinking back on Dad's observation that I did not have the patience to do business in Mexico, I realize that I had a lot of experience early, which was valuable in developing the cynicism and nerves of steel I needed for a long and fruitful career in international business.

CHAPTER 18

THE NEIGHBORHOOD

From 1964 to 1974, we were part of one of the most unusual neighborhoods anyone can imagine, with "neighbor" being defined as anyone within an hour's flying time. We were the last to join the group, and had the privilege of knowing many who were the original operators of their ranches. The individuality, hospitality and survivability of the Coahuila ranching community reminded me of stories of British East Africa before and after World War I. We not only learned about large-scale ranching, but also how to live and what kind of people we wanted to be. As the youngest members of the community, we had no feuds with anyone, and everyone was eager to teach and encourage us. It was an amazing way for a young couple to start their married life. This chapter is a thumbnail sketch of a few of the extraordinary people we knew. The neighborhood was unique in that each ranch's operations were very sophisticated and were so in a very pioneering environment. The owners were well educated, including graduates from Cornell, Dartmouth, Princeton, a private school in England, and Texas A&M.

Max Michaelis

Max was a character to end all characters, and was one of the few people I ever met who knew my grandfather, Ed C. Lasater. Max was more or less the godfather of the Charolais movement in North America, and the fact that my family is a leading cattle family created a bond between us. Max partnered with Alphe Broussard on the foundation herd of the Charolais breed in North America. Thirty years later, Alphe's son, Bill, and I beame partners on the descendants of that original herd. Max's son, Máximo, continues with their herd at Kyle, Texas.

The headquarters of Max's Fortín (Fortress) Ranch abutted the headquarters of the Phillips' Sierra Hermosa, with the two ranches lying end-to-end. Max was famous for his hospitality and for having a Cessna 210 constantly shuttling in customers and leading politicians, some of whom were allowed to shoot a buffalo while visiting. One day his pilot, Bud Glasscock, shot a gear-up landing in a new 210. I saw Bud several days later in Del Rio, and asked how he was. Although he had not been fired, he replied, "This shirt will probably last the rest of my life."

On a visit to the Fortín headquarters with Duke and Ruth Phillips, we encountered Max in front of the patio's whitewashed wall where he had a thermometer plastered on the wall on the sunny side. Although it was probably in the nineties, he was bent over reading the thermometer, fanning himself. As we walked up, he straightened, still fanning, and said, "My God, it's 109°," which gives a good insight into how some weather reports get started.

We were on Max's flight path to Del Rio, Texas. One day we heard him fly over, then back to land and drink coffee while the ground fog lifted in Del Rio. By then, we had decided to sell the ranch, and I invited him to see our top Beefmaster cows with calves that watered just off the north end of our airstrip. It was a beautiful day and the cattle were in great shape. When we drove up to the trough, he exclaimed, "These are good cattle! You can't leave them here." Although Mexico, at that time, did not allow the export of registered cattle, he went on to say that he was friends with Mexico's secretary of agriculture, and would get me a permit to take them back to the U.S. Max was as good as his word, but I could not swing the deal politically or financially. It has always been amazing to me that he would go to such effort to help someone who was a competitor.

Roger and Violet Sanford

Mr. and Mrs. Roger Sanford have already been mentioned several times, as well they should be. They not only helped us get started in business, they were dear friends and served as models of how we wanted our marriage and home to be. They were delightful, gracious people. As I have written, Mr. Sanford served as an officer in combat in France in World War I. From 1919–1926, he was involved in various activities in

Southwest Texas, including a failed oil venture that took many years to pay off. About 1926, he went to Coahuila, where he established a career as a quintessential cattle entrepreneur, buying and selling cattle and ranches, as well as owning a large ranching operation.

About 1932, Mr. Sanford and his half-brother, Judge Sanford, the Richie Brothers and Harvey Pollay acquired what became known as La Encantada Ranch (The Enchanted Place) from Bill Finan's father. The ranch, consisting of some 100,000 acres south of the Big Bend Park in Texas, became a highly successful enterprise, running some 2,000 Hereford cows. Their last shipment of 900 reputation Hereford calves to the U.S. was featured on the front page of the *Livestock Weekly* in the late sixties.

Violet and Roger Sanford.

We were living in Mexico when the ranch was divided and knew all the partners. I would guess that Mr. Ritchie was more of a financial partner, Mr. Sanford was probably the general manager, and Harvey and Sabina Pollay were the working partners. Annette and I spent the night at the Encantada with them as they approached retirement. Harvey could not wait to get to town with television and friends to enjoy. Sabina cried at the mention of leaving their beloved ranch. Mr. Sanford handled the division of the ranch and sale of the various parts. One *fracción* was sold to Alden McKellar in appreciation for the help his family had given Mr. Sanford when he was starting out.

Like most of the ranchers in Coahuila, Mr. Sanford was an individualist with a unique outlook on all matters. He loaned money to his friends at the prime rate in Mexico, which was ten percent at that time. He and his friend Bill George of the First National Bank of Eagle Pass, each loaned me $10,000, unsecured. This money amounted to significant operating capital for me. In 1972, the Nixon-McGovern election took place, and Mr. Sanford wrote a classic letter stating that if Mr. McGovern won, my note was due and payable. Fortunately, Nixon won and my note was renewed. When Mr. Sanford died, I paid off the note in full.

Mr. Sanford was one of Dr. Denton Cooley's first great success stories. Since he had been brought back to life by one of the early heart bypass operations, he willed his body to the medical center in Houston for research purposes. Annette and I are thankful that we were one of his last "projects." In 1972, I drove to his memorial service in Eagle Pass in a driving blizzard, which prevented me from returning home to San Angelo that day. Fittingly, at the gathering after the service, Alden McKellar, another Sanford "project," proposed a toast to our beloved friend.

Jesús and Esther Santos

"Nos sobró un toro."

—*Chui Santos*

I have already written in detail of our friendship with the Santos family. Their home became our headquarters in Múzquiz. Since there was no way for us to communicate to town from the ranch, we would arrive at their home, unannounced, and were always welcomed with open arms. Regardless of the time of day, something delicious to eat appeared immediately. I made most of my business phone calls from their living room. Although it was an imposition on Esther, she never complained. When we stayed in town, they insisted that we not stay in a hotel nor even in their guest bedroom, but only in their bedroom with the air-conditioner. The Santos family is typical of the Mexican people. Their home was next to the plaza and next door to an outside movie theater, so one was always aware of the teeming, bustling, happy life in a Mexican town.

When flying to Múzquiz, I would buzz the plaza, and the cab driver with whom I had an arrangement, would pull away from the cab stand to pick me up at the airport. My first stop was usually Manuel Padilla's office to attend to business, then the bank. Next the cabbie would drop me at the Santos house, and then spend several hours running errands on a list I gave him. I would make my telephone calls and have lunch with Chui and Esther or take them to El Club de Tiro (The Gun Club) or some other local restaurant.

Chui is very funny and an astute observer of the human condition. I had more laughs with him than any friend I have had. He kept us informed on the "goings on" and local gossip. He would not hesitate to tell some horrendous story on himself. Chui is a heavyset man, and his local nickname is *Chui el Gordo,* as distinguished from his cousin, *Chui el Presidente* (Fat Chui and Mayor Chui.) Whenever we left his house in his pickup, we always circled the plaza to see what was happening. In making that circle, we

Jesús and Esther Santos.

would pass Raul Yamamoto's butcher shop, Carnicería la Misión, where several locals gathered regularly to visit and drink beer with Raul. One day Chui told me that on my previous trip when we had driven by, one of the local wags said, *"Allí va el diez."* (There goes the ten; the one and the zero.) Chui was laughing so hard he could barely tell me the story.

He and I had many encounters. For years I ran my bull calves on his oat patch by the main highway, delivering them to the buyers as yearlings before the spring breeding season. Everyone driving into Múzquiz would see the bulls. The locals marveled at the fact that I contracted them in advance, with money down, in groups of ten. One year, we had forty bulls sold, four groups of ten. The buyers had made their selections, and the bulls were in four pens with the gates tied shut with bailing wire, and with four bobtail trucks lined up, ready to load. Thinking this was a done deal, I left for the ranch. On my next trip, Chui reported, "Lorenzo, I have good news, *"Nos sobró un toro."* (We had a bull left over.) To correct the mistake, we had to send a truck to Durango with one bull, at a price which consumed the whole price of the bull.

We received some wonderful lessons in manners from our friends in Mexico. After we owned a plane, we occasionally would go to Del Rio to spend the night at the Holiday Inn to make phone calls, eat pizza and watch TV. On one occasion, we had trucks due at the ranch, but they had not arrived. We flew to Del Rio, where I phoned Chui. As soon as he answered, I began questioning him about the trucks. He let me talk for a short while, and then interrupted, asking, "Lorenzo, how are Annette and the babies?" In Mexico, it is always first things first.

Annette and I had the experience of being included in a wedding when Chui and Esther's daughter, Esthelita, married. In that country, all important events are well and properly celebrated. We were *padrinos*, which means that, as close friends of the family, we pledged to support the young couple and signed the book at the civil ceremony in the family home. When the judge announced the names "Señor Lorenzo Lasater y Señora (Mr. and Mrs. Lorenzo Lasater)," we went forward to sign the book. It was a rich and meaningful experience.

In 1969 Chui and Esther drove and Ruth and Duke flew to Santa Cruz to help us celebrate Lorenzo's first birthday, a treasured memory for Annette and me. Our friendship with the Santos family has not changed in the forty years since we met. Although we do not see them as often as we would like, rarely does a week pass without some happy memory of them. We are fortunate to know such loving, gracious people.

Guillermo and Doris Osuna

We became acquainted with the Osunas about 1969. We had heard about them as they were intimate friends of Nelly and Bill Finan. Around that time, I sold Guillermo ten head of Beefmaster-Charbray cross bulls from the cows purchased from Mr. Sanford. Guillermo told me on the steps of Almacenes Múzquiz that was all the Beefmaster blood he needed.

When we started flying, we saw them more frequently and visited them overnight from time to time. On one trip, I pregnancy tested some Hereford cows for him, and he sold me the pregnant ones on credit. Guillermo is a Dartmouth graduate and one of the truly "brainy" people I have known. He is able to use his intelligence to give penetrating and valuable strategic advice. During one of our visits, he told me I did not need to own ranches on credit, but rather should advise people who already owned them but did not know how to manage them. He also told me to focus on marketing cattle for the same reason. It took me many years to absorb this advice, which has profoundly affected my business strategy. The headquarters where Guillermo and Doris lived is named Las Pilas, and is part of an older ranch known as El Infante (The Infant). Guillermo introduced me to the concept of "Terreno Privilegiado" (Privileged Land), meaning the best ranches in a given area. The Infante, the Valle Colombia, and the Lasater Ranch all fall into that category and each has unique characteristics that set it apart.

Photo by Watt M. Casey, Jr.

Doris and Guillermo Osuna.

In the case of Guillermo's ranch, the mountains, which form the south fence, run east and west, funneling moisture from the Gulf onto the ranch. It has the greatest diversity of flora and fauna that I have seen and is one of the most beautiful ranches. It also has a spring at the head of the valley that provides gravity for water by pipeline for the whole property. Guillermo, Bill Finan and my brother Dale have all used Allan Savory's ideas of Holistic Management since 1980 to improve their ranches.

Guillermo and Doris are the only bona-fide "jet-setters" Annette and I have known well. In visiting them, we were not only visiting one of the world's most beautiful places, but also spending time with very interesting people from all over the world. The Osunas continuously entertained. One highlight was spending New Year's Eve of 1971 at their ranch, accompanied by the Finans, Doris' brother and sister-in-law, and other family members. We toasted the New Year at midnight and enjoyed an elegant dinner afterwards.

The Osunas had four children, two boys and two girls. After we moved to San Angelo, their son, Ramón, was killed in a horseback accident. I attended the funeral at the ranch with Duke Phillips and Chui and Esther Santos. It was a heartbreaking tragedy.

On July 4, 1998, we were privileged to attend the wedding of the Osuna's daughter, Doris, at the Monterrey Country Club, a very elegant affair. As one of our friends was driving us to the airport the next morning, he remarked, only half joking, that the cost of our daughter Isabel's wedding would not have covered the tips on the one in Monterrey. It was a wonderful event and an opportunity to visit with many of our friends from Mexico.

Bill and Nelly Finan

I have mentioned visiting the Valle Colombia in the summer of 1960. Like many other pilgrims, I was awestruck by the quality of the ranch and cattle as well as the beauty of the home and family. There are few ranches anywhere in the world of this size that were founded and developed by one man who is still in charge. A friend in Monterrey told me that, after his first visit to the Valle Colombia, he returned home and told his wife, "My whole life has been wasted."

Any contact with the Finans is a summons to excellence. I was fortunate to visit them as an eighteen-year-old schoolboy interested in what they had to offer and in whom they took an intimate, personal interest. We toured the ranch extensively and discussed every imaginable subject, laying the basis for a friendship that continues to this day. Any contact with Bill is a challenge, and on a trip with Bill and Guillermo Osuna to look at a ranch in Tampico about 1969, Bill mentioned that I was overstocked at Santa Cruz, a situation of which I was not aware. He had surveyed the stocking rate when flying over our ranch on his trips to Múzquiz. After returning home, I studied the pasture conditions, and concluded he was right and reduced our cattle numbers. A year or so after our trip to Tampico, Bill and Nelly dropped by to spend the day. During the course of the visit, Bill mentioned that I needed cattle. I agreed but did not have capital to buy any. He said, "The trucks will be here at 3:00 p.m. tomorrow." Our first venture was very successful, but unfortunately, due to cattle markets plunging, we took big losses in 1974. We got along well as partners, agreed on nearly everything, and continued as partners until

2000, nearly thirty years. My brother Lane also had a wonderful, challenging encounter with Bill. When Lane told him he was thinking of practicing psychology and ranching, Bill's reply was, "great idea—that way you can be mediocre at both."

Bill told me that his father had looked from Canada to Mexico for a ranch that could be managed from the front porch. In 1917, he rode into the area that now comprises the Encantada and Valle Colombia, and knew he had found what he had been looking for. In 1930, Mr. Finan traded a piece of property in Durango to a family there for the Valle Colombia. In 1927, he entered into an arrangement with Judge Sanford regarding the Encantada. The agreement they had was kept in a lockbox in the Hotel Yolanda in Eagle Pass, which burned down. The terms of the agreement are not known to the survivors, but the Sanford group ended up with the ranch.

Bill and Nelly Finan in 2005.

In 1930, Bill Finan was ten when he rode horseback into the high country with Harvey Pollay, who was guiding hunters from San Antonio on the Encantada, and began developing that ranch as a working partner in 1932. Bill told me the ride from the Encino Ranch through the Alameda Canyon took four to five days. His parents drove up in a Model A, and they toured the ranch for several days, then Bill and his dad rode the horses home. Bill never intended to live anywhere but the Valle Colombia.

After his father's death in 1939, Bill took some 525 cattle (cows, calves, bulls, steers) to what was to become the Valle Colombia Ranch, one of the best ranches in Mexico. The different parts of the ranch, which consisted of 101,000 *hectares* (252,500 acres), are well known in Mexico: Las Cabras, La Gorriona, Valle Colombia, Valle Perú, Cimarrón, Santa Patricia and Rancho Nuevo. Bill celebrated his 20th birthday (September 24, 1939) camped on his new ranch. He hauled water for 34 years, first from Max Michaelis' San Felipe well and later from a tank on the south end of the Encantada. Bill's first significant well was dug on the Gorriona in 1942. The ranch consists of large valleys above 4,000 feet altitude, with no brush. It is very dry, fertile, alkali sacaton country. The main limiting factor is drinking water. Bill watered it with very large dirt tanks and deep wells (1,200 ft.). Laying out the pastures and improvements and operating off a master plan for nearly 70 years is a feat of ranch engineering without equal in my experience.

As a close friend since 1960, Bill had a positive influence on my career as a cattle breeder. In the early 1980s, he bought a colt from Walter Graham, a world-famous Hereford breeder, of Happy, Texas. We took my pickup and trailer from San Angelo, with Matt Brown driving, to get the colt. Listening to Bill and Walter discuss strategy was a turning point in my career. Basically, I realized that they got more calves out of their better bulls and that they used fewer herd bulls. After I came home, I reduced our breeding ratio to 1:25 (4% bulls) on cows and 1:16 (6%) on yearling heifers. I suggested to Dad that he do likewise. That fall, when Dale and I helped Dad sort the Lasater Ranch herd bulls, the mediocre bulls were eliminated, resulting in a noticeable improvement in Dad's and my herds.

On August 19, 1989, the fiftieth anniversary celebration of ranching was held at Valle Colombia. Several hundred people attended, arriving by pickup and some forty airplanes. I flew down from San Angelo with our mutual friends, Jack and Sally Grafa and Robert Cleere. Bill's close friend, Guillermo Osuna, gave an eloquent talk in Spanish, summarizing the ranch's history and paying tribute to the Finans. Guillermo ended his talk with this tribute:

"I have mentioned the cattle and the land, but there is another important aspect that has had great influence on many of us. When I came to Coahuila in 1958 to take charge of the ranch where we live, Bill was already a legend. I remember asking our manager, shortly after I arrived, who was the best rancher in the area. Without hesitation, he replied, 'El Bile' (the Billy). I said I would like to know him and visit his ranch some day. Somehow, Bill heard of this, and a few days later, a plane landed at the ranch. When I got to the strip, Bill was already standing by the plane. He said, "Let's go to the ranch." I got into the plane and went to the Valle for the first time; it was my first day at "Valle Colombia University," and the beginning of a wonderful friendship between our families.

It is not easy to learn at the University of Valle Colombia. The only professor does not like to teach, but prefers to lead by example. The few verbal instructions the students receive are almost always in code. New students usually need a translator, one of the old students. I say old, because at this school, there are no graduates. All who wish may continue learning because there is always something new to learn. I first came here thirty-one years ago (1958) and have never left without something new and useful.

Many of you have also been students at this school, which is not only for Bill's cattle friends; the cowboys, fence-builders, and everyone else who has come here to work, have left as better men, not only in their professions, but also in acquiring personal values that enable them to continue excelling. In this ranching community, the best reference is having worked at the Valle Colombia.

Bill has always been demanding of himself, his family, his friends and his workers, but always guided by a sense of justice and strong Christian love with which he has gained the respect and affection of all of us who have had the good fortune to know him."

Duke and Ruth Phillips

The Sierra Hermosa Ranch was an 83,000-acre semi-desert ranch lying in two big valleys, running north and south, with mountains on each side and a range of hills down the middle. The ranch was on the fringe of the better country, had brush and was always very dusty. It was an old, established *hacienda* with owner's home, barns, commissary, guest house, school and outbuildings, all whitewashed.

Annette and I spent more time with Duke and Ruth Phillips than with anyone else during our life in Mexico. Both Ruth and Duke were tremendous people. They had ranched previously at Laredo, Fort Stockton and in Venezuela, where they worked for the Rockefellers. Although they were twenty years older than we were, they had young children and were also starting a new business, so we had many interests in common. As was mentioned earlier, Duke was general partner in a limited partnership with Killam and Hurd of Laredo-Rio Bravo Cattle Co., Ltd. Our business setup was modeled on theirs.

The format of our visits was established early. At 6:00 a.m., Duke rolled whatever vehicle he was driving down the hill to his office, where the various foremen reported to get their instructions (cowboy crew, fence crew, pipeline crew, etc.), I would go down to the office at this time, and we would discuss the business of the day, including mineral supplements, pipeline problems, light-plant maintenance, and so on. Then we would go back to the house for a big breakfast. At 8:00 a.m., Duke talked to Guillermo Garcia's ranch radio network in Múzquiz, *equis uno de equis once* (x-eleven calling x-one), to arrange trucks and supplies and to get the local news and weather, *aquí amaneció despejado* (it is clear here). After finishing at the office, we would leave for a *vuelta* (circle) in Duke's most recent open touring car, the last being a Volkswagen "Thing," with dust-like talcum powder boiling throughout the three-to-four-hour round. We always made a tour to see a group of cattle or a ranch project in progress. Afterwards, we would return to the house to have cold Tecate beer and another delicious meal, enjoying the whole family and their boundless hospitality.

Possibly one reason our friendship meant so much is that we were opposite personalities. Duke was a pragmatist, and I am a visionary. Duke was less of a risk-taker than I am. Not only was our business model patterned on his, but I also learned about designing water systems and corrals, formulating a mineral supplement and countless other critical pieces of information. Our veterinarian for twenty years in West Texas, Dr. Bill Wohler, said our pens at the McAfee Ranch, which were modeled on the Sierra Hermosa pens, were the best designed in the area. Duke bought Beefmaster bulls from his longtime friend, Uncle Palo, and was interested in our breeding program, as well as my ideas on promoting and marketing cattle. It was a tremendously valuable friendship based on mutual affection and respect. His death in 2004 hit me harder than any other. Not only was it the loss of a very close friend, it also signified the end of a beloved era in our lives and the death of my own youth.

Duke was a wonderful listener and so accepting of everyone. He had no need to talk of his own exploits, unless asked, in which case he was perfectly open to discussing anything. As recounted earlier, Duke was my

DUKE PHILLIPS
APARTADO POSTAL 142
SABINAS. COAHUILA.
MEXICO.

August 26, 1969

Dear Laurie:

Have been putting the pencil to our high level rock phosphate ration, and
it looks like we have been way off base.

According to Faulkner's letter, as well as the book he sent me, breeding
cattle should not have more than 13.5 mg. Fluorine per lb. of total ration
(grain plus 20 lb. , plus or minus, of pasture grass) 13.5 mg. X 20 = 270 mg.
per day or about 1/4 lb. R.P. Rockphosphate Hemanas @ .0022 % = 999 mg.
Fl./lb. A 5 lb. supplement of grain at 5% R.P. would give 1/4 lb. R.P.

I certainly exceeded this last year, and wonder if it could in any way
relate to our present problem. Let's hope one year of this won't affect
either of us.

Our Cuchilla cows tested 88% p.g. Although this sure beats 57%, I am still
very concerned and plan t o call Faulkner when we go out later this week.

Yours,

Duke

P. S. Hope you were getting the rain last night that it looked like you
were from here.

mentor in aviation. Thanks in part to him, we bought the right plane for
the right price and flew safely for 30 years. Not once did he allude to the
fact that, in my wildest imaginings, I could never know what it was like
to fly in combat in the China-Burma-India Theater as he had. Sometimes,
when I am tempted to look down on someone who thinks on a different
scale than I, I remind myself that Duke never once mentioned how
limited my aviation experience was. Although he resembled movie actor
Gary Cooper, and exemplified the ideal rancher look, Duke was unaware
of the effect of his charisma on other people. His dry humor also was
typical of that prized in the cattle industry. One afternoon we were seated
on the veranda, facing east toward the airport, when a tiny rain shower
about a quarter mile away passed between the house and the hanger,
leaving a small rainbow over a dirt tank. As we observed the ending of the
shower, Duke said, "Well, spring rains are over."

When they were working cattle, Duke had an old bobtail truck that he used to haul the cowboys and saddle horses from Sierra Hermosa to his Bocatoche lease, a long drive by road through Múzquiz and Monclova. He

had an "X" painted on the roof of the truck so that he could track it from the air. If the truck stopped at a *cantina,* he could buzz the building, rattling the windows to get the men moving again.

At some point during our college years, Dale and I participated in a cattle working at the Bocatoche; we flew there with Duke. It was blazing hot, with no electricity or running water. We camped in some abandoned buildings at the headquarters, where there was a well and a set of pens. Duke had sent the bobtail the day before with the horses, camp, cowboy crew and various visitors, nephews, etc. Including all, there were at

Lt. Colonel Duke Phillips after service as a fighter pilot in the China-Burma-India Theater of World War II.

least twelve riders. After lunch one day, when Dale got ready to mount, there was one horse left, but it was not his; not only that, but the stirrups on the saddle were not the same length. One of the nephews did not realize that each man rode his same horse all day and that the stirrups could be adjusted to fit the rider correctly. About the second day, after gathering a large herd in rough country and flanking calves in boiling dust, we were hot, dirty and tired, Duke asked Dale if he would like a frozen daiquiri. Of course, there were none. Dale fell for the bait and both became obsessed with how good one would taste. When we finished the following day, the three of us jumped into the plane and flew straight to Sierra Hermosa. Without even washing our hands, we ran to the bar and made a pitcher of frozen daiquiris.

Ruth was a dynamic woman and fun. Like Duke, she loved young people. She was also a skilled pilot and handled most of their ranch errands, flying their Cherokee Six to Sabinas, Múzquiz or San Antonio. One evening, just minutes before dark, a plane landed on our air strip as we were sitting on the porch with Tom and Jan Newsome enjoying a gin and tonic. We watched in awe when it stopped at the south end, and with the engine still running, a lady pilot jumped out, unloaded a box, jumped back into the plane, and waved to us as she took off again. It was Ruth dropping off a case of tonic water while hurrying home before dark. Of course, we told Tom and Jan that we had a charter flight deliver our tonic water every month.

Ruth Phillips as a WASP during World War II. She trained at Avenger Field in Sweetwater, Texas.

Ruth and Duke sold out shortly after we did and their children scattered to various colleges; they divorced later. Duke ranched in Oregon and New Mexico before retiring in Colorado Springs, to be near his son and family. Duke, Jr., and his wife, Janet, had re-created a ranch much like the beloved Sierra Hermosa that they left behind in Mexico, on the Chico Basin Ranch, an 80,000-plus-acre conservancy. Ruth died in 2002. When I had my last visit with Duke in 2003, he was blind from macular degeneration but unchanged in appearance or outlook. He had some cattle on feed in South Texas and commented on how sweet it was. I am glad he lived long enough to see a good market.

When Duke, Jr., called in 2004 to tell us his dad had died, Annette and I were grief-stricken. Several months before, we had watched a rerun of *High Noon* with Gary Cooper. After the movie, I told Annette, "This is just a movie, but we know the real thing."

Texas was experiencing a blizzard on Valentine's Day 2004, the day before Duke's funeral. After having flights delayed and cancelled, I was finally able to fly to Colorado Springs. Arriving late at the airport, I decided to stay in a hotel in town rather than drive to their ranch. That evening, with everyone celebrating the holiday in a steakhouse/bar, I felt deep loneliness and grief. The other patrons must have wondered what had gone wrong with my love life. I was grieving not only the loss of my friend Duke, but also the amount of road behind Annette and me.

I feel sure that writing Duke's eulogy for the memorial service held at the Chico Basin Ranch and reliving our wonderful memories of Coahuila was a step toward starting this book in October 2004.

These many friendships and dozens of others made in the course of establishing our ranch in Mexico have enriched our lives immeasurably. They continue to enrich the lives of our children and our children's children.

CHAPTER 19

GONE TO TEXAS

"When can we start?"

—Bill Finan

In the 1960s, the cattle journals were full of stories about the growing cattle feeding industry on the High Plains. Joe Finley owned an interest in a feedlot at Blythe, California, and strongly urged Duke to get involved. I had seen the Finley 300-pound Hereford calves being trailed from their ranch to Múzquiz where they were loaded onto a train for the border, then on to the West Coast by truck or train. Mr. Joe said they were just *almas* (souls) when they got to Blythe. His strategy was to raise or buy a very inexpensive calf and to put on a lot of cheap pounds at the feedlot. He told Duke and me he did not buy cattle from his neighbors because he did not want to "hard trade" them. Being about 35 years ahead of the industry, Duke began preconditioning steers at Sierra Hermosa and started feeding cattle at the San Angelo Feedyard via the connection with Wade Choate and John Cargile.

After the fallout from our Kickapoo encounter, Annette and I were disillusioned to learn that we were not secure in our own home. In addition, I tried to get a permit to ship Beefmaster bulls to Costa Rica and was turned down. There were no consistent cattle markets, no feedlot industry, etc., in Mexico in 1970, so we decided to sell out. We immediately ran into two huge problems—the sale of the ranch and the fact that the government of Mexico would not let us export our Beefmaster herd to Texas. We would have to sell both the herd and ranch to buyers in Mexico. I thought the ranch, stocked with a top, successful herd of registered Beefmaster cattle would be salable, but I spent several years trying to sell it without success. One of my friends told me, "Lorenzo, nobody but you could run the business."

Yogi Berra is famous for his saying, "When you come to a fork in the road, take it." Whenever we have come to a fork in the road, Annette has encouraged me to "take it," and 1972 was a big year in that regard. We decided to begin feeding cattle in Texas, and sometime that spring, I wrote Bill Finan a letter suggesting that we each put up $50,000 in equity to keep 1,000 cattle on feed. My plan was to lease a feedlot in the San Angelo area and for Bill to buy the steers in Mexico, some of which would be preconditioned at Santa Cruz. When we flew to Valle Colombia, Bill shook hands and said, "When can we start?" It doesn't take long to make a deal with him. Our partnership was named Finan and Lasater. The heifers he had shipped to me on 24-hour notice the year before made a profit and were sold to a neighbor, Alberto Múzquiz.

Seeking a feedlot to lease, I ran some ads in the *Livestock Weekly* in the spring of 1972. The responses I received were from the San Angelo area. We flew there from Santa Cruz since we could stay in a motel and rent a car at the airport. I called Wade Choate, who had bought our calves in 1967, and who was the only person I knew in San Angelo. He had breakfast with me, and after I told him my plan, he mentioned that he owned an interest in a feedlot seventeen miles east at Miles, Texas. He suggested that I spend time working at the yard and feed some cattle before diving in and leasing one. Based on this good advice, I drove to the yard and met Roy Williams, the manager. Thirty-five years later, we are still doing business there. I met John Cargile, the principal owner of the San Angelo Feedyard, sometime in the fall of 1972. He welcomed us and invited us to finance our cattle at Central National Bank, of which he was a stockholder and director.

In July, we flew from Santa Cruz to Colorado Springs on vacation, stopping off in San Angelo to find a suitable place to rent. Upon returning in August, we signed a one-bedroom lease with Cielo Vista Apartments and began commuting weekly. We became friends with Wade and Martha Choate who were very helpful and even loaned us a black and white TV. Wade urged us to get a color television as soon as possible, saying that it was possible to watch some programs in color a viewer could not stand in black and white. Not having been accustomed to television, central heating and air-conditioning, we enjoyed the apartment very much and considered living there quite a luxury. Being only a one-bedroom apartment, Isabel, one year old, slept in a crib in a large walk-in closet and Lorenzo, four, slept in a bedroll in the living room. Because we were not used to living in such enclosed quarters, we kept the door open most of the time. It was easy to spot our apartment as it was the only one with the door open.

A local builder, Stuart Chancellor, was building a row of attractive town homes across from our apartment with beautiful views on Parkview Lake. Three months after we had rented the apartment, he had an open house, which we attended. Nobody paid any attention to us, although we were the only buyers present. We had never considered buying a new home, but after we saw these, I told Annette we were going to buy one, but that I would wait until the morning. The next day I called Stuart and met him at the site. He was very eager to make the first sale and was visibly shaking. I bought 2520 Lindenwood Drive with all the appliances and put down $3,000. The only mistake I made was not buying the whole row. Christmas was a happy one in our new home.

• • •

My book, *The Lasater Philosophy of Cattle Raising,* was published in 1972 by the University of Texas at El Paso. Carl Herzog, the editor, first told me that it was not a book that suited their press. He then told me that the press would only publish it because I was Ethel Matthews Casey's grandson. The trade edition was priced at $10.00, and a limited edition, signed by Carl, Dad and me, sold out immediately at $25.00. Little did Annette and I realize my book would go through more than ten editions over 20 years and be the most profitable book ever published by the University of Texas at El Paso.

As we spent more time in San Angelo, we began to meet people. John and Ta Cargile were gracious to include us in community events and introduced us to people. The Choates introduced us to Skipper and Dorothy Duncan. Through the Duncans, we met Andy and Bonnie Smith, as well as Charles and Kathy Probandt, all of whom became important friends and business associates. Bill and Joy Morehead and Jack and

Marjorie Bess Drake invited us to parties at their homes. Jack was a long-time partner at Producers Livestock Auction and one of the first people I met in San Angelo. Several friends invited us to The First Presbyterian Church. Since my family was Presbyterian, it was a logical choice and a perfect fit for us.

• • •

1973 was a memorable time in the cattle business. Just as Finan and Lasater's inventory in the United States and Mexico reached a peak, the market went way up. At one time, we showed a large paper profit. To their credit, Wade Choate and John Cargile did everything they could to restrain me. One day, while having lunch with I.W. Terry and others at Producers Auction, I mentioned Stratford of Texas' theory that no two pens of cattle, back to back, had ever lost money. As I left after lunch, I.W. followed me to the parking lot and advised me not to believe Stratford's theory. I will always remember his not wanting a younger man to be misinformed. In fact, fed cattle did lose money from September 1973 through March 1975—nineteen consecutive months.

Sometime during that period, fat cattle were listed on the Chicago Mercantile Exchange, and it became possible to hedge cattle on the futures market. A broker opened a little booth in the lobby of Producers Auction. I talked to various people about it, and the feedlot manager finally said, "Lasater, just go in there, hedge your cattle and see what happens." I placed the first hedge at San Angelo. We had a set of 100 cattle on feed that were making $100 on paper—the Holy Grail. I sold them on the futures for future delivery. Several weeks later, the market dropped, I lifted the hedge and the Merc sent me a check for $10,000. It seemed to me that having gone down so fast the futures might come back up, so I talked again to the broker. He suggested I buy the contracts, in effect, doubling our position, which is called a Texas hedge. I did, and several weeks later, when the market went back up, I sold the contracts back and made another profit. When we finally sold the cattle, they made another profit in the cash market. I was a happy 31-year-old man.

I made my first pasturage deal in the U.S. in the spring of 1973, on the Colorado River on the Robinson Ranch at Bastrop, Texas. We had some light Mexican steers on feed, and Roy Williams suggested we turn them out. I advertised and located some excellent pasture for them. A month or two later, I flew Roy to Austin to inspect the cattle for the bank. The cattle were on lush pasture and gaining two pounds a day with the market going up; Roy told the bank to find someone else to worry about.

• • •

I ran an ad for pasturage, and made a deal with Homer Haby to run our cows on his ranch at Stiles, west of San Angelo. Homer charged me $10-per-head, payable monthly in advance. The ranch had good pastures that had been rested and neighbored with Jack Ham and Billy Boyd. At some point, I cleared a short landing strip on a caliche road at Stiles. I kept a horse at the ranch and the Habys let me use an old pickup of theirs. One day, I was on horseback on the north end of the ranch and rode over to the home of Billy and Eldon Boyd to introduce myself. Eldon said it had been many years since anyone had ridden up to their house on horseback. They helped us immeasurably by keeping an eye on the cattle, checking the water and helping with the cow work.

Dick Springs and I contracted to buy 135 registered Beefmaster cows in the summer from the Musser Bros. of Delta, Colorado, who had used Lasater Ranch bulls since 1948. That fall I flew commercial to Grand Junction where Jack Musser met me. The Mussers' cattle were still in the high country, so we spent the first night at their headquarters near Delta and drove the next morning to Short Point, their cow camp in the Uncompahgre National Forest. My first trip to Short Point was unforgettable. It is a bachelor cow-camp, no electricity or indoor plumbing, set in spectacular surroundings right on the Continental Divide. On every trip, I spent time with Jack and Bernice, their son, Johnny, and saw Jack's brother Tom and their foreman, John Cunningham. The Mussers were real cowmen/cowboys. They broke their own horses, made their own chaps, could cook a roast and make cobbler that was out of this world.

When it was time for delivery, Dick could not come, so I selected his 35 cows. We drove to a large corral built of timbers cut on the ranch, and I was handed the reins to a saddled horse. I rode into a large pen holding some 250 pairs, bred cows, bred heifers and open heifers. I sorted out our cattle on horseback with the assistance of the Musser crew. As the cows were selected, they recorded the numbers for registration purposes. The cows were age-branded and number-branded with the Lasater code on the hip and the picturesque Musser holding-brands on the ribs: the X quarter-circle I, the LMJ or the Moon F. Everybody present could speak "cow." Gaddy Truck Line delivered the cattle to Stiles several days later, making the 800-mile trip over the Continental Divide without incident, and arriving within fifteen minutes of the appointed time. When I went to the bank to get the money, there was a mini-crisis. I earlier had told the young loan officer whom I was dealing with at Central National Bank that we were going to buy 100 cows. The banker had not understood what I was doing or had failed to inform his bosses, and the bank did not want to loan the money. John Cargile intervened, went with me to another bank, borrowed the money on his signature, and loaned it to me.

• • •

The fall of 1973 was an important time in my business career. The Beefmaster associations had split several years earlier, and the smaller breeders in our group needed help in marketing their bulls. By that time, the Beefmaster breed was on the rise, and I was selling many bulls. I made an arrangement with Skipper Duncan to start the FBA Consignment Bull Pool, with the bulls being pastured in one of his new Kleingrass pastures. It was a perfect location, handy to town and an attractive place to show the bulls. We received 200 bulls on consignment, and sold the salable ones in good order. Although a lot of refinement was needed, this was the first year of the Bull Co-op, which ran for thirty years, and was an important part of my being integrated into the U.S. ranching community.

After I had told Skipper about Santa Cruz, he wanted to see the ranch, so I took him for an overnight visit. The two-hour flight from San Angelo into the hinterlands was quite an adventure in itself. As soon as we landed, we got into the pickup to look around and encountered my foreman, Federico Arias, on horseback. Federico talked fast, and, of course, we were speaking real Spanish. Although Skipper spoke Spanish, he said he could not understand a word. San Angelo is sheep country, and coyotes were rarely seen. In Skipper's honor, a coyote killed a rabbit by the guest house window during the night. At the time, we had restocked the ranch with commercial heifers in partnership with Bill Finan and were breeding 800 heifers A.I., which were being penned in a big water lot at night. During the night, a mountain lion came to drink out of the trough and stampeded the heifers. The next day, Skipper said it was the wildest place he had ever been.

• • •

In 1974, I was president of the Foundation Beefmaster Association, Gene Newman was president of the Texas Cattle Feeders, and John Cargile was president of the Texas and Southwestern Cattle Raisers, so our city was well represented on the cattle scene. I later served with both of them on the board of the National Cattlemen's Association.

That year was one of the worst cattle market breaks in history, as well as the year of President Nixon's infamous price freeze on beef. The analysts said that we had a worldwide shortage of beef. They were half right: it was worldwide but not short. To make matters worse, the U.S. government sold wheat to the Russians in exchange for their help in withdrawing from Vietnam. This policy caused grain prices to skyrocket. When the price freeze was lifted, the price of cattle dropped. We saw steers bought and preconditioned in Mexico for sixty cents-a-pound, and fed at San Angelo for sixty cents per-pound-of-gain, sell for thirty cents-per-pound. They lost more than they cost. If we had shot them and burned them in Mexico, it would have saved time and money.

Sale of the Beefmaster Herd

At the same time I had contacted Bill Finan about partnering, I had offered our Beefmaster herd to Guillermo Osuna. That summer he and Isidro Lopez came to Santa Cruz to look at the cattle, and on September 1, Guillermo called to accept our offer to buy the foundation herd of the Beefmaster breed in Mexico. The transaction, involving 600 registration papers, was by far the largest to date in the breed and created a sensation in Northern Mexico. They moved the cattle to better ranches and carried on the program Annette and I had established. Bill and I bought out my limited partners and re-stocked Santa Cruz with 1,500 crossbred stocker heifers. Annette and I had paid off the ranch with interest in just under six years. When this sale was completed, we owned a 40% interest in a fine 31,500-acre ranch with no debt and no cattle.

The Sale of Santa Cruz

"I am going to sell you my ranch tomorrow."
—Laurie Lasater

On August 7, 1974, the cattle industry was in a state of collapse, and it was rumored that President Nixon would resign. I could see a firestorm coming. For several years, I had been negotiating to sell Santa Cruz to Vidal Gonzalez. Vidal was a neighbor who had bought bulls from us, and I had pregnancy-tested heifers for him. My crew and I would ride horseback to his headquarters, work the cattle, then drive home the non-breds to fatten and sell. I knew Vidal wanted a ranch for his son, Vidal, Jr., who was graduating from Texas A&M. I called Vidal one night and said, "I'm going to sell you my ranch tomorrow, how much will you give me?" He replied, "3,000,000 pesos" ($240,000). I said, "I'll see you at the Hotel Eagle at 10:00 a.m." I flew to Eagle Pass, where Vidal and I sat nose-to-nose in the Hotel Eagle Coffee Shop and negotiated from 10:00 a.m. until 4:00 p.m. That day he wired the money to Múzquiz to pay off the cattle loan Bill Finan and I had secured and wrote me a check for the difference, taking range delivery on our cattle. I slid our ranch deeds and Certificates of Inaffectability across the table, and we were finished in Mexico. Unbeknown to us, while Vidal and I were negotiating, President Nixon did resign that day—a big day for both of us. After the President's resignation, the international money markets crashed, and if we had not sold Santa Cruz that day, we would not have been able to sell it for years. On October 15, 1974, our cowboys had gathered and branded 1,495 of the 1,500 cattle we sold Vidal range delivery. I paid off the crew, and even now I am still sad to have left such good men behind.

That fall, we weaned our first calves in Texas, bought another 100 cows from the Mussers and received a large group of co-op bulls to sell. Finan and Lasater had survived, but just barely. In 1974 we had sold 3,500 cattle in the U.S. and Mexico, losing an average of $200 per head. After ten years in business and having paid off a ranch there in less than six years, my net worth on December 31 was a negative. Having seen these same events in the Depression and the fifties, Dad always preached against buying cattle speculatively. Unfortunately, people have to learn for themselves, and I am more of a risk-taker in Ed C. Lasater's mold. In 1974, we experienced the downside of that modus operandi. Finan and Lasater paid its bills, and Bill was not called on to cover the partnership's liabilities. We continued as partners for over twenty years.

There are 283,000,000 cattle in the six nations comprising the cone of South America, the largest concentration of cattle in the world, from where the future deficit in U.S. feeder cattle will be made up. As I write, our son Lorenzo is on his third trip to Brazil. That nation and its neighbors are the future of our cattle business. Thanks to our years in Mexico, we know the people, the culture and the language of that area, and our family is ready for the new frontier.

Our family after working cattle near Mertzon, Texas.

PART II

CHAPTER 20

THE 1970s

"You've got to write a book about the experiences you've had and the people you've known."

—*Guillermo Osuna*

In looking back over many years, there is a tendency to think that not much happened. The 1970s are an example. In writing these memoirs, I was fortunate to have three excellent sources of factual data: 30 years of flight logs, 25 years of a one-sentence daily diary entry and 40 years' records of our cattle sales kept by Annette. What emerges from these valuable records, aided by memory, is the fact that each decade was a hurricane of activities, many of which had far-reaching consequences.

When we returned to Texas from Mexico in 1972, we had valuable knowledge and experience. Having been closely involved with Joe Dawson, Roger Sanford, Duke Phillips, Guillermo Osuna, Bill Finan and Pomeroy Smith, we had a sophisticated understanding of finance and banking. Each of those friends had a lifetime of unique business experience, which he shared freely. We had borrowed money from two Mexican banks. We had learned to raise good cattle and to sell them in a difficult business environment, and we learned to operate with scarce resources. Above all, we had learned to solve problems under rugged circumstances and had confidence in our ability to meet any challenge. Now we would be utilizing all that we had learned as we started over buying cattle, leasing ranches and developing markets for Beefmaster cattle.

As I enjoyed the college football bowl games on January 1, 1974, I was unaware of three coming developments: that we were going to go broke; that the Beefmaster breed was going into a period of growth unequaled in U.S. cattle history; and that 1974 would mark the beginning of a downward spiral in the cow-calf industry in the United States that would last for nearly 30 years and devastate my generation of ranchers.

I have already described Finan and Lasater's feedlot and stocker losses. We had witnessed the Nixon price freeze, the Russian wheat deal and the housewives' boycott of beef. An old-timer told me that he thought the boycott was a joke, but he added, "those bitches nearly crippled us." It took the cattle industry many years and the passage of the Beef Checkoff to become proactive. Still to come was the prime rate hitting twenty percent on April Fools' Day 1980, a result of Jimmy Carter and Paul Volcker's decision to "wring inflation out of the economy." The continuation of these policies by Alan Greenspan has been successful, but the short-term results were disastrous for many. The Reagan Tax Reform Act of 1986 was described by my accountant, Mason Backus, as "the greatest redistribution of wealth in history." Although the reform was much needed, the immediate consequences, again, were rough with the collapse of cattle, oil, real estate and banking. In Texas, every major banking chain except Frost Bank failed or was acquired.

Along with numerous minor market bobbles, droughts, the Brucellosis program, the dairy buyout and other calamities, cattlemen faced the Great Drought of the Nineties, which started at San Angelo in May 1992, and ended in October 2003. John Cargile was quoted in *The Cattleman* saying that west of San Angelo, the nineties were worse than the fifties. From 1973 until 2003, ranchers saw 30 years of bad conditions. Many of my close friends in the ranching business lost their cattle and/or ranches during that time. Our fathers' generation saw their wildest dreams exceeded, while ours saw our worst fears surpassed. As far as this story is concerned, the good news is the unbelievable growth in the Beefmaster breed from 1973–1989. I was privileged to be one of the players in that period, which is why we were fortunate to recover partially from the losses sustained in 1974.

Starting Business in the U.S.A.

In 1973, I asked someone if he knew of a good bookkeeper. He recommended Sam Mabry, the comptroller of Mustang Chevrolet, who kept our books for 30 years until his death in 2003. At that time, we had two bank accounts in Mexico in pesos and two in the U.S. in dollars. We ran all recordkeeping in dollars through one set of books, and Sam kept it straight for $35 per month. He was knowledgeable and sophisticated, having kept books for many years for Frank Late, a renowned, hard-case oilman and car dealer. Sam was an exemplary gentleman who had served in World War II, played minor league baseball and was a poet and humorist. After our son Lorenzo went into business, Sam also kept books for him. When Watt (Laurence, III) was born, he told us, "I'll keep books for L One and L Two, but not for L Three."

Annette had handled our office since 1964, but as our business activities expanded and grew, she began hiring college students from Angelo State University to help her on a part-time basis. In the late 1970s, we had two students who were truly outstanding, Kayla Fletcher Weithauf and Mary Jansa Vaughn. Both have stayed in touch with Annette due to mutual affection. We were grief-stricken to learn at Christmas (2005) that Kayla, a pediatrician, had died of cancer. Cathy Gully followed Kayla and Mary as our secretary. She was one of our favorites, and she and Annette are still friends.

F-L Brand Meats

After we moved to San Angelo, Annette and I enjoyed regular visits from Bill and Nelly Finan. They continued to take an interest in our business and to offer encouragement as we worked to recover. Bill had always been in the meat business, and in 1974, we started F-L Brand meats, whereby we sold frozen beef from our cattle that had been properly cut and aged by Handy Packing Co. We sold meat directly to customers in San Angelo, and shipped it out of town by bus, packed in dry ice. Our biggest shipment was 2,000 pounds of steaks to the Fung family in Hong Kong. Although I had gone to Fountain Valley School with one of the brothers, I did not know the family, so I asked an acquaintance from Hong Kong about the difficulty of getting the meat imported. He told me there would be no problem: "When the Queen visits Hong Kong, she has tea with the Fungs." The business was developing well, but within a year, and for competitive reasons, a local retailer forced Handy to stop processing our meat, which ended F-L Brand Meats.

> *"Keep those and sell these."*
>
> —*Bill Finan*

On one of Bill's visits, we made a big circle, looking at cattle in several locations, including two groups of open heifers. In the course of telling him everything that was going on, I told him I planned to "keep these and sell those." When we got back to his plane at Mathis Field, Bill's only comment for the day was, "Keep those and sell these." After thinking about it, I realized that he was right on target as usual—that the older heifers would sell better and the younger ones were better to keep. Bill is a man of few words, but those words can be invaluable.

Ranch Leases

For us, after 1974, the decade of the '70s was spent in re-establishing our Beefmaster herd and selling large volumes of cattle to other people starting herds. I did not realize, as I began acquiring leases and making pasturage deals, that I would run cattle on more than 65 ranches during the first 42 years of my career. These were not stocker cattle, but registered cattle, requiring more finance, more labor and much more marketing effort than stockers. When I started making a list of the ranches we had owned, leased or pastured cattle on, I was amazed at how many there were.

The second Haby lease, near Menard, was very pretty, and Annette and the children would go with me to work the cattle. Isabel, at three years of age, sat on a corral fence and Lorenzo, age six, worked on horseback so that the cattle could see him and not step on or run over him. Possibly the greatest benefit to being in the cattle business is that the whole family can participate. Lorenzo and Isabel learned the cattle business from the ground up.

My cousin, Matt Brown, our first full-time employee in the United States and a top hand, came to apprentice with me for six months in 1978. He stayed nearly ten years, at which time we turned over our T-Circle lease at Eldorado, Texas, so that he could go into business for himself. He married Christy Cowden of Santa Rosa, New Mexico, in 1980; they have made an excellent team and have raised three fine children. Matt has been very successful with Beefmasters and Boer goats. Matt and Jimmy Autrey played key roles in teaching Lorenzo and Isabel the cattle business.

At some point in the 1970s, we began running cattle with Ralph Wilson and J.C. Doss on the Cedar Hill Ranch north of San Angelo. In the mid-'70s, John Cargile helped me lease the Doc Willeke estate on the west side of San Angelo from the (then named) San Angelo National Bank Trust Department. We had that lease for five years. Over the years, I had become friends with Robert Nickel, owner of the Twin Mountain Fence Co., and was able to lease his wife's ranch west of Mertzon. This gave us a solid operation of some 9,000 acres close together on Highway 67. Although Robert and Joyce later divorced, I continued leasing from Joyce and her new husband, Millard McAfee, for twenty-two years. Robert, as well as Joyce and Millard, are top business people, ideal landlords, and a pleasure to know. Due to the drought in 1996, we had to give up the lease—the ranch where our children grew up and where we developed the L Bar Beefmaster herd.

T Circle Ranch Partnership

In 1979, my Fountain Valley friend and fellow wrestler, Steve Cochran, called from Houston. His family had owned a ranch at Eldorado, Texas, since the 1890s, and he wanted some ideas on how to operate it. Steve's mother, Anne, a childhood friend of my mother, owned half and her cousin, Charlie Allen, and his family of St. Louis owned half. Charlie was their managing partner and a fellow Princetonian. We formed a partnership between Isa Cattle Co. and their group to develop the ranch to its maximum, using money borrowed from the First National Bank of Eldorado. Since we all got along well and they had owned the ranch for 90 years, it looked like a promising long-term venture. However, in

December 1983, Charlie announced that they were going to sell the headquarters portion of T-Circle Ranch, cutting the lease by nearly half. I have rarely received more surprising or untimely news. I knew I needed professional advice to solve the dissolution of the partnership amicably and without a loss to any partner, so I contacted and turned over the T-Circle problem to Mason Backus. I had been impressed with him personally, as well as with his financial acumen. Next to Annette, Mason has been my closest business advisor as well as a personal friend. Like many entrepreneurs, I have relied heavily on my CPA for business advice and analysis as well as tax and estate planning.

• • •

Having already established and sold a top herd in Mexico, I knew exactly what I wanted to accomplish in San Angelo. I bought a large number of Musser cows over the years, put them on a 90-day calving season and bred them A.I. and natural service to the best Lasater and Casey bulls. We culled everything that missed, including all cows that raised cull calves. Over the years, we took 1,200 cows bought from the Mussers and others and culled them on production alone down to 400 head. In 1985, we shortened the breeding season to 60 days.

In Mexico, I had the idea of grading the calves as well as weighing them individually at weaning. We graded them on a quality scale of 1 to 4 with 1 being the best and 4 being a cull, using the grade to eliminate weather variations from year to year. In evaluating them, we looked at weight-for-age, visual appraisal and age of dam. It would be hard to write a better formula for beef cattle improvement, and we have seen dramatic change in our cattle every year for over thirty years. Even though we were using less expensive cows as our base herd, I did not realize how costly this culling process was going to be. Just like improving a ranch, we were dependent on the cows increasing in value, and fortunately they did.

During the years after 1974, my business philosophy was also crystallizing. When I found out how illiquid a ranch can be, while in Mexico, I took the cure on owning land. In 1974, I experienced first-hand the hazards of speculating on cattle. When my banker commented to me that I was the only major cattle borrower who did not operate a family ranch, I realized that the great paradigm in the cattle business is the emphasis on the ownership of land, for many economic and emotional reasons, rather than the more sensible emphasis on owning or controlling cattle. A rancher does not have to own a bank to borrow money or own a ranch to run cattle.

My business interest, as well as my personal preference, was to own or to control large numbers of high-quality Beefmaster cattle. Our veterinarian of many years, Dr. Bill Wohler, once described me as an "entrepreneurial cattleman," and he was right. I own and manage cattle for profit and view cottonseed cake, money and grass as commodities to be acquired on the most favorable terms possible. The banking pressure on me as a non-landowner forced me to develop a viable business plan while riding a sinking ship. As my friend, Andy Smith, said with a smile on his face, "I used to feel sorry for you, but you son-of-a-bitch, you were learning to operate while the rest of us were going broke."

The Beginning of Isa Cattle Co., Inc.

In the spring of 1977, Charles Probandt, Annette and I drove to San Antonio for one of five meetings that took place among several members of the two Beefmaster associations. Since I had sold 110 females from the Musser and Spurlock ranches to Andy Smith and Bill Newsome in 1976, I mentioned to Charles on the way home that buying the Musser females every year would be a great opportunity, and he immediately offered to finance them. We began buying them for resale, thereby providing the Mussers with a market for their excellent females. In the fall of 1977, our *de facto* partnership purchased over 200 females at Delta, Colorado, and resold them. On January 1, 1978, Charles and I officially formed the Isa Cattle Co. Partnership, which the Probandts graciously named after our daughter. In 1979, the partnership sold 1,264 registered Beefmaster cattle. The partnership with Charles was going well and good profit margins in these cattle helped us to start our financial recovery. Charles was a good partner as well as a very caring man, and while visiting one day, he told me that one of his objectives was to see me get back on my feet financially.

The Mussers—Pioneering Ranchers

Our dealings with the Musser Brothers—Tom, Jack and Bernice, and their son, Johnny—of Delta, Colorado, gained momentum during these years as I bought many females from them. In addition to being great people, they provided us with a large pool of excellent ranch cattle to market—all Tom Lasater genetics. One of the things I realized on my first visit to the Mussers in the fall of 1973 was that they epitomized "The Cowboy Way" and represented the values that everyone in and out of our profession admires. I immediately decided to take Lorenzo there as soon as he was old enough to participate. When he was nine, we flew together in our plane from Colorado Springs, where we were on vacation, to Delta, Colorado. We took our saddles with us, so we were ready for action. We spent the first night at their headquarters at the mouth of Escalante Canyon, where Jack and Bernice lived. On the first morning of our visit, Jack drove us to the cow camp at Short Point, a spectacular piece of deeded ground surrounded by big hills and big aspen timber with the Continental Divide to the east and the La Sal Mountains in Utah 30 miles to the west. Upon arrival, Tom immediately turned Lorenzo loose with a four wheeler and a chainsaw in an aspen grove. His only instruction was not to drop a tree on the cow-camp.

> "Cows may come and cows may go, but the
> bull around here goes on forever."
>
> —cow camp sign

My nephew, Tom Lasater, is known for asking on his first visit to camp, "Where did you get all this old junk?" The cabin is tiny with every inch of wall covered with old pieces of equipment, a wash basin, a small mirror, a girlie calendar, a sign from the Denver Stockyards, etc. My favorite is a sign that says, "Cows may come and cows may go, but the bull around here goes on forever."

Jack and his brother, Tom, are the third generation of Musser Brothers. The first generation homesteaded in the canyon, and their son, Johnny, is the fourth. Jack's wife, Bernice, also grew up in the Escalante Canyon.

Each generation divided the work. Jack and Bernice lived at the Windy, ran the business and oversaw the irrigation. Tom summered at Short Point in the Uncompahgre National Forest. All hands participated in the cow work and everyone, including the hired cowboys, wintered at Windy. Tom's wife, Pat, lived in Delta in what they called the Gas House (because gasoline from a nearby service station had filtered into their basement). Tom visited Delta every few weeks to see his family and to get some clean clothes.

The Mussers are very interesting and unique. Although they are intelligent, educated people, they have their own self-contained culture and philosophy. They figured out in 1948 that Beefmasters would do better than Herefords in their extremely harsh environment. Their cows wintered on high desert government land, eating snow for water, with about ten percent dying each year. They understood and lived by "The Lasater Philosophy" as much as anyone ever has. They broke their own horses, butchered their own beef and made chaps from their own cowhides. Bernice told me that Jack, Tom and Johnny were the toughest cowboys in cowboy country. The Mussers perfected the art of the family partnership. Every morning they held an impromptu committee meeting in which they decided what to do and who would do it. Every opinion, including those of employees, was listened to with respect, and all volunteered for the hardest job. There was no complaining or recrimination for past problems.

From the Bernice Musser Collection

Short Point cow camp.

Each day at Short Point was delightful, with perfect weather, after a good night's sleep at high altitude. The first job every morning was to wrangle the horses, which were turned out into a large forest unit at night, so gathering them was no small item. Tom would prepare a terrific breakfast, including fresh biscuits, and then put in a roast to cook while the crew was working. After breakfast, we would leave to brand calves, break horses, fix fence flattened by snowdrifts or rotate cattle from one unit to

another, returning about mid-afternoon for roast beef with all the trimmings and homemade cobbler.

Everyone smoked, and the brands of choice were Lucky Strike and Bull Durham. Tom rarely went to a store and never saw a bill, but once he happened to see on the grocery bill what Lucky Strikes cost, so he began alternating "store boughts" with Bull Durham to lower his cigarette costs.

From the Bernice Musser Collection

Jack Musser, Tom Musser and their Uncle Don, "Unk," in 1952. When I was there, Tom looked like Unk and Johnny, Jack's son, looked like Jack. It is not surprising that the best cowboy picture I've seen was taken of the Mussers.

That is probably why cowboy shirts have two pockets, one for the Luckies and one for "roll-your-owns." I spent time with the Musser extended family at Short Point, the Windy and the Escalante Forks. I would not take anything for those visits fueled by good food, great company and plenty of Luckies and Johnny Walker Red. We talked about Beefmasters, their family history and ours, plus many items of personal philosophy. I was privileged to be part of their inner circle.

One of the interesting insights into their world regarded their uncle, Don Musser. Unk, as he was always referred to, taught Jack and Tom to cowboy, and more importantly, how to be men. The accompanying 1952 picture shows Jack and Tom with their uncle Don. When I spent time there, Tom looked like Unk and Johnny looked like his dad, Jack. One of the things that fascinated me about the cattle business was how the old-timers managed their financial and personal affairs so well with fewer tools than are available today. Tom and Jack told me how their father and uncle would allow the inventory to build up and then when the price was right, make a big sale. When I heard this, I knew it was the only way to optimize profit in a large-scale ranching operation. Regardless of how we choose to look at it, the cow-calf business is about inventory management, and any man-made timetable just will not work.

Tom told me that his uncle was a superman, noted for his feats of endurance and skill. He said that on some days in cow-camp everyone would get up early, cook breakfast and wrangle the horses in preparation for a hard day's work. But, afterwards, with no announcement, Unk might lie down and read a book or whatever. Without a word being spoken, the men with him would eventually realize that this was to be a day of rest and no work was going to be done. This legendary iron man knew how to take care of himself and husband his energies without the neighbors or people in town ever knowing he took a day off. As soon as I heard this story, I incorporated the valuable technique into my life. When I told this story to Guillermo Osuna, he said, "You've got to write a book about the experiences you've had and the people you've known."

My favorite story on Uncle Don took place when Tom and Jack were 8–10 years old. The Mussers had a large herd of big steers at the Escalante Forks, ready to be driven to town for shipment on the railroad to Denver, Phoenix or Los Angeles. Rather than waiting for the crew to come the next day for the eight-mile drive to the Lowe Place, Unk decided to go ahead and move them himself. According to Jack and Tom, not only were they no help, but their uncle was "babysitting" them during the drive. Unk knew the cattle and the terrain so well that each time the herd came to a canyon where they could turn back, a horseman was waiting. The steers never realized there was only one horseman, and he bluffed the cattle all the way down without losing one head.

• • •

The Musser families waged a multi-generation, running battle with the U.S. Forest Rangers. The government tried futilely to get an accurate count on their cattle and horses, which grazed on several allotments of a large national forest grazing unit in the Uncompahgre National Forest. The unit surrounded Short Point, a small piece of the Mussers' deeded land in the middle of the government unit. Tom and Jack had a large remuda, which they gathered out of the unit at daylight each morning and turned back into the unit after quitting time, so the rangers naturally thought the horses stayed on the deeded land and were not part of the official count.

One summer, when Lorenzo and I were visiting, the wrangler missed three horses in the morning. Just before dark, Tom decided to go find them in the unit, which was probably 15,000 to 20,000 acres of big timber. I went along to help him and to see for myself how he proposed to find the delinquents at dark. We rode several miles from camp and went straight to where the horses stood motionless, knowing he would be looking for them. Although one of the horses had a bell, Tom was hard of hearing. I had perfect hearing and never heard a sound until we were within fifty yards of them.

From the Bernice Musser Collection
Tom Musser on Whitewash (note the horse's blindfold).

One of the secrets of the Mussers' success was making every day fun, unlike life on the Lasater Ranch, where most days were concerned with the deadly-serious cow business. They always had several young men living with them working as cowboys or irrigators. These young men, including their motorcycles, love lives, etc., became members of the extended family. As I mentioned, the employees were part of all business decisions as well as making the daily plan. Most importantly, they received priceless training from the adults and helped the older people maintain their energy and youthful outlook.

In 1977, Charles and I made a gift of a Waggoner Ranch stud colt to the Mussers. I flew to Vernon, Texas, to make the selection, taking Skipper Duncan along to help me. We had one of the most interesting days. Wes O'Neil met us at the airport and drove us to the office to meet the general manager and then to one of their cow-camps for lunch. We selected My Kind of Man, an unbroken buckskin, two-year-old colt, from some thirty head. We were treated like royalty, and the tour alone was worth the modest price of the horse. It saddens me that now, 28 years later, this great pioneer ranch is being sold.

• • •

"Sort in haste, repent at your leisure."
—John Cargile

At the end of October, 1984, John Cargile and I flew to Delta, Colorado, in his Bonanza, to buy the Musser calf crop heifers to start his Beefmaster herd, and I bought the bulls. It was perfect fall weather, the day beginning cold in the morning but warming with bright sunshine. John enjoyed the Mussers and seeing a really "western" outfit. We drew up a contract on the calves after dinner and watched the new Beefmaster Association video. After the video, the conversation turned to loans for ranching, and knowing that one of the great men of the livestock industry was in their home, Bernice brought out their ledgers and laid them on the table saying, "Tell us what to do." John studied the records carefully and told them it was dangerous to owe large amounts of money in such a treacherous banking environment. Bernice is the archetypal ranch woman. I have known her sisters all over the U.S.—doing most of the hard work, pleading futilely with their menfolk to cut expenses, always with a big smile for everyone. Due to John's schedule, we returned in December to sort the calves on a one-day, round-trip (six flights) schedule from San Angelo to Grand Junction. It took seventeen hours and nearly killed both of us. While we were carefully sorting our calves, John quoted one of the great sheep-industry sayings, "Sort in haste, repent at your leisure."

The Beefmaster Associations

In the early '60s, various breeders prevailed on Dad to form a Beefmaster association so that we breeders could be competitive in exporting cattle. Until that time, there was no recordkeeping required. Because of Dad's good teachings, most of the breeders had excellent performance data. The new association, founded in San Antonio, Texas, was called Beefmaster Breeders Universal, named by my mother. South Texas politics were a problem from the outset, and when Archer Parr of Duval County fame started buying Beefmasters, Dad correctly prophesied the end of BBU. (The Parr family became famous when the county courthouse burned down with Lyndon Johnson's opponent's election ballots inside.)

Before long, a group of breeders began agitating to change the bylaws in order to sell their cattle at inflated prices. By 1968, a group of dishonest people seized control of the association by stuffing the ballot box at a convention in Corpus Christi. I was on the board at that time. Realizing it would be very time-consuming and costly to fight such a battle, a group of Dad's followers decided to split at the next year's annual convention in San Antonio. In 1972, we chartered the Foundation Beefmaster Association in Colorado, of which I was a founding director. In 1974, I succeeded David Kistner of Snellville, Georgia, as president.

Bull Facility

"Laurie paid all those debts with Beefmaster
cattle. Let him build whatever he wants."
—*John Cargile*

In the spring of 1979, we built our first bull test facility on San Angelo Feedyard property. In discussing the construction plans of the facility, the feedlot manager, Roy Williams, was concerned that the Brucellosis program was heating up, making it no longer possible to have breeding cattle in a quarantined feedlot. Roy talked to John Cargile about it, who told him, "Laurie paid all those debts with Beefmaster cattle. Let him build whatever he wants."

The first bull facility and its successor, built ten years later on the south side of Highway 67, near Miles, Texas, took our business to a new level. It improved our ability to evaluate the bulls, select herd sires and market the bulls. It also gave us a place for weaning and grading calves, breeding heifers by artificial insemination, and temporarily holding groups of cattle, such as those bought for resale or moved off pasturage that was poor or needing rest. It did away with the need to have the traditional ranch infrastructure and permanent employees, and was an outgrowth of how we learned to solve problems in Mexico. Given my unorthodox modus operandi, the bull facility concept is one of the innovations of which I am proudest.

It goes without saying that the key to the facility concept is the service given us by the San Angelo Feedyard for 34 years. The yard not only cares for and feeds the cattle and finances the feed, but also provides us access to a skilled nutritionist for special projects. It also makes available a consulting veterinarian for emergencies, of which we have had very few. It would be difficult to overstate the importance of the backing we have received from the original owner, John Cargile, and his managers, as well as from the current owners, Glenn and Mollie Polhemus. All are first-class business people.

The Isa Bull Test Facility near Miles, Texas.

• • •

I was looking at cattle on feed with Bob Carter at his feedlot at Plainview, Texas, in 1978, when George W. Bush, who was campaigning against Kent Hance for U.S. Respresentative that year, drove up. The three of us visited, standing together in the middle of nowhere. Later, while George W. was running for governor, Annette and I visited with him at a reception in San Angelo. I was amazed that he remembered me. Now, as the country watches President Bush struggling with overwhelming problems on all sides, I like to remember his pleasant, relaxed personality and ability to get along with everyone.

Isa Cattle Co. Bull Sales

"... trying to sell those damn bulls."
—Jack Williams

I had formulated my bull sale ideas from attending Jack Williams' sales with Bill Finan. Jack and I had a lot in common—both of us originated in South Texas, went to Mexico, came to San Angelo, and established great herds of cattle on leased land. We had a natural bond based on mutual experience and affection. After Jack sold his famous Hereford herd in a great sale, he started buying Beefmaster heifers from me in 1981 and joined Isa Cattle Co.'s Bull Co-op. Every time I saw him at the feed store, Jack would smile and tell me how much he enjoyed sitting in his easy chair watching television in the evenings, knowing I was on the phone "trying to sell those damn bulls."

Seeing that the demand for Beefmaster bulls was greater than the number of bulls I could raise, I decided to form a bull co-operative of several breeders of Foundation Beefmaster cattle. The first year of our bull consignment pool was 1973, and L.G. Hargis, Jr., of Waurika, Oklahoma, called to say that he wanted to bring bulls for it. Because I was out of town, Annette met him at the K-Mart parking lot in San Angelo. He followed her to Skipper Duncan's ranch where the co-op bulls were pastured. When they got to the pasture, L.G. opened the gate on his gooseneck and saw his bulls jump out of the trailer to disappear into the brush. When he returned home, his friends told him he would never see those bulls again. In fact, they did well, as did many successive groups.

By 1978 we had built a significant business at San Angelo. We had sold many cows and had customers needing markets for their bulls. We had our first bull sale on October 18 at the San Angelo Feedyard, using an alley and a small set of rented stands. We cataloged the bulls, pre-priced in sale order, with complete data. It was a family team effort. Lorenzo, age ten, helped Matt Brown bring the bulls up the alley. Before the sale, the buyers registered and were assigned buyer numbers. When a bull entered the ring, an interested buyer would hold up his number and enter a drawing. Charles Probandt handled the microphone and Uncle Palo (Watt Casey) and Trish Probandt handled the drawing, while Annette kept the books. When the first bull entered the ring, 22 buyers held up their numbers to buy the pre-priced bull. It was quite a memorable sale.

John Cargile, interested (but skeptical), watched the beginning of the sale. After about a third of the bulls had sold, he told Roy Williams that it did not appear that we needed any help and returned to town. Maurice Harrell, a Beefmaster breeder from Gonzales, Texas, came for the sale, arriving at noon. He could not believe we already had sold every bull at our price. The sale was a huge success, beyond all expectations. We realized that we needed to pay the Co-op members a bonus, which began a practice we continued until the Bull Co-op ended in 2003. It was exciting to work together in those early years with enthusiastic new breeders. The co-op breeders helped with all the bull workings and gave us great input. Charles suggested that all the cattle be run under one brand, which was a great idea that was never implemented. In retrospect, however, we should have kept control of breeding seasons as well as herd bull and semen bull selections.

One interesting example of valuable ideas from the Co-op (or the Bull Cartel as Frank Smith named it) was Skipper Duncan's idea for grading the bulls. We weighed them individually on a large scale at the feed yard. All the breeders stood around the scale and simultaneously graded each bull 1 to 4 by visual appraisal as well as weight and comparative test gain. Each man indicated his rating by extending the requisite number of fingers. The 1's would be in the first quarter of the sale, the 2's in the second quarter, etc. I had a top bull in the sale one year, and by prior agreement and for fun, they all graded him 4 at the working. This was a tremendous surprise to me and I reacted accordingly, which generated a lot of good-natured laughs.

Opening the International Market

In November 1964, Annette and I introduced the Beefmaster breed into Mexico. We took 35 bred cows and two herd bulls to the lease we had at La Lajita Ranch, Múzquiz, Coahuila, which was the beginning of our Beefmaster foundation herd in Mexico. Also, Dad agreed to sell me each year a group of bulls that he did not include in his annual sale contract. During our ten years in Mexico, we sold some 800 Beefmaster bulls to ranches all over the

Bill Finan and Guillermo Osuna.

country, as well as an equal number of females that established many registered Beefmaster herds there.

In 1972, Dale and I formed Lasater Brothers Cattle Co. to sell frozen genetics. That year we made an agreement with Guillermo Osuna to distribute our product in Mexico, an agreement that continues today with his son, Guillermo, Jr. In August, 1974, Obe Veldman, the manager of the Rhodesia Breeders Cooperative, came to San Angelo and contracted 16,000 straws of frozen semen. Obe was our first big customer outside Mexico. We delivered 11,000 straws via air in nitrogen tanks before the war there put an end to our doing business with that nation, renamed Zimbabwe. The semen we sent to Rhodesia made its way also into Botswana and South Africa, and formed the basis of the Beefmaster breed in Southern Africa, where it continues to flourish.

The destruction of Rhodesia is one of the tragedies of our age. A newspaper account, published December 5, 2005, reported that children in Zimbabwe were eating garbage to survive. Thirty years ago, the nation was an exporter of agricultural products, but today people are starving. The government of Robert Mugabe has been catastrophic. It is heartbreaking that the country did not have an honorable black leader. By contrast, the white population of Southern Africa reveres Nelson Mandela. Ian Smith, an exemplary person and leader, was Rhodesia's last white prime minister. In recent years, Annette and I had the privilege of having dinner with him at the home of Wendell and Debbie Schronk in San Antonio, Texas.

Opening the Florida Market

"Why not?"

—*Charles Probandt*

In 1975, Everett Boney, an old-time "cracker" cowman from Lorida, Florida, came to San Angelo and bought fifteen bulls. South Florida, like Southern Africa, would become an ongoing and important part of our lives. Eddie Lumpkin and Marvin Thomas, manager of the Allapattah Ranch, came to see our cattle operation in 1978. Marvin was the first of many Florida cowmen whom I would meet through Eddie, who was a key player in opening the Florida market for our cattle.

The next year, I received an impressive letter from Cordell Koch, manager of Seminole Sugar in South Florida, so I flew down to see their ranch operations. Cordell agreed to pick me up at the Sheraton Airport West Palm Beach on a given day at 6:00 a.m. In Palm Beach, the water fountains are not even turned on that early in the morning. Without a cup of coffee, I stepped outside the hotel as Cordell roared to a stop. We shook hands and headed for the ranch. It turned out that he did not eat breakfast and assumed the same for me. Fortunately, there was coffee at the ranch office. By lunch, I was really hungry, and it was then that I discovered that he did not eat lunch either. Needless to say, supper really tasted good. Cordell became an outstanding customer, buying over 100 bulls and frozen semen over the next several years. We also bred heifers at his Florida feedlot.

Cordell was from the Northwest, and had worked with John R. Scott in Montana. He was hired by Seminole Sugar to straighten out their feedlot management, and eventually became general manager of their cattle operations. Seminole Sugar was owned by one of the Jewish New York commodity families. Suspecting corruption, the family ordered an internal audit of their agricultural business. As a result, the Pinkertons showed up one day, escorted various employees to their cars, and told Cordell he was in charge. It was very educational for me to witness such dramatic events at close hand.

• • •

In 1976, Fred Barfield, of Immokalee, Florida, purchased our calf crop of Beefmaster bulls and heifers for $700 each. My bank, which was financing our cattle and thought they might be valued too high at that time, was astounded at the sale. This transaction did much to improve our situation with them by putting a value under the Beefmaster cows. In the summer of 1977, I visited Cordell and Fred and saw a lot of ranches with the largest numbers of cattle I had seen anywhere, including many outstanding Beefmaster Cross heifer calves. On this trip, Fred and I had lunch at Clewiston with Billy Rogers and saw his ranch at Lakeport, which I would lease several years later. We also saw Fred's bulls, including those he had purchased from us, on test on Purina Bull Developer for his sale that fall. Fred, who is a top cattleman and farmer, had built the best and most expensive set of working corrals for his sales.

In the fall of 1977, the sale, managed by Fred Thompson, still stands as one of the best. It was a memorable fall day at Barfield Farms with Florida and U.S. flags flying and a huge tent with steaks grilling and corn on the cob simmering. I attended the sale, because our L Bar bulls were in it. The cattle looked good and there was a big crowd. Before the sale, it was announced that Fred Barfield and Jack Dunn of Alice, Texas, the co-hosts of the sale, would be bidding on a bull in the offering. I did not realize that the bull was one of ours. The sale prices of the L Bar bulls blew the roof off. After the sale, I congratulated Fred, who told me he had made $700 on our calves. The sale was during the time the Beefmaster associations were factionalized politically, yet I caught a ride to the sale from the motel in Naples, Florida, with several members of the opposition, including Joe Hendrix. Our discussion in a small rental car became so heated that every half mile or so the car would swerve violently and nearly go into the bar ditch. Cordell Koch also had come to the sale with his crew from Seminole Sugar, so I joined them on the drive back to Florida's East Coast that evening, celebrating as we went. When I returned to San Angelo, I went by Charles Probandt's commodity brokerage office to tell him about my trip. I said that I had seen a real bull sale, but that I could not do anything like that. He asked, "Why not?" That moment was the birth of the Isa Cattle Co. Bull Sale.

Opening the Arizona Market

On March 15, 1978, Bert Reyes, the sale auctioneer, called from Duncan, Oklahoma, to say they were having an auction at 1:00 p.m., but that no one was there. I flew to Duncan in my airplane and was met at the airport. As I walked into the sale barn, someone handed me a catalog, and I sat down in the front row as the first animal came into the ring. I purchased the whole offering (42 females and 35 bulls) and shipped them to Ted and Pat Spurlock in Arizona.

Mr. R.C. Spurlock, their father, was a well-known cattleman, who knew my father and uncle, and was one of many western Mormon ranchers to recognize that Beefmasters were the answer to profitability in large-scale ranching. They had about 1,000 upgraded Beefmaster cows out of Lasater bulls. When I became acquainted with them, R.C. Spurlock and Sons had some 160,000 acres on both sides of I-40 at Navajo, Arizona. Their homes and offices were there, as well as the Navajo Inn, which they owned. On one trip, I landed on the abandoned railroad tracks behind their office and had an important meeting in my room at the motel. Ted, the oldest son, told me that they wanted me to market all of their Beefmaster cattle for $500 per head and to advise them on their breeding program. This was a great arrangement for me and for them. Like the arrangement with the Mussers, I would have another large pool of good, ranch-tough cattle to market. They hired Ron Nichols, a highly competent foreman/manager to smooth out the rough edges of their business. Ron implemented our suggestions and transformed the cattle in a few months, demonstrating the excellence of their operation. The program worked well, and we sold many cattle all over the U.S. After about two years, a promoter approached Ted and Pat and convinced them to join the other association, get rid of their Lasater bulls and sell their cattle, highly promoted, through their auctions. Shortly after they accepted the promoter's recommendations, the manager quit, their herd deteriorated, and R.C. Spurlock and Sons ceased to exist as a factor in the Beefmaster business. Things happen in life that are difficult to explain, and this loss is one I regret.

The story at Navajo is that the Spurlock brothers never saddled a horse after their dad died. Like many ranch children, they were burned out early. Mr. Spurlock believed in working 365 days a year. An example: one Christmas morning, the two brothers, each with eight young children, were celebrating together around 9:00 a.m., when their father arrived, wearing his chaps and spurs. After surveying the situation, he said he guessed he was the only one who cared about the ranch and walked out with Ted and Pat following closely behind. Unfortunately, their father did not give them enough business training along with the hard work to teach them how to keep the ranch together.

Pat, a big man with a big heart and a world of enthusiasm, became a close friend. He is one of those people who make life worthwhile. The year I went on the board, Pat and I were at a National Cattlemen's

Convention in Phoenix. We were staying in the same hotel and found ourselves in the sauna with a fellow from Indiana. The "hoosier" had never heard of Beefmasters, but when he came out of the sauna, he was a Beefmaster man forever. It is the custom at these conventions for someone from the hosting state to give the invocation at the opening meeting. When the lights were dimmed and Pat, in his pinstriped suit, came on stage and gave a truly beautiful prayer, I felt proud to know him. In dealing with the Spurlock, Flake, and Evans families and others, one is always aware of being with people of heightened spirituality who live their religion.

Opening the Nevada/California Market

In the late spring of 1979, Bill Maupin, manager of the IL Ranch at Tuscarora, Nevada, bought a truckload of bulls from Isa Cattle Co. The IL, estimated at 700,000 acres, ran 5,000 cows and 5,000 ewes. It was the only place I have dealt with that still had a toll station phone, which means that the caller says, "Operator, please connect me with the IL Ranch at Tuscarora, Nevada." After a minute of consultations, clicks and relays, I would hear Bill's wife Wanda's unmistakable voice say, "IL Ranch." As I have mentioned, Dad had a toll station number in the 1940s, "Lasater Ranch, USA," which he always regretted losing.

Bill Maupin was one of the great professional managers of large operations whom I have known. He followed the Lasater philosophy and developed a large cowherd well adapted to a demanding environment. Bill used our bulls to create a herd in Nevada that weaned 500-pound calves. He told me that in the fall they gathered 98% of the cattle they had turned out in the spring. In other words, the dead and missing count was only two percent, an unbelievable number on such a large ranch. Jack Sparrowk, considered the top cattleman in California, began buying IL steer calves to go to grass, and his success with them led in part to the popularity of Beefmasters in the West and Northwest. Many of our customers today had ties with Jack or Bill Maupin. Pearce Flournoy of Likely, California, uses Beefmasters because Jack recommended them, and Gary and Fillis Takacs of Winnemucca, Nevada, worked on the IL Ranch. Bill Maupin's arrival in San Angelo opened another significant chapter in my career.

• • •

Ron Florence, who owned the Bell Brand Ranch at Wells, Nevada, and bought 40 bulls a year, had been referred by Pat Spurlock. All of our negotiations were by telephone. Each spring I would phone him to sell him a load of bulls. After we had discussed the cattle business, and he had forced me to give my best spiel, which he enjoyed, he would buy a load. In 1982, I sensed that he might not buy bulls, so when I phoned him on March 11, I had my traps ready. As soon as Ron heard my voice, he shouted, "I am not going to buy any bulls this year whatsoever." As soon as he said that, I remembered that my former brother-in-law had told me that if you could get the other party to say no, the prospective buyer had left his cover and a sale could be made. We visited for 45 minutes. I explained that he could buy a load from me, two loads from a dispersal sale that was coming up, and average down his cost to only slightly more than his English bulls would bring for slaughter. He agreed to buy 124 bulls, the number he needed to replace his non-Beefmaster bulls. This was my greatest sale by telephone.

Baron—Lasater Brothers' Greatest Sale

"I thought that's what good bulls were bringing."
                                                                        —Laurie Lasater

In 1976, the Lasater Ranch had a bull calf for sale as a yearling off grass. As soon as I saw him, I realized he was something special. Dale had the second contract selection in Dad's bull delivery that year, and we decided that Lasater Brothers would buy that bull if the people who had the first contract did not take him. The night before the selection, I did not close my eyes. Because the bull was brownish/black in color, and the people wanted a red bull, we were able to buy him. Dale named him Baron.

The Harrell Cattle Company of Gonzales, Texas, BBU members, was starting to do business in a big way in the Beefmaster industry. I attended an auction they held to sell off part of the Homer Herring herd. (Homer was one of Dad's original customers.) A bull named Showboy sold for

$150,000 in that sale. At the same time, Baron was generating great public interest, and Dale and I had sold a large volume of semen from him. I had

Baron.

Baron at San Angelo, breeding him to some of Andy Smith's black-baldy cows to evaluate him for the Certified Meat Sire qualification under Performance Registry International. When the Harrell Cattle Co. expressed an interest in buying him, I remembered their recent auction and priced him at $150,000. Wallace asked, "Where in the world did you get that price?" I replied, "I thought that's what good bulls were bringing." The two brothers, Wallace and Maurice, came to see Baron's Beefmaster calves on the black-baldy cows at Water Valley. For the tour, Charles Probandt and I rented a van, which Charles drove. On the way back to San Angelo, Wallace offered me $50,000 for the bull. When I told him I was going to stay with my price, Charles nearly swerved the van into the bar ditch. After the Harrell brothers left, Charles asked, "Are you out of your mind?" I replied, "It's a done deal. They would not have offered $50,000 if they had not liked the bull." During the negotiations, I called Dad to make sure he would not object to the sale. After completing the sale just before Christmas, I called Dale, and as a joke, asked what he would take for his half-interest. The highest number he could think of was $10,000. I answered, "How would $50,000 each work?" We were both thrilled.

This sale put our cattle on the map. For the leaders of the opposing Beefmaster association to pay this kind of money for a Lasater bull was unbeatable public relations for us. The Harrell brothers syndicated the bull, renamed him Changer, and made good money on him, as they were entitled to. We had very pleasant business relationship with them. When Maurice died recently, his obituary showed a picture of him in his office in front of a picture of Changer on the wall behind him.

Closing the 1970s

1979, a big year in my career, started with a bang. Annette and I attended the International Stockman's School in San Antonio, Texas, sponsored by The Agriservices Foundation, of which Bill Finan and Guillermo Osuna were trustees. This popular school, founded by Dr. and Mrs. M.E. Ensminger, was a seminar where influential international leaders in world agriculture would gather to give presentations and speeches. Dad and Dr. Jan Bonsma of South Africa were speaking on this program. Because there were so many worthwhile presentations, Annette and I attended different ones. It is still unbelievable to me that Tom Lasater and Jan Bonsma, the two men who had the greatest impact on the world cattle industry in the twentieth century, appeared on the same program, easily accessible to anyone interested.

Lasater and Bonsma

The two principal influences on cattle breeding in the twentieth century were Tom Lasater, founder of the Beefmaster breed, and Prof. Jan Bonsma of South Africa, founder of the Bonsmara breed. They arrived at the same conclusions on cattle productivity, Lasater through practical experience and Bonsma through scientific study. Each was a great teacher and personality who influenced many.

Interestingly, they studied together under Dr. Jay L. Lush

Dad and Jan Bonsma speaking at Beckton Farms, Sheridan, Wyoming, in 1964.

at Iowa State in the early thirties, considered the founder of the modern science of animal breeding. One of Dr. Lush's papers was titled "Population Genetics," which is a byword in the Lasater philosophy. His interest in inbreeding and line breeding influenced Lasater and Bonsma in their creation of two composite breeds. The two students knew and influenced each other and the rest of the world.

I met Allan Savory at this same school in San Antonio. In 1980, he and his partner, Stan Parsons, accepted my invitation to settle in San Angelo and office with us. Annette administered their office and made arrangements for their first U.S. school on grazing and management. Every seat was sold and the attendees, who tied together our past and present, included people who were to be key players in our network for the next 25 years. They could not have had a more knowledgeable and diverse class.

It is hard to believe that so much was accomplished after 1974. All the training I received at home, plus the education and the tremendous business experience in Mexico, combined with a great wife and good partners, was bearing fruit. In 1979, Charles and I bought a new Piper Dakota (N2235C) from Longenette Flying Service. The Isa Cattle Co. aviation motto was *"a tailwind both ways."* It is evident that the motto was the truth.

CHAPTER 21

THE 1980s

Beginning with the market crash of 1974, the cattle industry was declining and suffered a body blow every six years—20 percent interest in 1980, tax reform act of 1986, onset of eleven years' drought in 1992, plus many minor droughts and market breaks.

Isa Cattle Co. in the '80s

On March 17, 1986, John S. Todd, Jr., came to work for Isa Cattle Co. as vice-president of operations. That same month, I was thinking of hiring Jimmy Autrey when his uncle, Delbert Autrey, came to buy bulls. I asked Delbert if Jimmy could handle the job. He told me, with tears in his eyes, that if he could afford him, Jimmy would never leave New Mexico. I hired him in May 1986, and he stayed nearly seven years, then returned to work for Lorenzo in December, 2004. I had leased the Noelke Ranch adjoining our McAfee lease, so his family moved there, taking over responsibility for 17,000 acres stocked with nearly 1,000 Beefmaster cows and heifers in five big grazing cells. I have been fortunate in having seven competent foremen during my 42-year career—Eugenio de la Rosa, Federico Arias, Luis Hernández, Matt Brown, Scott Phillips, Jack Sutton and Jimmy Autrey. The title I have aspired to is chairman, but the one I admire is foreman. Jimmy personifies the traits that the good ones possess—smart, athletic, a leader, and a problem solver with livestock and mechanical skills. An example of his problem solving occurred during one of our bull sales. Sometimes in the bull ring or the sale ring, a bull will find a *querencia* (safe spot) and refuse to leave it. During a sale, one of the bulls refused to leave the ring and no one could move him. After the bull's standoff, Jimmy, who was seated in the stands, came down to the pen, borrowed a paddle, whacked the bull twice and put him out of the ring.

• • •

Hugh MacMillan, a Princeton friend, loved to go to the ranch in Florida to look at the cattle with Jack Sutton. On one occasion, he took another Palm Beach lawyer with him. Hugh had a distinguished academic career at Princeton and Oxford, yet half way through the circle, he realized that he was the second-smartest man in the pickup and that the other high-powered lawyer understood nothing Hugh and Jack were discussing. One of my favorite stories about Jack Sutton exemplifies the physical prowess so admired in our industry. Jack was crossing a canal on our ranch lease at Fort Pierce, and as he stopped to open the gate, his cow-dog jumped out of the back of the pickup into the canal to cool off and was grabbed by an alligator. Jack grabbed a shovel, jumped into the canal, fought the alligator and rescued his dog. Florida cowboys love dogs more than anything.

• • •

After John Todd left, I advertised in a blind ad in the *Livestock Weekly* for a new vice-president of operations and received many promising responses. I had sold cattle to James Howell and his wife, Janet, of Midland, Texas; James realized that the ad was mine, and called me at home one night. Because Isa Cattle Co. could not pay the salary he was making as an engineer at Exxon, I told him that the job would not interest him. After I hung up, Annette observed that he had called because he was interested in the job, so I called James back and he came to work two weeks later, taking a fifty-percent pay cut. Our agreement was that he would upgrade Isa Cattle Co., Inc., and that I would teach him the cattle business. If I ever had any illusions about how poorly managed the Fortune 500 corporations were, I was quickly disabused. While being easygoing, always with a big smile, James was a perfectionist who came to work fifteen minutes early and left only when every task was completed. If I was working on a cow trade, an engineering study appeared on my desk, beautifully done in black ink on a white legal pad. If the Chicagoans or the New Yorkers needed some numbers, they received them immediately. If there was a problem on a pasturage deal, James went to the site and stayed until it was solved. He was not only a top employee, but he and Janet continued to buy cattle from us for their own ranch.

• • •

In April 1989, we hired Sheila Alexander, who typed this manuscript. Sheila, who has always been one of our favorites, worked for us for four years before moving to Arkansas, where her husband was called to be head pastor of a Church of God congregation. In addition to being an attractive lady and an excellent secretary, she taught us by example what being a Christian means. Ten years later, while we were fighting an eleven-year drought, she told me, to my great surprise, that her prayer group was praying for us. There is no question in my mind that is why we survived.

Buying Heifers in Florida

In 1980, business was picking up steam in Florida. Seminole Sugar bought fifty Beefmaster bulls and also financed us in buying 800 Beefmaster Cross heifers, breeding them to our bulls and selling us the pregnant heifers at a set price. Eddie Lumpkin had a buyer for them, saying that he knew the people well and that a contract was not necessary. However, the buyer did not perform on the heifers, which put Isa Cattle Co. in a significant financial crisis. We went to Glen Kerby of the Central National Bank and told him we needed a loan, which we would repay in 90 days. He loaned us the money, and in the following days, we sold the bred heifers to Andy Smith and Vernon Ryan of San Angelo, as well as to other buyers as far away as Alabama. They were fabulous heifers, and it was too bad that such a creative and successful deal was blighted by the buyer's non-performance and our misplaced trust in not drawing a contract with earnest money. Although we extricated ourselves with minor losses, this emergency put a strain on us and resulted in Charles Probandt withdrawing from the Isa Cattle Co. Partnership. Finan and Lasater bought him out in 1982, ending our successful association amicably. Although we were very different, Charles and I complemented each other, and we were highly successful in every venture.

Partnering with Throckmorton

"Sign 'em slow, Howard."

—*Bill Carey*

We moved into the big leagues in finance in the '80s. We did three cattle syndications, two in New York and one in Chicago, and made cattle deals with two members of the Forbes List of World Billionaires.

During my career, I have had four partners named Bill (Bill Finan, Bill Carey, Bill Broussard, and Bill Richey), each outstanding in his own way. Bill Carey, whom we met at the Savory-Parsons School sponsored by Isa Cattle Co., told me he was interested in learning how we operated, and he began financing us on large numbers of Beefmaster heifers being bred for resale. We had a successful relationship and partnership over many years in the most difficult cattle markets. Although we are both high-energy people, we are opposites in many ways: he is an Easterner and I am a Westerner; he is a money-man, and I, an operator and promoter; he is a non-risker and I, a risker. One of the basic differences between us was in our circumstances and objectives. I was trying to make a profit and needed accounting to know the breakevens for pricing purposes, and Bill used accounting to keep track of his family portfolio. Each of his ventures was named, with every tiny item posted with interest compounded daily, in a giant spreadsheet. The spreadsheets were pages and pages with hundreds of numbers in fine print. I once had a banker check one, who said Bill's program was more powerful than the one used by the bank. After we became good friends, I jokingly told him I was going to read his printouts someday while recovering from bypass surgery.

An example of our style: When a prospect was coming to look at the cattle, I would phone Bill, asking for the breakeven, meaning that the 361 remaining heifers were costing $672 per head as of 5:00 p.m. on Wednesday. Instead, I would get a four-page computer printout containing a sea of numbers. If I asked for the feed cost per head, the same thing happened. Although very articulate, Bill had a sense of humor, an example of which occurred one day after a hamburger lunch at their ranch headquarters, when Howard said he had to go back to the office to sign some checks. Bill replied, "Sign 'em slow, Howard." I came to admire Bill's financial skills, and I think he admired my knowing how to find and buy the cattle and get them sold, usually at a profit. Altogether, we handled over 5,000 Beefmaster heifers, mostly raised in Florida by us or by Lykes Brothers.

After Bill Carey met Howard Carleton at the Savory-Parsons school in San Angelo, Bill hired Howard as manager of the Throckmorton Land and Cattle Co., which was Bill and his sister's share of the historic Swenson Ranch (SMS) located near Throckmorton, Texas. Bill and Howard made one of the best management teams I have encountered. The combination of their teamwork, holistic management and Beefmaster cattle on that particular ranch was unbeatable. If I were allowed one phone call to ask a technical question about the cattle business, I would call Howard. I enjoyed working with Bill, his wife, Kip, and Howard. Their resources and management skills were invaluable, and partnering with Throckmorton for many years was an important part of my business life.

• • •

In 1981, I put together a group consisting of Bill Finan, Guillermo Osuna, Pomeroy Smith and Bill Carey to finance the purchase of a ranch in Florida. We hoped to purchase a large property adjacent to the Chamblee Ranch at Micco Bluff, north of Okeechobee. All of us were excited about the prospects, and in April the whole group, except Pomeroy, traveled to South Florida to see it. It was an outstanding group with strong finances and a lot of cattle and business experience. Bill Finan and I were currently partners; Bill Carey and I were partnering on cattle; Pom and I had been partners; and Guillermo and I had done extensive business. Bill Carey became the liaison between the rest of the group and me. Planning to stock the ranch, we began buying a sizeable number of Beefmaster heifers. It is interesting that just when I first started doing business in Florida, large numbers of Beefmaster Cross heifers became available for the first time. Later on, we realized we were not going to be able to buy the ranch, so in mid-February I went to West Palm Beach to liquidate the Florida heifer venture at a profit.

• • •

"The reds will beat them every time."
—the ranch foreman

Several years earlier, I had become acquainted with Arky Rogers of Lake City, Florida. He is a colorful figure, and certainly one of the outstanding cow traders in the United States, specializing in buying out herds of quality commercial females being dispersed. When there was to be a big herd for sale anywhere in the United States, Arky would pack his entire wardrobe, along with his draft book, in a giant leather suitcase, travel to the location and stay there, sometimes for several weeks, until the herd had been bought and resold at a profit. Like all good traders, he made his profit on the front.

In the spring of 1985, Hal Noelke, whose ranch joined my lease west of Mertzon, offered his ranch for lease to the first person bringing a signed check. John Cargile, who earlier had met Arky and arranged a female sale for him at Producers Auction, suggested that we lease the ranch and partner with Arky in buying crossbred females in Florida for resale.

John and I began negotiating with Hal, a difficult task. As John was planning to leave town, he told me, "I'm tired of fooling with this. You handle it however you want." After John left, I told Hal that we were not going to accept his terms. Hal replied, "I'll meet you in your lawyer's office in thirty minutes, and you draw the contract however you want." We leased 11,000 acres for five years at $5.00 per acre, including the hunting. Later, because of the complexity and potential liabilities connected with moving cattle out of Florida during the Brucellosis eradication program, John decided to end our partnership with Arky.

In May 1984, I had taken John to South Florida to see our cattle and the general area. We visited Bud Adams and Marvin Thomas, renowned Florida cattlemen, and had tours of those two great ranches. We also saw the Dudas' cattle at Indianlands, and John met Joe Duda and Jackie Bass. As a result of that trip, John and I contracted 700 Beefmaster Cross heifers from the Dudas for delivery the next year.

United States Sugar Corp. decided to sell their cowherd in South Florida in July 1985, so John and I flew down to meet Arky Rogers and look at the herd. It was one of the great herds of cattle in the United

States, consisting mainly of F-1 Braford and Brangus cows bred to Charolais bulls, and managed by Dr. Mike Milicevic. I knew Dr. Mike, who was sick about the impending sale, a typical bad corporate decision, and he did not even want to show them to us. As we saw various top quality groups, the most interesting stop was on what had been the Billy Rogers Ranch at Lakeport, Florida. U.S. Sugar raised its F-1 replacements in Mississippi, and Lakeport was stocked with 300 heavy-springing Brafords and 300 heavy-springing Brangus coming-three-year-old heifers. We were amazed by the good cattle on such a fine ranch. As we drove up the dike running through the middle of the ranch, we could see the Brafords on the left and the Brangus on the right. At that time, Dr. Mike, Arky and John were Brangus fans. It was dead quiet in the car, when the foreman touring with us spoke out, "The reds will beat them every time." I said, "Say that again; these fellows need to hear that," so he did. I was to be a working partner in the partnership with John and Arky providing the financing. We bid on 15,000 U.S. Sugar cows, but we were outbid. We did buy about 250 Second Cross Beefmaster heifers of very high quality that had come from Billy Rogers, which were sold at a profit.

A. Duda and Sons, Inc.

"You could wear out a new Oldsmobile and not
find any cattle that good."
—Andy Smith

The next day, we started receiving 811 Beefmaster heifer calves from A. Duda and Sons off the Indianlands Ranch south of Clewiston. The ranch lies along the highway that intersects Alligator Alley, which runs from Fort Lauderdale to Naples. It is the southernmost ranch in Florida, with no buildings or electricity. It is very wild and isolated and was reclaimed from the Everglades. Jackie Bass, Duda's South Florida Cattle Manager, had done the work of establishing this ranch from scratch, including the pastures and the cattle program.

The delivery itself was quite a spectacle. It was a hot Florida day, with the humidity shimmering little clouds above the ground. The Dudas were shipping their steer calves to Oklahoma and the heifers to us in Texas.

When we arrived, they had three pastures of 250 cows and calves lined up in pasture traps, ready to come into the pens. There were probably ten or fifteen cowboys, slickers tied on the backs of their saddles, with their dogs. The trucks were in line by the highway—Texas truck, Oklahoma truck, etc. The cowboys would bring up a herd to be sorted five ways: heifers; cull heifers; steers; cull steers; and cows. As they came down the chute, I would indicate the ten-percent cull heifers and the Oklahoma buyer did likewise on the steers. We could look behind us to see the cuts and the keepers in our respective groups, so it was easy to make adjustments. When they had loaded 50,000 pounds of heifers onto a truck, it pulled away and left for that state, a trip of approximately 36 hours. The process was repeated with a load of steers. The work was continuous, with all of the cattle being sorted, then weighed and loaded. The first day of a three-day delivery, we received 275 heifers with a pay weight of 530 pounds at $.66 per pound. All hands present were lifetime professionals, and it was one of the memorable days of my career. After the first trucks arrived at Andy Smith's ranch at Water Valley, Texas, I called him from Florida to see if the cattle had arrived okay. He said, "You could wear out a new Oldsmobile and not find any cattle that good."

The first day, the Duda employees put approximately 1,600 cattle down the chute. The trucks were in line, the herds were gathered as far as the eye could see, and everyone was working full blast. I was standing by the highway when a carload of German tourists stopped and asked me what in the world was happening. The Germans are very interested in everything related to cowboys, so I explained the whole process to them. When I finished, they drove slowly away, shaking their heads; the Wild West was wilder than they ever could have imagined. When we processed those 811 heifers in Andy's pens on July 15, they looked even better sorted off as a group than they had in Florida. The next day we also worked 370 bulls for the next two sales.

In August 1986, we started working the Duda heifers at Water Valley. They were bred 97.7% with 85% bred early. Aside from being fertile, productive cattle, their move to Texas from the Indianlands Ranch had upgraded their environment. They were a beautiful set of heifers on a fine ranch. During this period, most of the cattle work in Texas and Florida revolved around the Brucellosis eradication program. Both Texas and Florida were problems, and in the process of establishing some of the earliest certified-free herds in both states, we had to test everything nearly monthly. On September 14, with Isabel helping, we bled 425 cows at the T-Circle Ranch. While I was keeping count during one stretch of several workings, we bled 3,500 cows without our foreman, Matt Brown, ever letting one escape from our W-W portable squeeze chute.

• • •

The summer of 1983, J.D. Cage and I flew from San Angelo to Okeechobee in his pressurized Cessna T210. I will never forget the San Angelo tower saying, "Cessna N210CR cleared R-NAV direct to Okeechobee, Florida, via the Lampasas VOR." The new technology enabled pilots on an instrument flight plan to fly directly to their destination, with technology moving the navigational aids in line rather than going via the on-ground aids. At that time, we were planning to feed the FTX calves as bulls, so the next day we met Bob Carter of Plainview, Texas, and Joe Duda for breakfast and to see our calves at Fort Pierce. Both liked the cattle, and Bob laid out a simple veterinary program to prepare the male calves for shipment to the feedlot. From Fort Pierce, we flew to Clewiston with Joe in his company's Aero-Commander to see the Duda's cattle at their Indianland Ranch. Those cattle, as fall-calvers, had been marked and branded, so it was impressive to see such a large number of good cattle. That visit, including Joe Duda, Jackie Bass, Bob Carter, J.D. and me—all seasoned professionals in the industry—was a real turning point. Bob said, correctly, that the Beefmaster bull calves would outperform anything in the feedlot, and we already knew the heifers were the best.

FTX Ranch Co., Ltd.

"Don't worry cowboy. We'll handle the IRS."
—New York lawyer

Hugh MacMillan, our Florida lawyer, had formed a partnership with a New York lawyer-CPA, who had a stable of investors, including one member of the Forbes 400, for whom he put together tax shelters. Under the tax rules at that time, the cattle business lent itself to the leveraged tax shelter structure probably better than any other. It was legally possible then to form a syndication at year-end, take ten percent investment tax credit, a full year's depreciation, and prepay significant expenses, thereby achieving a first-day loss of five times the cash investment. Leverage was achieved by borrowing against letters of credit signed by the wealthy investors. When Hugh talked to me regarding forming a company, Bill Carey and I had an inventory of Beefmaster heifer calves on hand, which gave the New York firm time to put the deal together.

In our first meeting with Hugh's partner, I told him that I wanted all legal, accounting and management fees agreed to beforehand, a good move on my part. I asked him who would be the partner on tax matters, and he said, "Don't worry cowboy, we'll handle the IRS." His whole concept was based on using letters of credit to provide equity and also to establish the "at risk" requirement for tax purposes. His grasp of finance was brilliant, and we worked well together. In one of our meetings, I gave him a one-page proposal, which he studied for ten minutes, made a fifteen-degree adjustment and the deal took off. He taught me one of the most important things I have learned about negotiations: Always get what you want and give the other fellow what he wants—and remember, they usually are different.

At midnight on May 26, 1982, Hugh called, committing on a cattle syndication starting with 956 heifers. The project, named FTX Ranch Co., Ltd., would be completed by year-end with Isa Cattle Co. as managing general partner and investor. Setting up FTX Ranch was exciting. I still have our brand, FTX, registered in Florida. We made a pasturage deal for some 1,300 heifers (on the Al Brown Ranch at Fort Pierce) and bought some more groups, including some from A. Duda & Sons., Inc., and Bright Hour Ranch.

Our program, the first and biggest of its kind, consisted of raising three-quarter Beefmaster heifers from one-half Beefmaster cows. When I wrote the bylaws for the Foundation Beefmaster Association, I established a program for registering three-quarter Beefmaster females whose offspring would be seven-eighths or full blood Beefmasters. The program worked as we had hoped; the bull calves would be fed as bulls in Texas for slaughter and sold to Safeway stores, and the females could be sold as starter herds for people wanting to enter the Beefmaster business. The FTX management contract gave us the ability to incorporate as Isa Cattle Co., Inc. We kept fifty percent of the stock and sold fifty percent to investors. The board of directors consisted of J.D. Cage, Watt Casey, Dale Lasater, Garland Lasater and me. Ronnie Goodwin did our legal work and Mason Backus was our accountant and a key business adviser. The Central National Bank extended us a revolving

FTX Commercial Beefmaster heifers near Fort Pierce, Florida, purchased from A. Duda & Sons, Inc.

line of credit. Things could not have looked better in spite of bad market conditions in 1982.

1983 was eventful on all fronts. I was heavily involved in getting FTX Ranch Co., Ltd., running smoothly. During my trips to Florida, I learned from Jackie Bass that the Dudas were considering selling their cross-bred cows on a Miccosukee Indian lease in South Florida. I could see an opportunity for another cattle syndication. That year I had lengthy negotiations with the Dudas and the New Yorkers. We finalized an agreement to buy the 3,500 cows with owner financing, with the Dudas pasturing the cattle on a turn-key basis and Jackie Bass serving as manager. It appeared to be a perfect fit for all parties.

On October 28, Hugh and I met to close the deal with Joe Duda and Jackie, along with Duda's lawyer and others. We could not get it closed, however, because their lawyer could not understand it and was not familiar with cattle tax law. It was a tremendous blow to our group. I had already delivered 140 Beefmaster bulls to Indianland, which Joe bought at a fair price, showing what honorable people they are. After the collapse of the deal, I had numerous talks with the New Yorker, who suggested we syndicate our cattle in Texas. Annette and I met with him on November 21, our anniversary, after which the two of us had dinner that evening at the famous Plaza Hotel. It was very easy to make a deal as we followed the same format that we had for the Duda deal: Finan and Lasater and T-Circle Ranch Company sold their purebred Beefmaster herds with owner financing to FTX Ranch Co. II, Ltd. We contracted to run the cattle on a turn-key basis with Isa Cattle Co., Inc., handling the marketing. As things often turn out, it was a better arrangement than the previous one.

In July 1985, Hyman B. Fox, CPA, came from New York over the Fourth of July weekend to audit the FTX I and II herds in Texas and Florida. Hy was a smart, handsome six-footer who became a favorite of everyone in Texas. Neither Hy nor his wife, Lynne, had ever been on a ranch before, so we had fun touring Eldorado and Water Valley. Hy, Lynne and I left the next morning for Palm Beach. I furnished him a list of the numbers of the cows in each group, and he quickly realized that he could read ten or so numbers in the pasture, and if the numbers were on the list, it was certain that the list was correct. We met our foreman, Jack Sutton, at Fort Pierce, Florida, who drove us to the ranch. The cattle were easy to see, but when we came to the last pasture with 200 head of 2,000 left to be accounted for, it became quiet in the pickup—there was not a cow in sight. Then Jack drove around a little strip of woods and there they were, bedded down as happy as could be.

• • •

When I was summoned to New York on October 23, 1985, I was concerned about what was in store. After looking over the P&L for a few minutes, the New York lawyer announced that he had decided we should go public. Even though this possibility had been in the mill for some time, I was surprised and pleased with this new direction, as going public seems to be the dream of every American entrepreneur. On this same trip, Bill Carey and I agreed on our financing formula for the Beefmaster heifers: Throckmorton would finance them at WSJ prime plus one; Isa would receive $25.00 per head toward its overhead, and we would split the profit or loss.

We began amalgamating FTX I and II with Isa Cattle Co. to go public as an integrated company with registered and commercial Beefmaster cattle, leading into a branded beef program of some type. The Isa Cattle Co. board of directors, along with our accountant, Mason Backus, met several times during the first six months of 1986. Although the group was outstanding, with a unique blend of cattle experience, business and financial experience, and Wall Street experience, we were 15 years ahead of our time.

That same month, June, Jackie Bass called from Florida to advise me that the U.S. Sugar Ranch at Lakeport (formerly Billy Rogers') was up for lease. Hoping to lease it, I flew to South Florida, arriving late. A copy of the proposed 30-page lease document had been left for me at the hotel desk. It was the most lawyer-infested mess I had ever seen, with everything slanted their way. I immediately called one of U.S. Sugar's managers,

FTX cows nears Lakeport, Florida.

who told me not to pay any attention, that it was just how they did business. I took his advice and ignored it. When I met the next day with five executives, accountants and lawyers for the company, I had three items written down on a 3" by 5" card that were "make or break" for me. They accepted my terms and we made a deal. Our foreman, Jack Sutton, moved our cattle there, and it was the best, most profitable ranch I have operated.

Our FTX I herd was really flourishing at Lakeport, and I looked forward to each of my monthly trips. In January, I showed the new operation to Bill Carey, Hugh MacMillan and a friend. It was gratifying to show them such an outstanding operation. U.S. Sugar had the ranch for sale, and I gave a lot of thought to buying it. Because Bill was already financing the purchase of the FTX I heifers, he was thoroughly familiar with the situation. We discussed buying the herd but reached no conclusion on the ranch for sale. I did not propose buying the ranch because I was afraid to take on such a heavy interest burden. When I visited the ranch in 2005, it was worth many times more. That was the only situation in business where my nerve failed me.

U.S. Sugar had given us notice in October that our lease at Lakeport would terminate on April 30, 1989. This necessitated a decision on the disposition of the FTX Ranch Co., Ltd., cowherd. Since the business was in good condition, I advised the New York firm to liquidate it. Although all parties knew that time was running out, I could not get a response or advice from them. Finally, in desperation, I asked Pat Hall, a San Angelo friend and lawyer, for help. He wrote the New Yorker, with a copy to each of the investors, that his refusal to meet his responsibilities was jeopardizing the assets of the partnership. When that nuclear bomb hit New York, the consultation problem was cured forever. The reply was, "Sell the cows, but make a tax-free exchange so as not to trigger the tax liabilities, and no more letters from Pat Hall."

The buyer of the Lakeport Ranch in Florida was Jenaro Calle from Colombia, South America, who already owned another large ranch west of Okeechobee. U.S. Sugar had checked him out carefully and Jack Sutton had met him at the ranch. He spoke limited English, so all our negotiations were in Spanish by phone to Florida and Colombia. Although I did not meet him until we closed the deal, the fact that I could speak fluent Spanish created a bond of trust, and we negotiated a mutually satisfactory sale. He bought 900 First Cross Beefmaster cows and our bull battery. We kept the calves and later sold him 200 Second Cross heifers. In accordance with the instructions from New York, the sale money went to Throckmorton Land and Cattle for 720 bred Second Cross heifers in Texas, owned by Isa/Throckmorton. Like all good deals, this one was good for all parties. We paid off our operating loan at the First Bank of Indiantown. The bank president, Ed Appleton, was sick to lose us as a customer. Having the cows as collateral and our selling the calves each year to "zero out" the debt was the bank's best loan.

At the end of April 1989, I went to Florida and closed the herd sale with Jenaro. The weather was perfect and the cattle were in peak condition. The total transaction, including herd bulls and calves and the tax-free exchange, involved over 2,500 head of cattle, all breeding stock except for the steer calves—easily the biggest day of my career and one of the happiest. The problems with FTX II continued throughout 1989 and seemed to get worse with time. Annette bought 180 registered Beefmaster heifer calves from the partnership to help keep it afloat and also as an investment for herself. Those 1989 heifers would be the backbone of our herd for years to come.

Due to the tremendous leverage at high interest rates, managing the FTX I and II partnerships was difficult. We were in a monthly struggle to keep the bills paid. The two were fundamentally different in one regard: in FTX I, the partnership owned the cattle and I could borrow operating money against the herd; in the case of FTX II, however, we were financing the cattle and also periodically billing the partnership for pasturage. These payments were subject to capital calls, which usually were deposited several months late. In January 1988, due to late capital calls, we were having one of our periodic crises. The New Yorker and I were co-general partners, and I was to consult only with him on key matters; however, I never received a reply to any of my consultations sent by fax. The lawyer knew that we prized our reputation and would never be late on any payments, even if we had to lend the money, which we often did.

At the same time, the New Yorkers were having no success in formulating an Initial Public Offering. And, although the lawyer had assured this cowboy that they would handle the IRS, they had been audited, and the first I heard was a frantic SOS from them that the IRS had ruled that the cattle did not exist and that the entire business was a sham. I turned the matter over to Mason, who resolved everything with the IRS without any problem or penalty. From then on we had no more communication problems with New York, and whatever Mason said was golden. From utilizing the professional skills of Pat and Mason with such success, I learned to use accountants and lawyers in all important big-city negotiations.

As if the foregoing were not enough, Hal Noelke was taking bankruptcy and we would ultimately lose most of our principal ranching base in Texas. When John Cargile and I leased the ranch, it never occurred to us that Hal would lose it. Our lease was subordinated to his creditors, who made no effort to help us. In fact, just the opposite; they started stalking, unannounced and unauthorized, around the ranch.

Lykes Bros.

In April 1985, Carroll Adams, working for Lykes in South Texas, came to San Angelo and bought 55 yearling bulls to be delivered to Florida. These bulls were to be bred to some of their plainer cows and produced some of the best calves on the ranch. When that invoice hit the head office in Tampa, the shock waves reverberated throughout the company. Those were the most expensive bulls Lykes Bros. had ever purchased, and some questioned whether the company could survive. Carroll Adams was a story unto himself. He was a big, powerful, weather-beaten man with his blue jeans tucked into 16" stovepipe-topped boots. When I took him to lunch at Bentwood Country Club, here in cowboy country, a hush fell over the room when we walked in the door.

On my trips to Florida, I had become acquainted with Charlie Lykes, Jr., who was taking over a lead role in the management of the cattle operations. Charlie and I discussed cattle extensively, and he became interested in trying some Beefmasters. Lykes Bros. had run a traditional operation, using fairly low-quality crossbred cows to produce big steers for slaughter off grass. I was spending the night with Charlie in Florida when the orders came from Tampa office headquarters to transform the ranch into a modern operation. Charlie hired Mike Milicevic, Jr., one of the outstanding young cattlemen in America, and together they created one of the world's great ranching operations. They eventually converted their Wild Island division, with some 8,000 head of cattle, to all Beefmasters. One of Mike's accomplishments, coming in as a young man, was winning over Lykes' cattle division employees, many of whom were long-time employees. On one of my visits to Wild Island, one of the employees, Glenn Sapp, showed me where the cowboys had camped when he went to work for Lykes at about thirteen years of age. Having worked nearly 50 years, he said he had never drawn a check from anyone but Lykes Bros.

• • •

One year, Bill Carey and I contracted to buy 1,500 Beefmaster Cross heifer calves. The Lykes' cowboys rode out 1,700 cows with heifer calves for us to pick from—just a routine job for their cowboy crew. This delivery was a highlight in my business relationship with that organization.

Doing business with the great ranches in South Florida, including Lykes Bros., Inc., and A. Duda and Sons, Inc., has been a key chapter in my education as a cowman. I have been privileged to see the behind-the-scene facts, figures and information on how some of the lowest-cost operators can produce some of the best calves in the world. I have bought thousands of cattle from them, sired by bulls they bought from Isa Cattle Co. Together, they have bought over 1,000 Beefmaster bulls, and not a single one has been turned back—not because they never bought a bad bull, but because they are quality people who appreciate our cattle and the service we offer.

Directors and Association Meetings and Speeches

In January 1982, Annette and I flew to Phoenix for my first meeting as a board member of National Cattlemen's Association, representing the Beefmaster Association. Of course, I was excited, but John Cargile assured me before leaving San Angelo, that it would not amount to much. He was right as to substance, but any gathering of the colorful individuals who comprise the U.S. cattle industry is a spectacle to behold.

• • •

At the end of February, Annette and I drove with Andy Smith to the Broadmoor Hotel in Colorado Springs for the Foundation Beefmaster Association convention. Ken Monfort of Greeley, Colorado, gave an outstanding talk explaining that the cattle feeding industry originated as a means of disposing of surplus corn. "After they fed their hogs, burned it in their stoves and made whiskey, someone suggested they try feeding the piles still left to cattle." Bill Farr, also a cattle feeder from Greeley, explained to me on another occasion that the farm program, designed to save the "family farm" during the depression, destroyed the family ranch through chronic overproduction of beef, pork and poultry. Cheap grain equals cheap cattle.

• • •

A month later, John Cargile called from Fort Worth to say that I had been elected to the board of directors of the Texas and Southwestern Cattle Raisers Association, following in the footsteps of my grandfather and father. Because the new directors are introduced at the TSCRA convention every year, he suggested to Annette that we should come for the board meeting, but I was at the ranch delivering bulls to Nevada, so could not attend.

• • •

Each March, the NCA board of directors meets in Washington to lobby Congress. In 1982, I attended my first Washington meeting and was officially welcomed to the TSCRA board by John Armstrong, John Cargile, Frates Seeligson and J.E. Birdwell, all well-known Texas cattlemen. After two days of meetings, J.E. and I were going home on the same flight, and although he was detained, I waited for him. We did catch the plane, fortunately, and that trip home together and the fact that I had waited for him cemented our friendship.

• • •

The Foundation Beefmaster Association was in the process of making a video, a project in which Dale and I were prime movers. My concept was to interview Tom Lasater, Watt Casey, Humberto Garza, the Musser brothers and O.D. Butler of Texas A&M. To that list were added John Armstrong of the King Ranch and Forrest Bassford of *Western Livestock Journal,* both friends of Dad's and students of his career. The film crew also interviewed Charles Probandt, Andy Smith and me, and videotaped some of Andy's Beefmaster X Black Baldy Crosses.

• • •

"My God, Laurie, you killed him!"
—an Australian rancher

In 1984, I was to give one of the talks at the World Brahman Congress in Houston, having been invited by Wendell Schronk, a friend who later became executive vice-president of the Beefmaster association. I was paired with Angus breeder Henry Gardiner of Kansas. He was speaking on the Open Herd (bringing in genetics), and I was speaking on the Closed Herd. At the breakfast beforehand, it was suggested that we have some kind of debate. I said, "Let's just each tell our story and let the audience draw their conclusions." Henry went first and with all his slides, etc., used up all his time and half of mine. In his talk, he mentioned that selecting for growth had resulted in some calving problems. When I finally got to speak, they had opened the bar in the back of the auditorium, so conditions were less than perfect. In the course of my speech, I remarked that Dad calved his heifers unassisted in a 6,000-acre pasture. Afterwards, I went back to the bar and met an Australian rancher who said, "My God, Laurie, you killed him!"

Several days later, I gave two talks at the Florida Beef Shortcourse on "The Lasater Philosophy" and "The Origin of the Beefmaster Breed." I was honored to be on the program with Bud Adams of Florida, founder of the Braford breed. I said in my talks that Florida had the opportunity of selling replacement heifers to the rest of the country. Our customer, Wes Williamson, Jr., of Okeechobee, was there and told me that they developed a program of selling bred heifers that was adapted from that shortcourse.

Private Treaty Cattle Sales and Purchases

Sammy Baugh (of Washington Redskins football fame) had bought bulls for several years, but I had not met him. He called one day, and I met his wife and him at the bull facility. I had a large number of bulls on hand and he needed forty head. I made him a proposal of sorting 40 head from the total group, and to accept the sale, he, in an old-fashioned manner, extended his hand to shake.

• • •

The most unique cattle delivery we made occurred when I sold twenty registered Beefmaster cows, topped out of the herd with calves and bred back, to the Kipukai Ranch on the Island of Kauai, Hawaii. The cattle were trucked to California, flown by air to Honolulu, shipped by barge to the island, and then loaded in boxes to be hauled by truck over the mountains to the ranch. Later, Alex Franco, Brian Caires and Jay Nobriga from Hawaii came to San Angelo to select 53 yearling bulls to go to commercial ranches there.

> *"Don't they have Christmas in Texas?"*
> —Cherry Ann Sutherland

Our family went to Hawaii in December 1988 for a Christmas holiday and to see our new customers there. We were supposed to arrive at the

Marriott Maui on the 23rd to tour ranches, but because American Airlines had mechanical problems, we missed our connections and

arrived a day late in Maui. Although I did not think it a good idea, the Hawaiians insisted on our making the ranch tour on Christmas Day, and like a fool, I agreed. The last stop was at Lindy Sutherland's home, and when I entered, I saw unopened presents stacked under the Christmas tree and I heard children in

L Bar Beefmasters on the Kipukai Ranch in Kauai.

another room. When I met his wife, Cherry Ann, she shook my hand and asked, "Don't they have Christmas in Texas?" We left Maui two days later to fly to Kauai for several days. As we were landing at the airport there, we could see the Kipukai Ranch, owned by Lindy, where the cows were that we had sold him. We stayed at the Waiahai Hotel on Poipu Beach, an all-time family favorite. Annette and I had breakfast each morning on the beach while watching the sun rise over the Pacific Ocean. We toured the island, including the Kipukai Ranch, with Lindy's employee, Daldo Torres. We saw wonderful sights, learned many new things and Hawaiian words, my favorite being their Merry Christmas. Each year, when I wish the family, *"Mele Kalikimaka,"* I enjoy great memories of that trip.

• • •

That summer, Bobby Straub, from Pearce, Arizona, brought Rudy Johnson from the Mexican state of Sonora to look at our bulls. Rudy said that he was interested in several hundred bulls. We spent two or three days looking at cattle, but the only purchase he made was a $5.00 plastic pipefitting tool. At the end of the sojourn, as we were having a glass of iced tea at Rudy's motel, I said, "Just for my edification, explain to me what we have been doing the last several days." He said, "It has been just wonderful—I have seen your fine cattle, become acquainted with you and learned about the beautiful San Angelo area." I replied, "I guess if you are happy, I am too," and sent them on their way.

• • •

In May 1989, George Denny, a Harvard Business School graduate and venture capitalist, and his wife, Joan, from Boston dropped by San Angelo on their way to Arizona. I met them at the airport and drove them to Mertzon where Jimmy Autrey had grouped 300 cows with calves on a hillside. George began buying Beefmaster cattle that month, starting with 318 Mariposa heifers from South Texas. He bought 700 females from me during the summer.

I flew to California in August to spend time with him, and to see his farm/ranch operations at Goose Valley near Burney, California. While there, he asked me to look through a stack of résumés. Bill Maupin's (manager of the IL Ranch in Nevada) was on top, and I told him to look no further. George interviewed Bill and his wife, Wanda, and offered them a job, but they decided not to move to California. George later hired Shana and Dusty de Braga, who have done a good job managing Denny Cattle Company, with ranches in California, Nevada and Oregon.

I learned in November 1989, that the investors in FTX Ranch Co. II, Ltd., were not going to make their capital call, so after two weeks of intense negotiations, I sold George our mature cow herd and herd bulls. That year, he established the world's largest registered Beefmaster herd, including 1,200 head purchased from me. He contracted to leave the L Bar herd in Texas under our management, with those bulls going into our October sale and the top-end bulls from his California herd into our February sale. We also had an agreement to market the sale females from his herds. However, he later decided he wanted to manage and sell all of his cattle himself in California.

• • •

When Alberto Bailleres of Mexico City, a member of the Forbes List of World Billionaires, called from Colorado Springs, he said, "I'm up here with your dad and brother and they won't sell me any cattle. Will you sell me some?" Needless to say, I said I would. On August 16, Alberto came to San Angelo from Mexico City in his Gulfstream with the Mexican flag on the tail. I met him and part of his family at the airport where their arrival created quite a sensation. I showed them our cattle, and they contracted 85 bred heifers to go to the Margaritas Ranch at Múzquiz (where I had visited the Spence family in 1960). In October they returned to select the heifers and for Isa Cattle Co.'s bull sale.

• • •

Throckmorton and Isa owned some bred heifers for sale. An acquaintance I knew well in East Texas recommended a young man from the Ennis area as a prospective "farm system" breeder. I sold him 240 heifers for $300,000 with the understanding that Bill Carey would finance them. Not wanting to leave any loose ends, I had a lawyer draw a contract and note and file a lien on the cattle, which were individually numbered and eartagged. Due to the large transaction and financing, Bill even offered to consolidate the buyer's financing into one note. We went along normally for a period of months, with the rancher delivering his bull calves to San Angelo. At the same time, Throckmorton had an order buyer who was buying cows at auctions for their operation. By chance, the cattle buyer bought a cow the man had bought from us. The cow's I.D. number is how we learned that the cattle had been stolen from us by the customer, then sold and the money applied, not to our cattle loan, but to his secured real estate loan. When the smoke cleared, with payments received and cattle recovered, our partnership was out a large sum of money. We hired a lawyer, spent a lot of money pursuing the debtor, who took bankruptcy hoping to get out of it. Bill took it upon himself to start a multi-year endeavor, not only to collect the money, but also to take the individual out of business. He hired the Vinson and Elkins law firm, bought out all the other creditors listed in the bankruptcy, foreclosed on the ranch, stocked it with cattle until he sold the land and cattle at a profit and sent me a check for half the amount. As I said, the beginning loss was large, and by the time the process was completed with buying out other creditors, legal fees and interest, there was a tremendous investment. This was an extraordinary example of a partner's staying the course.

• • •

When Tom Newsome called to tell me that his father, Bill, our longtime friend and cattleman, was dying of a brain tumor, I flew to

Dallas to see him. His wife, Frannie, served us lunch and we visited in their library. As we said our goodbyes, Bill asked me to buy his Beefmaster herd and I said I would. Bruce and Stuart (Bill's grandchildren) later showed me the cattle and handled the delivery. Although they were only high school students, every detail was flawless. Bill and Frannie, like L.G. and Frances Hargis, were people whom Annette and I loved and who gave us important advice and encouragement.

Bull Sales at Auction

On September 15, 1979, we worked 332 bulls in inventory. For some twenty years, starting with our first bull sale, through all the Brucellosis testing on our cowherd and the thousands of bred heifers we were selling, Dr. Bill Wohler was our vet. We worked huge numbers of cattle through the chute. In 1987 we decided, as an experiment, to sonogram the ribeyes on John Cargile's yearling bulls. John suggested we do this as a public-relations measure to demonstrate our being progressive. As usual, he was right on target. We sold 281 bulls and had 55 buyers from ten states, including our partner-to-be, Bill Broussard from Melbourne, Florida. The average was a disappointment, but it was a tremendous accomplishment to sell this number of bulls during a severe stock market break and such terrible economic environment.

• • •

Because we were doing so much business in Florida, I decided to put on a bull sale at the Okeechobee Livestock Market. The bulls were gain-tested and processed at the bull facility in Texas and shipped to Florida a week or so ahead for the sale on October 30, 1987. On sale day, the sun was shining, the bulls looked good, and we had a big crowd. As always, we started the sale with a top bull, and a buyer was there from Texas to buy him. The bull brought about fifty percent less than he should have, and the sale went down from there. It took me a few seconds to recover from paralysis. I asked Eddie Lumpkin, who had assured me everything was set, "What the hell's going on?" Of course, he had no idea. Although Okeechobee is a big market, the facility itself is very cramped and the seating is crowded, with the audience looking down on the ring. The only access to the auctioneer's box is by crawling on a two-by-twelve foot board over the ring. After the auctioneer sold the ninth bull, I crawled across the ring, took the microphone, thanked the crowd and told them the bulls would be for sale afterwards. To stop the auction was one of the hardest things I have ever done, and one of which I am very proud. Many of the people attending were offended, a reaction which greatly pleased me. After the sale, I met Mr. Reuben Carlton, whose son and grandson are still customers, who bought 31 of the bulls at a fair price. Our foreman, Jack, hauled the other bulls to our lease at Lakeport where we sold them in good order. I learned later that someone from the auction had called one of my friends, as well as others, and spread the false rumor that the bulls were no good.

• • •

In February 1987, as we prepared for our first spring bull sale in San Angelo, Bill Maupin came from Nevada to visit. Several years later, Bill told me that a neighbor had said the IL Ranch had the best cowherd in Nevada after using our bulls. After he saw our cattle at San Angelo, I had a pilot fly Bill in my plane to the Panhandle to see our Beefmaster steers on feed. He liked what he saw and gave us an order for 40 bulls from our upcoming sale.

• • •

On September 29, 1989, we were working 400 bulls for the biggest bull sale held in Texas to that date. Working, sorting and cataloging that many bulls is a huge undertaking. James Howell, participating for the first time, was having trouble keeping track of what was happening. I told him, jokingly, "James, they are just like members of your family. Look at them and remember their numbers and which pen they are in." The next day, he came to the facility with the bulls scored and ranked in order on a computer printout. Since that day, we have used his system to catalog the bulls. On October 7, we sold 381 bulls.

California Cattle Syndication

In September 1984, Isa Cattle Co. formed a partnership with Max Watkins to promote the Beefmaster breed in California. Each partner bought a $50,000 C.D. and deposited it as collateral with Security Pacific Bank, which extended us a $500,000 line of credit to trade cattle. I went to California on January 9, 1985, to spend time with Max and to learn about the area. One of the ranches where Max pastured cattle was in the Santa Ynez Valley, where I had visited years before. It also was headquarters for a famous trail-riding group named *Rancheros Visitadores,* which included many actors and other celebrities.

Max was a one-of-a-kind individual and a super salesman with lots of charisma. I learned about public relations and marketing from him. He was a unique and personable man who knew many of the top cattlemen in the West and visited their ranches to help brand calves (a big tradition in California). He was a Gold Card Roper. He always told me, "You Lasaters need to put on a better act. You are the real cowmen, not like all these 'cake-eaters' in their neckerchiefs and handmade boots." Knowing I loved good hats, Max encouraged me to buy a 100X cowboy hat.

The premise of our partnership was that we would help Max introduce Beefmasters into California and the West, using Isa Cattle Co.'s proven methods of selling large volumes of quality cattle with little overhead. In theory, Isa Cattle Co. was to provide the management and administrative structure. We could have run the business from San Angelo with no additional cost whatsoever, but since we were in his territory, Max ran it in California. Max never understood that to trade cattle successfully meant having no additional overhead, just the trader and his existing phone, car and office. Every few months, there was a new item of equipment or an employee added to the overhead. Max was very successful in promoting the cattle, but we could never get the expenses under control and he did not want input, so I sent John Todd to California in April 1986 to liquidate the Lasater and Watkins Partnership, bringing our half of the cattle home. Although we lost $80,000 on that venture, Isa has a strong presence today in the California-Oregon-Nevada bull market.

• • •

Now, in my sixty-fifth year, it is amazing to look back on my schedule in my prime at forty-five. In addition to managing large ranching operations in Texas and Florida, the international frozen semen business, and a trading company in California, I was traveling extensively both commercially and in my own plane. In addition to putting on several auctions a year, I made numerous private treaty sales of both females and bulls.

• • •

"Any new ideas today?"

—*John Armstrong*

In May 1985, John Armstrong and Scott Kleberg arrived in the King Ranch jet to spend the day. We had a good tour of ranches at Mertzon and Eldorado, Texas. Continuing Dad's friendship with John, we had an intensive discussion of cattle breeding and marketing, both in regard to our program and to the King Ranch. John and Dad had been close friends and exchanged ideas as young men. They referred to themselves as the "schoolboy ranchers." Their standard salutation was, "Any new ideas today?" During the 1940s, they formulated what they called "the Five Essentials," the origin of John's "five points" brand. Around 1949, Dad added Hardiness, and the list became the world-famous Six Essential Characteristics: Disposition, Fertility, Weight, Conformation, Hardiness and Milk Production. John told me that the acceptance of Dad's ideas was the best thing that ever happened to the cattle industry.

A short time later, Tío Kleberg invited me to help judge the King Ranch sale bulls. Annette and I drove to Kingsville on October 9 to join a prestigious group: Bill Farr of Greeley, Colorado; Dick Yeager of the Waggoner Ranch; Jim Leachman; and Don Butler, president of NCA. Later the King Ranch hired Jim as a consultant on their cattle program. I was surprised because I had not realized they were looking for outside management when they visited with me in San Angelo. When The King Ranch let Leachman go, I realized I had dodged one more bullet.

The Chicago Connection

I do not remember how Bill Sanders and I met, but we developed a significant relationship. He was interested in what I was doing and vice versa. I have met few people who reminded me of either Dad or Dale, but Bill reminds me of both. He looked like Dad as a young man, wearing English-style clothes and shoes. He is a brainy guy who did things his own way. He was the founder and chairman of LaSalle Partners in Chicago, a commercial real estate firm he later sold to Japanese investors. He bought a ranch south of Santa Fe, New Mexico, and the first time I visited him there, we looked at his cattle and then went to dinner in nearby Lamy. He asked me what I thought of his herd, and I told him, truthfully, that they were some of the worst cattle I had seen. After he recovered from that blow, he realized that I could and would help him; I became his advisor on ranching, and he advised me on business. Bill did everything in sequence of priorities, and he used to call me on Sunday afternoon to talk about ranching as his chauffeur drove him to O'Hare Airport.

• • •

The year 1985 seems to have been a time for memorable trips. In October, Lorenzo and I traveled to Chicago so he could see and interview with Northwestern University and the University of Chicago. The next morning, as we walked down the steps, along with several hundred other people leaving O'Hare, we saw a Cadillac double-parked at the foot of the steps and a man waving to us. It was Bill Sanders' chauffeur, Huey. We introduced ourselves and headed for Northwestern University. Bill's secretary had typed Huey's instructions on 3" x 5" cards, i.e., "leave airport, go north on 182nd, turn right on Northwestern Avenue, do a U-turn and park in front of the admissions office at 10:15 a.m. sharp." After Lorenzo's interview, we headed downtown to the Chicago Mercantile Exchange, where cattle futures are traded, for a tour and lunch with Bill's brother. After lunch, we went to see Bill at LaSalle Partners, the company he founded.

Bill gave Lorenzo and me a tour of his company that was worth a semester in graduate school. After we saw his office, which was very formal with wood paneling, fine art and very little office equipment or filing cabinets in evidence, he took us to a room accessed by a coded card-key, which contained the nerve center of the company. In that room, every city block in every major city of the United States was described in a black loose-leaf binder—the present use of the property (warehouse, parking lot, etc.), its highest and best use (hotel, apartment building, office building, etc.), the current revenue, and the potential future revenue. He selected at random a city block in Seattle, opened the book on the counter, and explained to us what the potential earnings were from that real estate. I have rarely seen such a virtuoso performance. Until then, I don't think I fully understood what the term "Information Age" meant. Bill's clientele consisted of the CEOs of the Fortune 500 companies, which have vast commercial real estate holdings scattered all over the country. His company offered their clients a means of consolidating and getting control of their enormous holdings.

At the end of the day, we left LaSalle Street bound for Bill's home in Hyde Park on the University of Chicago campus overlooking Lake Michigan. Bill was a trustee of the university. There we met his wife, Cita, also from El Paso, and their four children (now five). After dressing for dinner, Bill told me the guest list: Mr. and Mrs. Gaylord Freeman (chairman of the First National Bank of Chicago; Mr. and Mrs. George Ranney (chairman of Inland Steel); and Mr. and Mrs. Mike Koldyke (chairman of Frontenac Ventures). As we stood by the piano, sipping a scotch, Bill asked me what I wanted to discuss. I asked, "What do you mean?" He said, "These people all have ranches in New Mexico and are coming to meet you and to talk about the cattle business." Although his secretary had phoned before I left San Angelo, asking me to bring ten copies of my book and the new FBA video, I had not realized the evening was to be devoted to cattle. As the guests arrived, each was given a cocktail and a copy of my book. As everyone was seated, we watched the video. At the end, someone said, "Play it again."

> *"He is a nice young man who is not interested*
> *in the University of Chicago."*
> —*University of Chicago Dean of Admissions*

The next morning, after Bill and I had dropped Lorenzo at the University of Chicago admissions office for his interview with the dean, we went back to Bill's home to talk about business. Bill's strategy was simple: formulate an idea and hire top people to multiply it, i.e., commercial real estate management based on the information he had shown us in the secure room of his office. Bill said I should hire a top MBA for Isa Cattle Co., and gave me pointers for dealing with the New Yorkers. Later in the morning, as Bill and I were discussing the cattle business, the dean called Bill to report on his interview with Lorenzo, saying, "He is a nice young man who is not interested in the University of Chicago."

NewBeef, Inc.

In September 1986, I finalized a feeding program for Garland Lasater and one of his partners. We were using this as a vehicle to gather carcass data on Beefmaster steers and to establish a market. That month I bought 270 steer calves from J.D. Cage at Muleshoe that weighed 535 pounds at 73 cents per pound.

November 1986 was another busy month. Mike Koldyke, a leading venture capitalist, had put me in touch with a potential underwriter in Chicago for our cattle feeding program. John Todd had made a consultant arrangement with Mike Bowles to help us line up a feedlot-packer arrangement for our branded beef program. Mike recommended a prominent feeder in Oklahoma. I had been warned that the feeder was not up to par, but went with Bowles' recommendation. On November 11, John, Mike Bowles and I drove from Amarillo to Oklahoma to check the cattle on feed. I was riding in front with the yard manager when we finally found the steers we were looking for, with ice caked on their backs and many sick ones in the pen that had not been doctored. Seeing our cattle sick, I blew up and wanted to move the cattle right then. Bowles talked me out of it. The owner sat in the back of the suburban and kept humming "Stormy Weather." I guess he thought it was funny; I did not. There was one significant experience that day. At that time, the Certified Angus Beef program was running ads implying that the CAB cattle were being fed in that yard. I told the yard manager, who was in the ads, that I would like to see the cattle. I quickly learned the truth as he told me there were no cattle on feed, but that they just eyeballed the carcasses at the slaughterhouse. As a leading cattleman said later, "The program was a brilliant advertising success, based on smoke and mirrors."

In February 1987, we sold our first formula cattle to Excel at $1.01 on the hot carcass weight. We had fed many outstanding Beefmaster calves, including Lorin McDowell's (Garden City, Texas) bull calves and many

FTX bull calves. Lanny Binger was vice-president of Excel, and we developed a pleasant business relationship with Bill Harrison and him in negotiating a pricing formula. Lanny spoke to the Texas and Southwestern Cattle Raisers board and challenged them to bring Excel better cattle. He told me later I was the only breeder who actually bought large numbers of breed-specific cattle to feed and sell to Excel. In May of that year, we agreed on a formula-pricing mechanism that would reward superior carcasses.

I visited with cousin Garland in Fort Worth in July regarding the possibility of Isa Cattle, Co.'s going public. He loved to illustrate his points by putting on a dialogue in which he skillfully played both parts. He expressed the belief that going public was an expensive way to raise capital because of ongoing legal and accounting costs and also explained that the endeavor was not big enough in fees to generate public interest. Although I am sure Garland realized it was not attractive to the investment bankers and that I was not suited by temperament to run such a business, he put his heart and soul into helping Isa go public or raise capital for a branded beef program.

On October 14, Mason Backus, Garland and I flew to Chicago on Midway Airlines. We stayed at the Chicago Club, an all-male private club of which Bill Sanders was president. (When U.S. Grant brought Mrs. Grant to Chicago after the Civil War, the Chicago Club doors were opened to ladies for only that visit, which was the last time for over one hundred years.) After dinner, the three of us spent the evening strategizing for our breakfast meeting with Mike Koldyke. The next morning, as Mike started laying out his proposal, I pushed my breakfast aside and started taking notes. He asked if I did not want to eat, and I replied, "We have food in San Angelo." He named our company NewBeef, Inc., and proposed that Isa own fifty percent of the company. The investors would put up money in the form of convertible debentures with no interest for five years and then six percent and five-year amortization if they opted not to convert for fifty percent of the stock. A Chicago law firm would draw a prospectus; we were to have quarterly board meetings and be audited by a Big Eight firm in preparation for going public. The premise of the venture was to document the feedlot and carcass superiority of Beefmaster steers to raise capital to maintain 12,500 cattle on feed, with Isa Cattle Co., Inc., guaranteeing the debentures. He laid out the whole proposition in simple terms, and it was agreed to by telephone on December 8. Mason, Garland and Pat Hall, one of my lawyers, advised me not to guarantee the debentures, but I did, convinced this was the answer for Isa and the promotion of the Beefmaster breed.

The NewBeef offering was completed in May 1988, with most of the capital coming from our side: Jack Modesett, Jr.; Throckmorton Land & Cattle; the Lasater Ranch; and Isa Cattle Co. Four Chicagoans, including Bill Sanders and Mike Koldyke, invested. Seven of the eight investors constituted the board of directors.

We started a program (named the "Farm Program" by Mike) for investors wishing to come into the Beefmaster business on an entry-level basis, providing bulls for our February sale. Jack Modesett joined Mike Koldyke and Richard Smith (Stowers Ranch) as well as John Todd, George Denny and others in that program.

Also in May, John and I negotiated a deal with Lanny Binger for ten loads of Beefmaster steers at 77½ cents per pound, less discounts, which was two cents over the market price of bulk choice steers, as reported weekly by the Texas Cattle Feeders. When NewBeef came on line, we already had a large ongoing program established with our FTX I bull calves, plus tax feeders and our personal cattle on feed. In the summer of 1988, I bought two-and-a-half truckloads of yearling Beefmaster steers, weighing 725 pounds at 80 cents from Don Morrison of Pampa, Texas.

In August, we began feeding cattle at Friona Feed Yard at Friona, Texas. The yard was managed by Walt Olson, who did an excellent job with our cattle. Excel had a plant less than ten miles from the yard. After feeding cattle for sixteen years, we had our program perfected. We fed them a corn-based ration. On arrival, the calves were sorted by size in pens of about 90 to 100 head. Each pen was sorted once by topping off a load of finished steers and giving the second half of the group extra days to catch up. We fed the cattle to yield 65 percent on the hot carcass weight. We soon had 3,500 cattle on feed at Friona, all lined up and sorted by size, in pens fronting on the highway. Anyone driving down the highway could see the excellence of the steer calves our bulls were generating. Once, when I was standing in the pens looking at the cattle, a car on the highway slammed on the brakes and stopped. Two men got out to look at the cattle. They possibly had never seen that many good cattle in one place—very few people have. One day, when I was in Excel's Friona plant with the manager, a group of our cattle came down the line looking like "peas in a pod." He said that if we supplied 500 head per week, we could name our price. We perfected our pricing formula with Excel. All the Beefmaster cattle that we fed netted two cents-per-pound over bulk choice steers, based on liveweight, with some bringing as much as seven cents over the market.

NewBeef partnered with Friona on the cattle and also promoted other rancher and investor cattle into the feedlot. We located all the cattle, which made money, and received a $15-per-head management fee on arrival, which is how we financed our operations. Everyone in the organization was surprised at the feedlot performance and the premiums the finished cattle brought. In 1989, when the owner of the feedlot got into legal difficulties, they hired a Harvard Business School graduate to run the company. When we met, he told me they had no interest in continuing the program. Sometime later, someone told me Friona Industries was starting a premium calf program themselves and I replied, "They sell feed and medicine and lend money, and any other claims are hot air."

On October 20, we had our second NewBeef quarterly board meeting at Amarillo, Texas. As part of the meeting, we took the directors to Friona to see our cattle on feed. It was blowing snow and sleet, and when the cowboys came into the office to get warmed, all the city people got a first-hand look at the realities of the cattle business. In spite of the weather, the cattle looked terrific and enthusiasm for our project was high. In March 1989, we had a board meeting in Chicago and decided to raise, by private placement, $1,200,000 to keep 10,000 cattle on feed to provide Excel with 500 finished cattle per week. NewBeef, Inc., was set up in accord with Mike Koldyke's instructions; a memorandum prepared by a Chicago law firm, quarterly board meetings and Big Eight audit. The combined cost of these items was $70,000. We also hedged all of the cattle on the options market, an expensive item, which was company policy.

In June 1989, we moved NewBeef's cattle feeding from Friona to Great Plains Feed Yard. We had a very difficult board meeting in July. The market had turned down, and some of the cattle lost money. When Mike told me to "demonstrate the superiority of Beefmaster cattle," he had not understood that cattle could perform well and still lose money. NewBeef, Inc., was set up to allow the venture capitalist to get an inexpensive look at an industry and to exit if he did not like what he saw. As mentioned, we were top-heavy with administrative expenses and hedge costs, in addition to the normal ups and downs of the cattle business. It had become evident that we could not raise the capital. On September 1, Mike resigned from the board, effectively ending the project. It was a tremendous blow to me, personally and financially. I will never forget James Howell, Bill Carey and Dale comforting me after the meeting, knowing what a beating I had taken. They worked hard for several years helping me keep NewBeef afloat, but it was doomed, and although we were not legally responsible, Annette and I personally paid off the debentures with interest during the Great Drought of the Nineties.

None of this is a criticism of Mike Koldyke. There is not a nicer, more honorable person anywhere. We came from different cultures and brought different assumptions to the deal. I had been in business 25 years and had already survived experiences outside his realm of understanding. It never occurred to me that someone would walk away from a venture that had just started. The problem with NewBeef was the historic timing of my idea of owning the cattle to control the inventory, the product quality and flow—a typical "cowboy" concept.

• • •

In June 1987, Bob Kingsbery and I had collaborated on a short book titled *Welcome to the New Cattle Industry*. In that book, I correctly predicted that the ranching industry was breaking up into its four parts: ownership of land; ownership of cattle; management of land; and management of cattle. These functions could be carried out by one to four entities. Our particular interest was, and is, the management of cattle, i.e., genetics and marketing. This division in the industry was not really prophetic since our business had already evolved in that direction. The old-timers had an apt saying, "You can live off a ranch, you can improve a ranch or you can pay for a ranch, but you can't do all three at once."

That summer, Bob and his wife, Kerri, put on a Texas Grazing Conference in San Antonio. It was a family event as Matt Brown and I were speakers and Annette, Uncle Palo and Aunt Dosia were in attendance. When I got up to give my talk, I saw an individual sitting in the middle of the crowd who had come to San Angelo some months before, apparently interested in buying a lot of cattle. I showed him everything, priced everything and he returned home. When I called later to see if he was still interested in the cattle, I was informed that he had died in emergency surgery. Obviously he had not died; he had wanted to check out our program and get some prices—nothing more.

Closing the 1980s

The 1980s was one of the most difficult decades in the history of the U.S. cattle industry. In addition to high interest rates, government interference, periodic drought and bad markets, we were saddled with the Brucellosis program, based on an imperfect vaccine and an imperfect test. We bled many thousands of cattle each year, and every test was a risk. We even had a spurious reactor on a bull just before one of our bull sales. In spite of the best efforts of our industry leaders, this program was the biggest problem and cost that I have encountered in 42 years in the cattle business. It was all negative energy because Brucellosis can be controlled easily by universal calf-hood vaccination.

With the Tax Reform Act and the dairy buyout, 1986 was a terrible year in the cattle business. On Christmas Eve, the phone rang; it was the international operator from Zurich, Switzerland. I told her she had the wrong number and then heard John Cargile's frantic voice saying, "No, no, operator, that's him." Due to market conditions and psychology, John had become concerned about the Duda heifers, and wanted to run them through Producers, saying he would not charge a commission on their sale. I managed to reassure him that we were in good shape on the cattle, and he agreed to hold them until 1987.

• • •

May 1989 was the twenty-fifth anniversary of the introduction of the Beefmaster breed into Mexico by Annette and me. I was invited to speak at the Beefmaster convention in Monterrey, and flew down from Del Rio with Guillermo and Doris Osuna. At that time, Guillermo had the screwworm eradication contract in southern Mexico and was entitled to a plane with diplomatic status, which meant it did not have to clear Mexico Customs or Immigration. We flew to Monterrey International without benefit of papers and walked through customs and immigration without a problem, quite an experience for an old border-jumper! We were taken to the fairgrounds in a bulletproof car. We spent the afternoon seeing old friends and looking at the exhibits. After a long day of drinking beer in one-hundred-degree heat, we had dinner at 2:00 a.m. The next day I gave a 20-minute speech in Spanish, followed by two hours of questions and answers. My friends, the Sillers, who arrived late, came to the podium to read my speech, then sat down and joined in the discussion. Only in Mexico!

Notwithstanding the problems, 1988 was a year of great professional satisfaction for me. The quality of our cattle was evident in the outstanding feedlot and carcass results we were seeing in the Panhandle, the quality of bulls and bred heifers we were selling, and the quality of our customers. If the cattle are good, I am happy, as I know everything else will probably sort itself out eventually. With some 7,000 cattle in inventory, and approximately 3,000 registered Beefmaster females in our co-operator herds, we had achieved my longtime ambition of having an outstanding, vertically-integrated business that could support a branded beef program.

The year 1989, which started badly with the loss of key leases in Florida and Texas, ended by being a pivotal year for us with the sale of 3,122 Beefmasters (by far our biggest year in female sales) and nearly 800 bulls. Just reading of the events of 1989 is difficult. If I were not reading a diary and records, I would not believe that people could survive while operating in such a bad business environment, ranging over a tremendous area.

LA SALLE PARTNERS
Incorporated
11 South LaSalle Street
Chicago, Illinois 60603
(312) 782-5800

June 30, 1986

Mr. Henry Singleton
Chairman and Chief Executive Officer
Teledyne, Inc.
1901 Avenue of the Stars
Los Angeles, California 90067

Dear Henry:

The weather certainly has been good for New Mexico. I believe that it rained all of last week. Our family will be at the ranch over the Fourth. It should be exceptionally green.

Attached you will find a book written by Laurie Lasater entitled The Lasater Philosophy of Cattle Raising. If you have a sincere interest in the livestock end of ranching, you really owe it to yourself to read this book. It is clearly the best of its kind. It will give you a very simple exposure to the important principles of cattle ranching.

After reading the book a couple of years ago, I was so impressed with it that I have gotten to know Laurie Lasater very well. He is truly one of the two or three most innovative leaders in the cattle industry. You are welcome to keep the book as I have my own copy.

I hope all is well.

Cordially,

LA SALLE PARTNERS
INCORPORATED

Bill

William D. Sanders
Chairman

WDS:bp

Enclosure
    As Stated

bcc: Laurence M. Lasater

Corporate Real Estate Services · Chicago · Cincinnati · Dallas · Denver · El Paso · New York · San Diego · Washington, D.C.

Letter from Bill Sanders to Henry Singleton.

CHAPTER 22

THE END OF AN ERA

In early August 1986, Bernice Musser called to report that the bank that financed their cattle operations had sold, and the acquiring bank was having difficulties and was forcing its customers with equity to sell out. She asked me to help and sent me their financial statements on August 14. I began working on various ideas, including syndication or the Mussers' partnering with someone and their moving with their cattle to a new location.

Bill Sanders had put me in contact with a neighbor who ranched in New Mexico, Henry Singleton, Chairman of Teledyne, and the first of the great conglomerators (the subject of a cover story in *Forbes* magazine). The letter, pictured here, is an interesting insight into how business is conducted at the highest levels. The eventual sale and delivery of the Musser herd to Henry Singleton was one of the highlights of my career for several reasons: I was able to help the Mussers in a desperate business environment; I made a commission, which I needed, and became intimately acquainted with one of the great businessmen of the twentieth century. However, I also witnessed the end of an era in our nation's history, as well as the history of the cattle business.

On September 3, 1986, I flew to Los Angeles to meet with Henry Singleton at the headquarters of Teledyne at 1901 Avenue of the Stars. Their offices were above the Century Plaza Hotel, where I stayed. I went to negotiate the sale of the Musser herd with certain expectations of how things might transpire. Although he had very little experience with the ranching business, Dr. Singleton had already acquired large ranch holdings in California and New Mexico. I thought that the Mussers might move with their herd to his newly purchased Lobo Ranch at Encino, New Mexico, and that Isa Cattle Co. might be involved in marketing his Beefmaster production. I assumed that these would be complex negotiations, dealing with lawyers and accountants. None of these expectations materialized.

Dr. Singleton was an electrical engineer by training and founded Teledyne with a partner after World War II. After a period of years, he and his partner learned they could make more money buying companies than building a company. He became the first great conglomerator and was one of the early members of the Forbes List of World Billionaires. Dr. Singleton was a very friendly, accessible man, who was hard of hearing (a handicap which bothered him). He used high-tech equipment to overcome his handicap. I was determined to learn all I could from him, and, in this, I was not disappointed. I have been privileged over and over to participate in business transactions at the highest level, worldwide, and this was another instance.

Henry Singleton

Forbes magazine cover story of July 1979 describes "The Singular Henry Singleton" as one of the towering figures of this business era, equal in accomplishment to Alfred P. Sloan, Jr., and David Sarnoff. Dr. Singleton founded Teledyne in 1960 with partners George Kozmetsky, who went on to be dean of the college of business administration at the University of Texas, and Arthur Rock, one of our greatest venture capitalists. During my dinner with Dr. and Mrs. Singleton, they told me of his experiences with Arthur Rock as founding directors of Apple Computer. *Forbes*, in the highest

Henry Singleton on the cover of *Forbes* magazine.

compliment they could pay, says that Teledyne, a multibillion dollar company, is run in an entrepreneurial innovative way.

"Like the people, like the product, buy the company."

—Dr. Henry Singleton

Dr. Singleton's office was nicely furnished, but nothing excessive. He had an administrative assistant whom he could buzz when he wanted to dictate a memo or have her make a phone call. Stacked beside his desk were 28 blue, loose-leaf binders containing the financials of the companies that comprised Teledyne (Teledyne-Continental, Teledyne-Water-Pik, etc.). In his shirt pocket, he carried a 3" by 5" card for every business, with five numbers, no words, for each company. These were the monthly operating figures for each entity. If he needed more information, he referred to the loose-leaf binder. In a closet off to one side, he had a miniature stock exchange with stock ticker running. He was managing $500,000,000 in cash.

I asked him how he selected companies to buy, expecting to hear some complex Harvard Business School evaluation baloney formula, and he replied, "Like the people, like the product, buy the company." I asked, "Dr. Singleton, how do you learn about these businesses?" He replied, "I tell them I don't understand their business, so they explain it to me and then I understand." Only a genius like Tom Lasater, Bill Sanders or Henry Singleton can give a simple, one-sentence, plain English answer to a complex question. Although he was an engineer by training, Dr. Singleton knew that all business was about people.

Our discussions during my first trip followed the Singleton formula. He told me that he did not understand our business so I explained it to him. We talked for three or four hours. I explained specific subjects to him, such as the origin of the Beefmaster breed and his marketing options. He listened carefully, asked a few questions and did not interject his opinions or personality. At the end of each subject, he buzzed his assistant, who came into the office to take notes as he dictated a memo on that subject, demonstrating that he had understood it perfectly. There were no interruptions. He had not checked his calendar; he had no other appointments that day; he had not once mentioned how busy he was, nor had he needed any help from lawyers and accountants in dealing with me.

He is the only high-level businessperson I have dealt with who never had a "pressing" engagement or took a call. At the end of the day, he invited me to accompany him to his home in Beverly Hills to meet his wife, a delightful lady. We had a glass of wine before going to dinner at their favorite neighborhood restaurant, Valentino's.

Nine days later I returned to Los Angeles to conclude the deal. The negotiations were pleasant. Dr. Singleton knew he was buying valuable cattle in a distressed situation and did not abuse that in any way. On September 12, 1986, we made a deal to sell 1,275 registered Beefmaster cattle. I was surprised that he did not want to see the cattle, but Bill Sanders explained that Henry Singleton's decision to buy the Musser herd was not a big item in his year and was like my deciding whether to buy an Oldsmobile or a Cadillac.

The negotiations followed the same pattern as in our previous meeting. As we agreed on a segment of the deal, such as herd health or delivery, he buzzed Helen, the administrative assistant, and dictated a memo. We valued each class of cattle individually. As we concluded negotiations, I told him that in the cattle business, an earnest money check was customary. He blew up. I felt sure he was playacting, although I will never know, but he startled me with his outrage. (You whippersnapper, do you know who I am?) He said, "What could go wrong?" I replied, forthrightly, "You might die." Then he really did get mad. I thought our deal was blown up. He grabbed the phone, called the unsuspecting banker in Delta, Colorado, and said, "This is Henry Singleton. I am buying the Musser herd. Do you require a down payment?" The banker said, "No." Henry slammed down the telephone, having dealt with the last irritant, and we signed the agreed-to contract. The banker immediately called the Mussers and said he had made a terrible mistake. Henry and I stayed in touch, talking once or twice a year on the telephone, but I never saw him again before he died.

On December 11, 1986, I helped Jack, Tom and Johnny Musser and their foreman, John Cunningham, bring 640 bred females seventeen miles down the canyon from the Escalante Forks to the Windy. They already had brought down 390 calves and 35 herd bulls. As we rode behind those wonderful cattle on a beautiful fall day, I could not help thinking that their having to sell their cattle and ranch was a tragedy. I was witnessing another sad ending in the history of pioneer ranching. Greedy financial people overreached themselves and put their stockholders and borrowers in trouble. Sacred trusts were violated—sins which will be answered for on another day. No one would ever know or love this ranch as the Mussers had, and there would never be a herd of cattle like theirs. This herd had served as the basis for

The Musser cow herd leaves the Escalante Forks for the last time.

the spread of Beefmasters from the Continental Divide to the Pacific Ocean, not to mention their having served as the basis for our great herd of cattle at San Angelo, which now forms one of the three major herds of the Beefmaster breed. As we rode down the Escalante Canyon that December day, I did not realize that over the coming seventeen years or so, I would witness, time and again, those whom I considered to be the best of a great industry either forced out of business or quitting in disgust.

We loaded the cattle at the Windy, Henry Singleton wired the money and Gaddy Truck Line hauled them to Encino, New Mexico. That day (as with Duke Phillips' death) marked the end of one of the favorite chapters in my life, as well as the end of a period in American history that began one hundred years earlier when the homesteaders came to Western Colorado.

Lorenzo readying for a round-up.

CHAPTER 23

THE 1990s

Each decade of my career was loaded with important events. That is probably not surprising, given that ten years is twenty percent of a 50-year career. The seventies and eighties were difficult times, but unbelievably, the nineties were the most difficult time of my 42-year career to date. Two incidents dictated that fact: the start of the Great Drought of the Nineties in May 1992, and the failure of the Central National Bank in San Angelo, Texas, in 1990. Three of my closest ranching friends lost their cattle and part or all of their ranches during that period. All are top ranchers and sterling individuals, but years of ultra-high interest rates, capped off by eleven years of dry weather hurt them and everyone else financially.

Lorenzo's Joining Isa Cattle Co.

The most important development of the '90s was Lorenzo's joining our business. Before I entered business, I remember thinking when I was young that my father had "finished the job." Later, I realized there were a few things to do, and finally it dawned on me that Annette and I had not scratched the surface. Lorenzo graduated from TCU Ranch Management School, full of energy and ideas, ready to go to work. He updated our cattle recordkeeping and sales catalogs and also implemented the policy of dehorning both bull and heifer calves. On a more profound level, he began advocating selection for greater uniformity and consistency in our cattle, which was the right thing to do at that point in the history and evolution of the breed. He and I agreed that the cattle were very good but that it was time to make them more acceptable.

Beefmaster Breeders United

In 1996, after several meetings with members of Foundation Beefmaster Association and Beefmaster Breeders Universal, all of the details of merging were agreed upon. It was decided to merge under the new name of Beefmaster Breeders United to keep the acronym BBU. Our first convention on October 25, 1996, was in Corpus Christi, Texas, forty miles and 65 years from where and when the breed was founded.

Bank's Failure

On March 22, 1990, David Hill, of Central National Bank, called me at home early in the morning. He told me that the loan committee had renewed Isa Cattle Co, Inc.'s operating loan for one year, then hung up. Later in the day, I heard on the radio that the bank had closed its doors. That telephone call and the directors' all-night efforts to protect their customers probably saved us.

Central National Bank was acquired by the Gerald Ford Group (not the president). In my *naiveté,* I thought the new owners would continue to operate the bank and would need customers. Some days later, however, I was asked to meet with David Hill and Gary Fletcher, the hatchet man sent to liquidate the bank. Fortunately, I took Mason Backus, my accountant, and James Howell, Isa Cattle Co.'s vice president of operations, with me. Fletcher told me that the bank wanted to be paid with interest in 90 days. Mason, demonstrating his business skills, immediately responded, "We'd like to see the minutes of the loan committee meeting of March 21." Having had his bluff called, Fletcher agreed to give us until March 1991. This situation set into motion a chain of events that did not end until October 2000. We were put in an immediate financial crisis by having our approved revolving credit, with which to run our business, changed so that we were making principal and interest payments each month. This was very difficult for James, Annette and me. James was a help in holding the bank at bay, but the strain on him was great. In October, knowing we could not afford him but would not let him go, he resigned to run their family ranching business.

We had to scramble to reorganize and refinance our business. A large part of the bank line had been used to buy the co-operators' bulls. In September 1990, Bill Carey agreed to finance the bulls. In December, my partners in the Lasater Ranch Partnership made me a loan, and in February 1991, I borrowed some money against my Shackelford and Throckmorton County minerals from the First National Bank of Albany, Texas. Also, the then Southwest Bank extended us a revolving line of credit, negotiated by Mason Backus with Mike Boyd, president of the bank.

I later learned that some of the bank's borrowers had negotiated to pay off their loans for pennies on the dollar. When the Gerald Ford Group bought the bank, they picked the low-hanging fruit and stuck the U.S. taxpayers with the balance. Closing the bank served no purpose and hurt the borrowers, the stockholders and the taxpayers. At some point, Gerald Ford came to San Angelo to speak to the Chamber of Commerce. Someone asked if I were going. I replied, "Hell no and I hope the S.O.B. gets crippled on the trip." Dad always told me, "Beware of the fish-eyed money men," which was very important advice. I have taken care never to allow a bank or a partner to get the upper hand where they could do me financial harm without hurting themselves.

• • •

Because Annette and I did not want to return to Colorado, it was clear to all of the family for years that I was not interested in taking an active role in the Lasater Ranch Partnership. Upon Dad's retirement, Dale took over the management of the family ranch in May 1986. Although Dale and I are brothers with different talents and interests, we took the pledge as young men not to fight over money. I am proud of the fact that we have combined our efforts and provided business leadership for the family with no disagreements or unpleasantness of any kind. The events already described led to my withdrawal from the partnership, which took place over ten years. On November 28, 1994, Dale and I agreed on an overall valuation for the Lasater Ranch Partnership. We each wrote down a number on a 3" x 5" card. Dale's figure was higher than mine, which tells the fairness of both brothers/partners.

The Great Drought of the Nineties

In my 42-year career, six events have had serious business consequences for us: the drought of 1966–67 at Santa Cruz; the market break of 1974; 20% prime rate in 1980; the Tax Reform Act of 1986 (which ended our two syndications and closed that avenue for raising capital); the failure of the Central National Bank; and the Great Drought of the Nineties.

In the fall and winter of 1991–1992, a 117-year record for rainfall was broken in the San Angelo area. The mud at the Bull Test Facility was so deep that we had to move the bulls to pasture. In May 1992, however, it stopped raining, and we did not have a normal spring or fall growing season until October 2003—a period of eleven years. May, June and September in San Angelo are the rain months, and if it does not rain enough, everything goes dormant in the summer due to heat and after frost in the fall (about November 15).

We were in drought condition by the fall of 1992. Neither our long-suffering cattle nor we knew that we had embarked on an eleven-year odyssey. I estimate that our registered cows were moved fifteen times between 1992 and 2003. The moves and the readjustment period were very stressful on the cattle and expensive for us. This "unnatural" selection put great fertility pressure on our cows, with those that could not breed back being sold. The young cattle that could not live and reproduce each year with less-than-normal nutrition were also sold. The Drought of the Fifties had forced Dad to move to Eastern Colorado to buy a ranch. Seeing that the drought made his cattle even better genetically, as well as financially improving the family business, we knew we could not sell out. The Great Drought of the Nineties did the same for us. We came out of it with a smaller, better herd of cattle and a more profitable, less risky business. That eleven-year ordeal, coupled with Lorenzo's coming into the business in 1993, bringing talent, energy and much-needed new ideas, helped us to develop what is now recognized as one of the world's great herds of cattle.

In the summer of 1998, while in the struggle to stay in business through the drought, I met one of my neighbors, Johnny Wales of Irion County, at a social function. In our visit he said that he was going to have to sell some of his excellent Brangus heifers. I offered to help him, and in that process, picked up very smart business insight. Johnny said he did not count anything as profit until it was taken out of the cattle business and invested in securities. Having always done the opposite, it was easy for me to see the wisdom of his insight. The cattle business consists of unique individuals who have developed shrewd techniques as they work to survive.

In a Liquidation Mode

I have always been a builder and an entrepreneur, and given that fact, it is interesting to look back and see how many years I have spent in a liquidation mode due to external circumstances. I have already described the tremendous business we had built using capital from partners as well as passive investors. In the nineties, we liquidated those businesses and stopped using anything but partner capital and bank financing.

In 1993, FTX Ranch Co. Ltd., had a herd of some 500 five-year-old cows pregnant with their fourth calves. Several years earlier, I had established a program with Producers Auction whereby we would sell a featured lot of quality commercial replacement females in conjunction with the weekly sale. Producers would promote the cattle, as would Isa. If the cattle did not sell, we paid no commission. We were able to make this type of arrangement as a new marketing effort due to the volume of business we were doing at that time.

We consigned 300 bred cows to Producers in June 1993. The cows originated as heifers purchased from Lykes Bros., and were very good. Lykes' cattle manager, Mike Milicevic, had seen them at San Angelo and could not believe how well they had grown out. All of the cows were officially calfhood vaccinated for Brucellosis and had been blood-tested several times, but an hour or so before the sale, John Cargile told me that Dr. Bill Wohler had found a Brucellosis reactor on the card test. Instead of taking that cow off the consignment for further testing, they stopped the whole consignment. I was shocked that they did not offer to take the one cow out, as was usually done. Ten minutes before the sale started, it was announced, with no explanation, that the featured lot would not sell. I had a buyer there from California. We took the cattle back to the ranch, and, fortunately, sold them as well as another 200 to the buyer (with no commission). The cow in question was slaughtered, her glands harvested and sent to Ames, Iowa, for testing in the federal lab. As was obvious all along, she was exonerated as a vaccine reactor. This is just one of many horror stories arising from the Brucellosis Eradication Program. The 500 cows just mentioned triggered another tax-free exchange for Isa/Throckmorton. FTX had developed a valuable business of buying bred heifers from our partnership, putting them in production and then selling them for maximum price as five-year-olds.

As general partner, I had signed the FTX operating loan. As the situation deteriorated, due to drought and low cattle prices, my exposure increased, triggering the decision to sell out. We sold the last of the cows in small groups at Producers Auction. In October 1996, we paid off the note. The liquidation of FTX Ranch Co., Ltd., ended a happy chapter in my career. We had pioneered several successful programs, selling three-quarter Beefmaster heifers, feeding bull calves and making tax-free exchanges of prime-age cows for bred heifers. The cattle were good and the ideas were sound, but the partnership could not overcome the terrific leverage built in at high interest rate nor the onset of a killer drought.

Our thirtieth wedding anniversary, November 21, 1994, took place at a difficult time in business. The NewBeef project ended and Isa Cattle Co. had lost $100,000 on three bull sales in Florida and $80,000 in California. Our loss in NewBeef was $225,000 in debentures, plus Isa Cattle Co.'s investment. These events put the company in a negative net worth situation. The normal practice would have been to bankrupt Isa Cattle Co., Inc., and walk away from the debentures, but Annette and I never considered not paying. When I wrote Isa Cattle Co.'s stockholders of the situation, some of them elected to surrender their stock in order to take the loss of their investment for tax purposes. Those who stayed were J.D. Cage, Matt Brown, Tom Newsome and Henry Martinez. Sometime during those years, Annette and I made a tacit agreement: Annette would pay the bills and I would generate the income, and since that time, I have not looked at a bill, signed a check or made a budget. I get up early every morning to figure out how to make some money, and Annette gets up early to figure out how to stretch the money. It has worked. Too bad we did not know that in 1964! In January 1999, Isa Cattle Co., Inc., paid off the debentures with interest. Annette and I loaned the company the money to make the payments and those loans were paid back with interest by 2004, at which point the company had a positive net worth. Those stockholders who faithfully stayed with us will eventually get their capital back—better late than never!

Learning with Bill Sanders

As I wrote earlier, I had a significant business friendship with Bill Sanders, former chairman of LaSalle Partners, Incorporated. Bill came to San Angelo with his friend Howard Beasley, who was chairman of Lone Star Steel. During the visit, Bill and Howard advised me not to go public, something I was working hard to do at that time. (Ironically, Bill did go public later, with mixed results.) After we became acquainted, Bill began developing a Beefmaster herd on his ranch at Santa Fe, New Mexico, and through me, he hired Duke Phillips, III, who did a great job in developing Bill's infrastructure and cattle program. Duke had been in the Beefmaster business all of his life and had judged bulls with Uncle Palo. Because Bill felt only numbers and statistics counted in selecting cattle, he had already picked the bulls from Isa Cattle Co.'s catalog in his computer in Chicago, and when he sent Duke to buy bulls for his registered Beefmaster herd at our October sale in the late 1980s, he would not allow Duke, who was attending the sale, to select the bulls. When I saw the list, I told Bill he was wasting his money.

In 1989, Bill asked me to interview a potential employee, James Fuller, who had previously worked for Clayton Williams, a renowned Midland oilman. After the interview, I told Bill that if he did not hire James, I would. Bill hired him, and later that same month sent James to San Angelo to buy cattle. We drove a 550–600 round-trip in one day to Hearne, Texas, where James bought 350 heifers belonging to Isa/Throckmorton. On the way home, James asked if I had received many speeding tickets. I said, "No, never, why?" He replied that we had not gone under 70 mph since leaving San Angelo. I asked if he wanted to drive, and he said, "Yes."

Bill later hired Jim Sammons, the son of our friends James and Joan Sammons, who had been working for Guillermo Osuna in Mexico.

When Jim came to buy bulls at our sale in October 1992, we had just started using the new technology of cattle DNA, being the first large ranch anywhere to DNA calves. The bull, Lasater 513, was very influential behind our herd genetics, and he had three sons, identified by DNA, at the top of the sale. Everyone present, including me, ranked the bulls 1, 2, 3, which was how they sold. Jim had been given severe budget limitations by Bill, so he bought #3, L Bar 1167. We found, accidentally, when we bought the Sanders herd later, that L Bar 1167 had turned out to be the best of the half-brothers, and I apologized to Jim for criticizing his selection.

In March 1992, I went to Santa Fe and made a deal with Bill Sanders to pasture his cattle in Texas, market the production of 275 of his registered Beefmaster cows at San Angelo and partner on 130 yearling Beefmaster bulls. Before Bill went public in October 1993, he offered me his Beefmaster herd, which indicated that he had given up on his lifelong dream of going into the cattle business.

In September 1990, over coffee in Santa Fe, Bill and I visited about each of our present and future business plans. Bill had sold LaSalle Partners and was working on taking Security Capital public. When I asked what his business plan was, he said that his company would buy properties that yielded ten percent unleveraged and then leverage them—shades of Tom Lasater and Henry Singleton! Bill invited us to invest in Security Capital before it went public, a courtesy I appreciated.

Doing Business with Denny Cattle Company

George Denny was one of many interesting people I have dealt with. He identifies an opportunity and moves fast in a big way. I believe his firm in Boston manages capital for the Harvard Endowment. George has been very successful in the cattle business by buying land and cattle when they are cheap. Our getting together was unusual—he had read my book and called to meet me. George told me that he wanted to model his business on ours and be the dominant Beefmaster breeder on the West Coast. After I saw his ranches in California, I knew he was financially capable of becoming the largest Beefmaster breeder in the world. I took him at his word and hoped to be a part of that process.

Our sale of 1,200 registered Beefmaster cattle to George in 1989 went very smoothly, and the plan was to leave the L Bar herd with us in Texas. His bulls from our herd would be sold through our October Bull Sale and his other Beefmaster bulls were to sell in February's event. He also would be generating large numbers of desirable young registered females. His main market for bulls and females was in Texas and Mexico through Isa Cattle Co., Inc. The first setback arrived by fax in late 1991 when he wrote that he had changed plans and was moving the L Bar Herd to California in a year. According to George, he could run them more cheaply "at the margin" in California. In fairness, he may have been afraid of the harshness of this environment in West Texas.

All our business was done by fax. I think he enjoyed negotiating with me and also used this transaction as a means of learning about the cattle business. Every negotiation with George was a struggle involving numerous faxes (I have a boxful of them). Having moved the cattle to cut expenses, he did not want to consider that the freight back to Texas was part of the cost of being in California. He wanted to split the gain over the cow's commercial value, less freight, but I wanted to be paid a flat fee. I am convinced Harvard has a course titled "Using Bogus Numbers for Negotiation." In every fax he sent, the starting premise was that the value of his cows or the freight charge was unacceptable. I finally learned that the only way to deal with him was to give him a price delivered to the point of sale, and then mark it up $200 per head. Without exception, every financially-oriented person I have dealt with has been unwilling to make the effort to be successful in the registered cattle business. The 2,000 registered Beefmasters that George originally bought are now commercial cattle worth $1,500 less per head than our herd in Texas. His bull customers now buy from us. When I read in the San Francisco Chronicle that he had sold a conservation easement on his Inks Creek Ranch at Red Bluff, California, for $3,000,000, I could at least understand the economics of his thinking.

Since coming to San Angelo in 1972, I have made four herd sales in the $1,000,000 category to buyers who were investors and who needed help managing and marketing their cattle. I planned to help them, but none was interested and none of those important herds survived as a competitive force in the seedstock business. The time and effort to raise and market breeding stock did not meet their profitability criteria.

Pasturing Cattle

"Don't open the gate. Get me to a phone to
order trucks to get these cattle out of here."
—Laurie Lasater

In April 1996, when I wrote a letter to our bull-cooperators to see if anyone wanted to pasture the bulls for the Isa sale the first Saturday in October, J.D. Cage phoned that he was interested in the business. He and his son, Jay, have done a fabulous job taking our bulls and sale to another level. The Cages are wonderful cattlemen, and on their own initiative, they have made improvements to the program, reduced our overall costs and helped us improve our cattle. Lorenzo is the third generation, and Jay is the fourth of our families' friendship.

• • •

As the heifer business with Bill Carey grew to involve large numbers, totaling over 7,000 heifers bought from FTX, Lykes and Dudas, we were forced to move eastward into higher rainfall country. We ran cattle in the area of College Station, Texas, for several years. In 1990 we had a large number of heifers pastured on the J.T. White Ranch at Hearne. Carlton Eckert and Jay Nixon, both having done business with Isa Cattle Co. and Throckmorton Land and Cattle Co., had put the pasturage deal together for us. On January 9, I flew to Hearne for my first tour and "look-see." It was bitterly cold when Eckert and Nixon met me at the airport. We drove to the headquarters of the White Ranch, which was leased by an Italian nobleman named Giovanni Vaselli. We drove to see the cattle with Dave Keeling, the (supposed) ranch manager, driving a suburban with me in front, Nixon and Eckert in the middle and Giovanni in the third seat. When Keeling drove up to a gate and stopped, I could see several hundred cattle in a small field with nothing to eat. Nixon and Eckert fumbled to open their doors, and I said, "I've seen the cattle. Don't open the gate. Get me to a phone to order trucks to get these cattle out of here." In the ensuing melee, Giovanni and I discovered we had a common language,

Spanish. He immediately realized that I was the man and told me in Spanish, "Ignore these dogs. Tell me what to do and we'll do it." Unfortunately, Giovanni, overwhelmed by his lack of experience in this country, was preyed upon by the local thieves and the Farm Credit System. One day when his wife, María, who spoke no English, was at the post office, the Farm Credit System seized her car and left her to walk home. It made me embarrassed to be an American. I prevailed on Bill Carey to loan Giovanni $12,000, secured by his hay crop. Of course, Giovanni fed the hay crop to our cattle, but he had to take bankruptcy. We never got paid, but he had assured me that when the family estate in Italy is settled, we would be, and I have a letter from his American lawyer assuring me of that. The Vasellis are wonderful people, and have gone through one of the worst financial ordeals I have witnessed.

At Bill Carey's suggestion, we moved our pasturage operation to Andy Adams, Jr., with even worse results. Andy also ended up owing Bill money as the cattle did not perform well. But, in Aggieland, the third time was charmed. We pastured cattle with Robbie Thigpen on a lease at the intersection of Highway 6 and the OSR (Old San Antonio Road). Robbie is a first-class individual, and except for me, was Bill's main Texas ally. We did well there, and I enjoyed flying regularly to College Station, where Robbie's foreman, Tommy Baros, would meet me. One year we delivered 705 Lykes Bros. heifer calves, and a year later we had 700 live heifers there. On a particularly beautiful day, I took Jack Grafa to see the cattle. We drove into the pasture just as the heifers were meandering in to water, and I told Tommy to stop as they were parading for us. We parked under a shade tree and saw the 700 walk by, one at a time. One of life's perfect moments. Aside from the risks of pasturage and conception rate, it became harder and harder to sell bred heifers. All the big heifer-sellers in the country, including Arky Rogers, John Cargile and me, gave up about the same time. It seems a shame the large and valuable enterprise Bill and I had created over fifteen years disappeared without a whimper.

Pasturing Cattle with Bob Page and David Krieg

Pasturing cattle has been a way of life for us since moving to San Angelo in 1972. As we became better established in the community, we were offered chances to pasture cattle with people who are a pleasure to know. Playing on the First Presbyterian Church softball team, I became acquainted with Bob Page, a good athlete who got a kick out of the fact that I played competitively. He is a top cowboy, who handles horses and cattle beautifully, and does not want to be anything else. He also helped us work cattle at the bull facility and other locations, sometimes bringing his daughters, Courtney and Suzanne, who were good help. Bob inherited a ranch at Orient, north of San Angelo, from his mother, Helen Marie Page, as well as a family lease on the Steen Ranch at Christoval, south of San Angelo. Having the cattle on a pretty ranch close to town was important for our marketing. It enabled us to show a valuable demonstration herd to people wanting to see what Beefmaster Cross females looked like and what kind of calves they produced. The females were Lykes Bros. heifers out of our bulls.

Bob had been pasturing cattle for Jimmie Powell, who purchased a ranch in Nebraska and moved part of his cattle there. At the time we were moving the FTX Ranch Co., Ltd., operation to Texas in 1989, this opened an opportunity to pasture cattle with Bob. He made a proposal to run 400 animal units for us on both the Orient and Christoval ranches, which was a successful arrangement for both parties. Unfortunately, the drought made it difficult for him to make a profit pasturing cattle and he ended the arrangement in 2000. When he decided to stop leasing the Steen Ranch, Bob recommended to David Steen that he lease us the 6,600-acre ranch. David did so, which we still enjoy operating today.

One day I went to the ranch to check on the cattle. Bob was not there, but his mother, Helen, was home and invited me in for a glass of tea. During our conversation, we touched on estate planning, which was of interest to their family at that time. I later told Bob how my mother had called a family meeting in the Denver office of Claude Maer, known for estate planning, to formulate an estate plan. I suggested he could do the same with Jim Carter in San Angelo. Shortly afterwards, Helen and Wilson unexpectedly died in the same year. Bob told me that having an estate plan saved the ranch he inherited, as well as the one his sister received. In 2005, Bob sold his ranch at Orient and bought a small ranch in New Mexico.

• • •

"Damn! These are good cattle!"

—*David Krieg*

Over the years I have referred many bull buyers to producers of other breeds of cattle. At Jack Grafa's recommendation, I referred a Florida buyer to Krieg Herefords, and the buyer bought ten bulls. Shortly afterwards, David Krieg came by the office with a gift certificate from M.L. Leddys, which I used to buy a winter coat. Some twelve years later, when it was bitterly cold at our October bull sale, I gave the coat to Jimmie Philman, a Duda employee from Florida, and told him that since the coat had sentimental value to me, I wanted him to have a warm feeling when he thought of his friends in Texas.

David came to the office several months later and said he was interested in some of my ideas on how to make a living in the cattle business. We visited at great length and made a deal that day for him to pasture some of the FTX cows on a lease near Eden, Texas. Over the next eleven years, we would pasture every class of cattle with the Krieg Ranch, including cows, heifers, sales bulls and steers. As I recall, the cattle were run on three locations the family owned and eight more that they leased. All this activity took place while we were scrambling to keep grass in front of the cattle under impossible drought conditions—the circumstances were difficult for him and for us. David was involved in several of our most important transactions. One was receiving Bill Sanders' herd in 1992 from New Mexico at the Mustang Ranch, where he was pasturing our cattle with Ben and Ann McCulloch. Because of the Brucellosis program, legalizing those cattle in Texas required much work and time. In 1994 he also received the Broussard Beefmaster herd from Florida. David offered me pasturage on the Price Ranch, a beautiful, well-improved ranch where he had built a set of pens modeled on our pens at the McAfee Ranch. At that time, Lorenzo and I were making a deal with Bill Broussard to partner on his Charolais herd, so I told David we would put those cattle there. He was not pleased, but when the Florida trucks unloaded, he immediately called, saying, "Damn! These are good cattle!" Of the people I have known in West Texas, he took the biggest interest in my ideas on cattle marketing and finance. David is one of the most effective people in getting a lot of work done with few ripples and is one of the few who is both, cowboy and cowman. He and Andy Smith are two people, outside the family, whom I rely on for bull selection.

In 1999, David's mother, Emilie, had some money to invest, so she asked David if they should get advice from Lasater. David asked, "You mean Laurie?" She replied, "No, no, the boy, Lorenzo."

Pasturing Cattle at Paris, Texas

In January 1994, Annette and I went skiing, making the mountain drive via Creede to Telluride, Colorado. While we were there, Lorenzo called to say the drought situation was critical and we needed to move cattle. He had located pasturage in East Texas and had checked references on the man involved. We drove straight home, and the next day Lorenzo and I flew to Clarksville, northeast of Dallas. The individual we were meeting arrived approximately ten minutes later in a new diesel pickup with a trip-hopper cake feeder on back, pulling an Easley trailer with a good-looking gray horse on board. As he drove up the strip, Lorenzo and I turned to each other and said, "We need to move over here. We have found the mother lode." The day was beautiful, the man was impressive, the pasture was good and the price was right, so we made a deal.

The aviation map shows Clarksville has gasoline, but no one was there to sell it. Flying to Clarksville consumed a lot of our fuel, leaving about a 45-minute margin of fuel on the way back. On our flight home, I called the Coleman Unicom, but no one answered. I did not want to land and not be able to buy fuel, so we continued to San Angelo. The Piper Dakota has tanks in the right and left wingtips, and the prescribed technique in this situation is to empty the right tank, and then land using the left tank with all the remaining fuel. As we neared the San Angelo airport, Lorenzo was sleeping peacefully as I started a ten-mile descent to runway 210. About five miles out, the engine coughed as the right tank went dry and I switched to the left tank. Although we landed without further excitement, that was the end of that siesta.

The first indication that something was "bad wrong" at Clarksville came in the form of a late-night call from Oklahoma. The caller asked if

I was the Laurence Lasater pasturing cattle on the Harts Bluff Ranch near Cut-Hand, Texas. I said I was. The story unfolded: He said that he was pasturing cattle with the same man that we were, and explained that he had made that decision based on seeing our cattle, which were doing well. His cattle, however, were starving to death, he said. A Texas and Southwestern Cattle Raisers inspector later told me that the man we were pasturing with was a notorious con man they had been trying to put in irons for years.

Fortunately, I earlier had met Ed Atkins of Paris, Texas, where he and his brother, Jack, operated the Atkins Ranch and Spring Creek Natural Beef. After I talked to Ed about possible pasturage, he went to the lease personally, loaded our cattle and took them to his ranch. In June 1994, we made a deal with the Atkins brothers to pasture a significant number of cattle. As the drought got progressively worse in West Texas, Ed and Jack helped us greatly by pasturing a large number of our cattle. The brothers owned a duck-hunting slough that had formerly belonged to the Hunt family of Dallas. It was reputed to be the best. The brothers put on an annual duck hunt in January that we enjoyed—unbelievable hunting, food from Ed's Rocking W Barbecue, poker, squirrel hunting, crow hunting and all the trimmings. Ed and Jack had a collection of guns, and when I mentioned that I was looking for a twelve gauge over and under shotgun, they gave me a beautiful, Spanish-made trap gun they were not using. The brothers had an outstanding natural beef program based on Belgian Blue cattle. We ultimately bred all of our (Bill Richey's) commercial cows to Belgian bulls and sold them to the brothers. Those calves were some of the best I have seen. One year, when Ed was president of the Belgian Blue Association, I spoke at their convention in Kansas City. It was fun doing business with them, and we hated to have it end.

Partners

Having great partners has been one of the keys to my career. In the nineties, several of my longtime partnerships ended, and three new ones started in response to a specific opportunity. Because of the quality of the people involved, these partnerships have lasted a long time. My partnership with Bill Finan lasted over thirty years, and with Bill Carey, sixteen years. The one with my brother Dale lasted thirty years.

In November 1991, I spoke at Allan Nation's grazing school in Jackson, Mississippi. The program was oversold, so the speakers were asked to stay over a day to repeat our talks. Allan had a terrific crowd, and it was a fun event. My topic, "Ranching with Minimal Capital," was recorded on tape and circulated all over the world. Among those buying the tape was Bill Richey of Miami, a lawyer specializing in international bank fraud and money laundering. When Bill's secretary called asking how to get access to these ideas, I suggested that he invest in some cattle with us. Bill did, starting with a small investment in commercial cattle. Although we did not meet for four years and have been together only three times in 14 years, we have been partners in a series of larger investments, eventually owning 350 cows plus bulls. Those cattle were sold in the nineties, after which Bill made three other investments with us. Bill called in 1996 to ask what I would charge to advise him on his Florida ranch real estate. I told him to mail me an airplane ticket. He did, and I stayed at the Miami Intercontinental Hotel next to his office. Bill and his wife, Linda, took me to dinner that night and introduced me to stone crab, which is special, and the next day, we looked at ranches east of Okeechobee. In due course, he bought several small ranches near Stuart, and has caught the unbelievable Florida boom of the last five years.

• • •

I had known Bill Broussard for a number of years. Bill is a founding partner in a large medical practice, with eleven doctors, named Florida Eye. It is the main HMO in Melbourne, a booming area on South Florida's Atlantic coast. Although he started buying bulls in 1982, we did not become friends until he called in October 1993 and asked me to sell his Beefmaster herd. I flew to Orlando and drove to the Crescent J Ranch near Yee-Haw Junction, where his foreman, Billy Davis, showed me the cattle. Billy is a classic Florida cracker cowboy/spurmaker. I was surprised at how good the cattle were. That night, Bill was involved with a medical meeting so I had the evening to myself at the hotel, which gave me time to think. A band was playing in the lounge, so I went in, and as I thought over the day, I realized the cattle were too good to sell. Bill, a lifetime cattleman from Louisiana, had followed Dad's philosophy and had used only Lasater and Casey genetics. The next morning, we met for breakfast and I showed him the inventory counts with prices of each group. I suggested that we partner on the cattle, with him financing the venture at six percent interest, and us pasturing the cattle and handling the marketing, and he agreed. The partnership was supposed to make annual payments, but because of the drought in Texas, we could not make a payment for four years. When one bull crop sold well in October 1997, we were able to pay off everything. After the sale that day, Bill and I were enjoying the wonderful day, standing in the pasture at the Steen Ranch. In the middle of our conversation, he shook my hand and congratulated me on my tenacity. I replied that if he had made a margin call, we would not be standing there.

In the summer of 1998, I realized I was not receiving my monthly *Florida Cattleman,* so I asked for the back copies. The evening I received them, I was sitting in my chair riffling through the back issues when I saw an ad announcing that Bill was selling his Crescent J Charolais herd in an auction at the ranch that fall. As soon as I saw Bill's ad, I knew the cattle could not be allowed to evaporate. I went straight to the phone and called Bill, who answered on the first ring. When I told him the cattle market was bad and that the sale could be a fiasco, he agreed. I said, "Why don't we partner on the cattle?" Bill was pleased. Although I had seen the herd as well as their progeny on other ranches in Florida and knew how good they were, I wanted Lorenzo to see and okay the cattle, so we flew to Orlando. The cattle were better than he expected, and that night Lorenzo and I concluded a deal with Bill, a venture that has worked well—we sell the bulls every October along with our Beefmasters. (The Charolais X Beefmaster cross is, by far, the best of all the terminal crosses.)

The Crescent J Charolais Herd

A Frenchman named Jean Peugibet exported Charolais cattle from France to Mexico before World War II. Alphé Broussard, Bill's father, purchased the descendants of this herd, and brought them to the U.S. in 1952. The Mexican shipper did not have the proper export permits, so the cattle were returned to Mexico amid an international scandal. Mr. Broussard served a year at Angola, later to be pardoned by President Eisenhower. He established a partnership with Maxey Michaelis, our neighbor in Mexico, and together they were able to recover part of the cattle. Our Charolais herd is directly descended from the foundation herd in North America.

Shortly after the Broussard Charolais came to Texas, Billy Davis, a classic Florida cracker cowboy/spurmaker, left the Crescent J, but we stayed in contact. I next saw him in 2006 when Tommy Mann and I visited the Rollins Ranch where Billy was working for Bill Gray, the new general manager. Billy told us of a classic conversation that went like this:

Billy: "Mr. Bill, I need a day off."

Bill G.: "Billy, why in the world would you need a day off?"

Billy: "I've got to buy my wife some clothes. When I leave in the morning, she's in her nightgown and when I come home in the evening, she's in her nightgown. She has nothing to wear."

• • •

"These are beautiful animals."
—*Scott Marsh*

In December 1995, I moved the financing of the Sanders herd to the San Angelo Banking Center, where John Childers agreed to finance our breeding operation. Two years later, Scott Marsh, my Princeton roommate, having sold his commercial cattle in 1997, agreed to buy a one-third interest in our purebred spring-calving Beefmaster herd. Later the partnership purchased Annette's cattle, and he bought another one-third interest. He enjoyed his few trips to Texas, and on one of his visits, we were touring the McAfee Ranch, and as we drove up on a cow and calf grazing in a pretty glade, he exclaimed, "These are beautiful animals."

• • •

I have written of our partnership with Bill Carey, which ended on a positive note when he finally foreclosed in January 1996 on the ranch belonging to the man who stole $100,000 worth of cattle from us. Throckmorton Land and Cattle stocked and operated the ranch for a year before selling the cattle and the land for a profit. The ranch, by coincidence, sold to Obe Veldman, my old Rhodesian connection. That multi-year ordeal ended on July 16, 1997, when Bill sent me a check. Later Throckmorton sold 10,000 acres of wheat land to the Mormon Church, and sold the ranch's remaining 30,000 acres to Ross McKnight at an unbelievable price in 1999. Bill traded his Texas ranch in a tax-free exchange for a ranch in Oklahoma and some hotel properties in the East. He moved his ranching/farming operations to Oklahoma. At the same time, Lykes Bros. decided not to sell any more Beefmaster heifers, thus ending another interesting chapter in my career.

Selling Bulls in the '90s

My core business, and that of Isa Cattle Co., has always been selling bulls. I like raising good bulls as well as helping others to do so, and then selling the heck out of them. Generally, this operation has been profitable for me. As president of the company, however, I misinterpreted my assignment. I thought I should run as far and as fast as possible with the company's capital, when I should have protected it and stayed with the core business. The mistake was not putting on bull sales in Florida, partnering with Max Watkins or starting NewBeef, the mistake was taking all the risk. Those losses were my responsibility, and I regret them. Fortunately, there are no unpaid creditors lurking in the brush, as is often the case.

The decade of the 1990s was an eventful time in the evolution of our bull-selling program. In February 1990, we had our last bull working in the old pens at San Angelo Feedyard; the company had built us a new Bull Test Facility on the south side of Highway 67. The new corrals were dedicated in August 1990, at which time various people important in my career were honored. The facility incorporated the best design ideas of John Cargile and Glenn Polhemus, as well as our own. By a creative means of financing, Isa Cattle Co. paid half the cost of the construction by a check-off fee on all bulls tested there. I was thrilled with the installation. I mentioned previously that James Howell developed a scoring system to rank the bulls quickly and easily on paper. In February 1991, we used his system to catalog 300 bulls in the new facility, and our secretary, Sheila Alexander, entered the scoring data into a redesigned sale catalog.

As the Great Drought of the Nineties tightened its grip and widened into more western states and Mexico, I could see that our spring bull sale, which was aimed at customers in the Western U.S. and Northern Mexico, was going to be in trouble. We held our last spring sale in 1994, and it was one of our best sales with 217 bulls. The González brothers from Hermosillo, Sonora, bought 45 head, the largest single bull purchase at one of our auctions.

Volume Bull Buyers in the '90s
(10 or more bulls at one time)

Juan Diaz—MX

Eddie Lumpkin—FL

Morrison Cattle Co.—TX

Mabry Carlton & Sons—FL

Alberto Bailleres—MX

Ted Richardson—TX

Mahone Cattle Co.—NM

C-Farr Ranch—FL

A. Duda & Sons, Inc.—FL

Durando & Paris—FL

Ramos Land & Cattle Co.—NM

Karl Ronstadt—AZ

Eduardo Gómez—MX

Hubbard Ranch—OR

Triangle Ranch—NM

Daniel Boone—MX

Ricardo Salas—MX

Bob Dickerson—TX

Drgac Bros.—TX

Fernando González—MX

Throckmorton Land & Cattle—TX

Willowbrook Ranch—MS

McElroy Ranch—TX

Bright Hour Ranch—FL

Vic Choate—TX

Monroe Short—MS

T.G. Lee Farms—FL

Lykes Bros., Inc.—FL

McDaniel Ranch—FL

Enrique Perez—MX

Blue Oak Farms—TX

Agri-Beef Co.—OK

W.W. Jones—TX

Louie Guazzini—NV

González Bros.—MX

Rocker B Ranch—TX

Rio Ranch Corp—FL

Ramón Corona—MX

Albert Cano—MX
Rodolfo Johnson—MX
Barlite Ranch—TX
Cow Creek Ranch—FL
Six L Cattle Co.—CO
Mariposa Ranch—TX
Tom Cooper—NM
Alamo Ranch—NM
Pearce Flournoy—CA
Wilson & Swink—MO
Horacio Hinojosa—MX
Bill Zunino—NV
Lee R. McCormick—TN
Rob Beard—TX
Crescent TS Cattle—FL
Petty Ranch—TX
Alfonso Caballero—MX
Jesús Yurén—MX

Denny Cattle Co.—CA
Jones Ranch, LLC—TX
Triple S Ranch—FL
Alberto Nava—MX
Baugh Family Ranch—TX
Fritz Stein Farms—FL
Riley West & Co.—AZ
San Emigdio Cattle Co.—CA
Wedgeworth Family—TX
FTX Ranch Co.—TX
John King—AZ
Joe Goff—AZ
Roy Thompson—NM
Joe and Jo Ann Mendiburu—CA
Arturo Siller Group—MX
John Cargile—TX
Rafter T Ranch—FL

"All I'm going to say is I am using his bulls to pay for land."

—Jody Wedgeworth

It is a real cause for celebration in our family when a customer appreciates our cattle and uses our ideas to good advantage, as is the case of Pearce Flournoy in California, and the Lykes and Dudas in Florida. In 1990, the Wedgeworth family from Carthage, Texas, appeared on the scene. They began buying conservatively, but have changed to buying 15–20 Beefmaster and Charolais bulls off the top of the offering each year. They now feed their steer calves and sell their surplus females for replacements. One year, Jody Wedgeworth invited me to Carthage to speak at their winter Cattlemen's Banquet and gave a great introduction: "You all know this man. All I'm going to say is I am using his bulls to pay for land."

• • •

Dick Jones of Corpus Christi, Texas, began buying bulls in 1992. The Jones Ranch is one of the historic ranches of South Texas, lying between Falfurrias and Hebbronville. The bond between our families began when our grandfathers were neighbors. Dick quickly became one of our key volume buyers. The Jones Ranch is divided into three divisions, with the Alto Colorado being closest to Falfurrias. I made my first trip there in September 1995, landing on their ranch strip. During the course of the visit, I told him that the cattle market looked bad for our October 7 sale and that he might consider taking advantage of the opportunity to upgrade his bull battery. He bought 60 bulls, and after being delivered to the Alto Colorado division, the bulls became sick. The cause could never be identified, and Dick and I agreed to split the cost of the treatment and death loss. This was very gracious on his part, and is representative of the high-class person he is. His son, Whit, and our son, Lorenzo, are active now in the Texas and Southwestern Cattle Raisers Association.

• • •

Dwight Bertrand of Lake Charles, Louisiana, bought for the first time in 1999. We had done little business in that area, and thanks to his efforts, that state is now one of our key markets for bulls and females. Dwight is a retired Air Force colonel and teaches at McNeese State University. I have spoken to his students and have become friends with him. I visit regularly, enjoying the hospitality of Dwight and his wife, Julie. As in other neighborhoods, it has been a pleasure to become acquainted with many nice people there.

Sales and Auctioneers

"The industry we thought we were in never existed."

—Skipper Duncan

Both of our early auctioneers, Ron Ball and Skinner Hardy, were World Champion Auctioneers. In April 1995, I was searching for an auctioneer and telephoned Pat Goggins of Billings, Montana, assuming his auction (PAYS) sponsored the annual auctioneer contest. The Goggins family are the top Angus breeders in the U.S. and have several related businesses, including PAYS (Public Auction Yards). Pat told me that the contest rotated, but that his son, Joe, was a good auctioneer. I asked Joe to send a video and hired him for our sale in October 1995. Joe is a real cowman, who connects with our clientele. That year, Joe and Lorenzo started together and earned their pay by keeping the sale going and selling all the bulls. Joe went on the ranch tour after the sale, and was amazed that the cattle were doing so well in such a difficult environment. Before the sale, Skipper Duncan and I were visiting in the lobby when he told me, "The industry we thought we were in never existed." The lights came on for me at that moment.

In October 1996, Lorenzo and Joe's second sale was a great one—the kind that renews one's fighting spirit. Lorenzo had redesigned the sale catalog and received many compliments. Before the auction, I was walking on the catwalk at Producers Auction when one of their cowboys trotted by on horseback with the new catalog stuck under his belt in his back pocket. He waved and said, "This new catalog is sure better than the old one," not realizing he was talking to the man who had designed the "old one."

The last three bull sales of the 1990s were very successful. Our 36th sale in 1997 was dedicated to my uncle, Watt Casey. This was the sale in which L Bar 5502 was sold, and he and his classmates from the fall-calving Broussard herd averaged $3,100.

John Cargile and I discussed cattle marketing continuously for over 30 years. At a time when I was seeking new outlets for commercial and registered Beefmaster cattle, he was looking for new business for Producers Auction and new enterprises for the West Texas ranching community. We agreed to have a Beefmaster female sale, sponsored by Producers Auction, on the Friday before our bull sale on Saturday. The First Annual Beefmaster Fiesta in October 1991, seven months before the drought, was very successful. People from all over the United States and Mexico were there to buy the cattle. No one could believe how successful the sale was.

• • •

I met Juan Diaz for the first time at Producers before the Fiesta sale. He is from Hermosillo, Sonora, Mexico, and he and his brother, Pepe, are of

Spanish descent. They own and operate Café Combate, which manufactures and distributes instant coffee all over Mexico. Their father got his start in Chihuahua delivering milk in an "express" pulled by a mule. Juan is an outstanding businessman and cattleman. Under his management, everything is done with meticulous care and every bill is paid when presented. We sat together at both the bull and female sale. Juan bought 120 females (the largest female purchase at our sales) as well as 32 bulls, the second largest dollar purchase at a bull sale. Each time Juan bought one, another animal he liked came into the ring, so he bought it also.

• • •

In February 1992, Gustavo Ybarra, who was married to the sister of the secretary of public works in Hermosillo, arrived in San Angelo and began buying large numbers of registered cattle. In addition, Eduardo Gómez, representing a world-renowned Mexican big-game hunter, began buying large numbers of cattle. The González brothers (who were close friends of the leading presidential candidate at that time) had been added to the group. I traveled to Hermosillo in September 1992 where we had a tremendous tour of all the ranches and a dinner for some twenty guests at the Valle Grande Hotel, after which I gave a talk in Spanish, "The History of the Lasater Family." They were very large ranchers and owned the Chrysler dealership. We also discussed starting a marketing group (Isa de México, SA) to sell Beefmaster cattle in Mexico and Central America. Members of the group were to buy stock, and I would run the company. The cattle, the people and the financial and political resources were in place to be successful. When I made a second trip to meet with the group in 1993, we had our first bull-judging event at Juan Diaz' ranch, El Rodeo, located on the highway between Hermosillo and Nogales. We weighed and graded his weaned bull calves. As I weighed the bulls and explained how the cattle would be numbered and the sale order established, Juan had a waiter serving Chivas Regal to all attending. By the end of the next year, Luis Donaldo Colosio, the presidential candidate, was assassinated, the drought got worse, interest rates went up and Mexico devalued its currency forty percent. As all loans were pegged to dollars, the devaluation of currency on December 20, 1994, meant that everyone's debts increased by forty percent. Everyone went broke but Juan Diaz, and that was the end of Isa de México.

While doing business in Sonora, we had two humorous experiences. The first occurred after a bull sale when a buyer from that state became ill at the sale. I told Lorenzo to take him to Community Hospital and "don't let him die because he has not yet paid for his bulls." When Annette went to check on him at the hospital, the buyer was lying on a gurney smiling and saying, "This is the nicest hospital I have ever been in." Among his personal possessions was a huge roll of cash he carried in his front jean's pocket, along with a pocket knife and laptop computer.

The second incident occurred at the Charlie Michelini export pens in Nogales, Arizona. A Mexican buyer had made a large down payment on a group of registered cows, which I delivered to Arizona, that were in the pens awaiting our payment by wire transfer. About five days before the down payment was consumed by the cows' yardage expenses, I faxed the buyer that I was sending trucks on Monday to bring them home. The buyer called on Friday and said he would wire the money on Monday and asked if I could release the cows to save the weekend's expenses? I told him, *"No hay problema,"* (No problem) and immediately called the export pens to leave instructions not to release the cattle until I personally called to release them. The money was wired on Monday, the feed bill was paid, and everyone lived happily ever after.

Travels with Lorenzo

One of the most enjoyable parts of my career has been traveling extensively with Lorenzo on a variety of short and long trips. We have looked at ranches, attended cattle and deer-breeding events and called on customers. Two trips we made together were memorable and demonstrate the breadth of our activities. In the 1970s I had begun calling on customers systematically. In August 1994, we flew to West Palm Beach, Florida. We visited Rio Ranch Corporation, which had bought the Lakeport Ranch and the original FTX herd. The next day, we visited the Lykes Bros. office, and Mike Milicevik took us on a short tour to the Wild Island division, which was stocked with Beefmasters. (If I were telling a martian about the ranching business and had one place to visit, it would be the Wild Island division at Lykes Bros.) It is hard to beat a beautiful ranch under great management, stocked with fabulous cattle. From their office, we drove to the Bright Hour Ranch, near Arcadia, Florida, another very large, historical ranch stocked mostly with Beefmaster Cross cows. (In ten years, that ranch would sell for several times more than anyone would have thought possible in 1994.) The last stop was at the A. Duda and Sons, Inc., office at Rockledge, Florida, on I-95. The Dudas were building the city of Viera, Florida, on their ranch, and a few years in the future would sell 15,000 acres to the State of Florida. While we were visiting there with Jimmie Philman and Malcolm Lavender, it was pouring rain—a nice way to end the trip. We flew home on Sunday, having called on ranches with over 45,000 cows.

Buckaroo Country

Pete Crow, publisher of the *Western Livestock Journal,* his father, Dick, before him, and Forrest Bassford have been students of and supporters of the Lasaters since about 1950. Pete introduced me to Bob Baesler of Roswell, New Mexico. Bob, in turn, gave me a telephone introduction to Pearce Flournoy of Likely, California. At that time, Pearce was preparing to sell a load of Beefmaster heifers and called me about feeding them. I told him to put them in the NewBeef program with Clay Birdwell at Hereford, Texas, which he did. In June 1995, he and his son, Lanny, came to San Angelo, and I hired a pilot to fly us to Hereford. Pearce's 500-pound heifers were the best cattle in the yard, and after expenses, netted $50.00 per head or ten-cents-a-pound profit. That October, he attended our bull sale and bought his first bulls from Isa Cattle Co. Since 1996, I have visited Pearce and his family every year. The Flournoy family founded the town of Likely in northern California in the1880s, and Pearce is a great buckaroo and cowman. Like Billy Davis in Florida, Pearce exemplifies the best of cowboy humor.

The Great Basin is defined as Nevada and the counties that join it. That area is where the "buckaroo" culture exists. (Buckaroo is a bastardization of the Spanish word *vaquero,* cowboy.) The buckaroo culture is different from our vaquero culture in Texas. Here, the better hands help the less capable, knowing that they need their help to get the work done. In the Great Basin, where the ranches are enormous and the distances vast, cowboys often work alone, and trade secrets are carefully guarded to increase employability. For example, if there is a trick to getting on a horse, the buckaroo might go behind the barn to mount up, so that no one can see how he does it.

In June 1999, Lorenzo and I flew to Reno, Nevada, rented a car and drove north 175 miles to Likely, California, which is centered in beautiful mountain country with trout streams everywhere. My only concern about taking Lorenzo to Likely was that he would refuse to come home. After seeing how good Pearce's heifers were at Hereford, our mission was to help him set up a program to sell his surplus Beefmaster Cross females. He had originally bought Watt Casey bulls from Max Watkins. The day after we arrived at Likely, we loaded three saddled horses and drove forty miles to the Flournoys' Willow Creek Ranch, northwest of Alturas, California. We rode out his sales females and sorted them into two groups, with one to go on

Pearce Flournoy, holding my horse—a wild horse named *Handsome* for his Roman nose.

the Western Video Sale. Lorenzo and I wrote the description for the video catalog. I told Pearce to tell the representative he would "no sale" them if they did not net $700 per cow. The "rep" told Pearce that was impossible. The cows brought $735, netting Pearce $710. Surprise! Surprise! In a short time, Pearce learned from us how to feed his cattle, when necessary, and how to sell his surplus females at a premium. In addition to being a close friend, Pearce has become an effective spokesman for our cattle and our ideas in the Western United States. In a nutshell, that is how we have built our markets.

• • •

Next, we flew to Bakersfield, California, to see the San Emigdio Ranch, another unique and beautiful property, originally a Spanish Land Grant, which joins the famous Tejón Ranch. It also has been called the Kern

County Land Company. The geography is unique, characterized by huge, round hills covered with grass. As an old, established ranch, it had a wonderful character, much like Sierra Hermosa in Mexico, and about the

With Bill Boyd on San Emigdio Ranch near Bakersfield, California.

same size. Bill and Merna Boyd, the managers who had a working interest, reminded me of Duke and Ruth Phillips, and the headquarters had the same relaxed Spanish Colonial feeling. Bill's son, Craig, a top hand, lived at a different headquarters and was in charge of the steers. Kurt Thomas, one of the financial partners in the San Emigdio Cattle Company, met us at the Bakersfield airport and drove us to the ranch. Kurt is a Harvard Business School graduate and active in several agribusiness ventures in the area. As soon as we arrived at the ranch, we left on a long tour with Bill. The defining characteristic of the San Emigdio was the water system, the operation of which was very complex. Bill had worked on it for several years and was the first manager to get the system functioning perfectly. The ranch was stocked with good Beefmaster Cross cows, some purchased from Joe Mendiburu, as well as many #2 Mexican steers.

That night, the Boyds had an impromptu party for us on the lawn at the main house, attended by the three other couples on the ranch. All the men but Craig had been to our bull sales, so we discussed the cattle business at length. There was a pasture of cattle to work, so the next morning Lorenzo and I helped behind the chute. I noticed that some of the cattle showed signs of iodine deficiency. Bill asked me to explain it to the crew, so we had a short seminar on nutrition, in which I explained that protein, phosphorous, vitamin A and iodine were critical to herd health and reproduction and were almost universally deficient. We also shared with them our ideas on selling commercial replacement females at a premium. A year or two later, we helped two valued customers by arranging the sale of some San Emigdio heifers to Karl Ronstadt in Arizona. The Boyds gave us two classic books about the Southern California *vaquero* history. When David Stoeckleins' beautiful book about California cowboys was published, San Emigdio and the Flournoy family were featured.

The Boyds had moved to San Emigdio to work until the end of their careers, and Craig was slated to take over from Bill. Suddenly, without warning and for no reason, the lease was terminated by the owners, who had established some sort of conservancy and were ignorant of the care being taken of the ranch and the value of the Boyds as a reservoir of the cowboy culture. It is hard for me to reconcile the heartbreak suffered by people who are admirable and who personify American ranching values.

• • •

When we left, Bill drove us into Bakersfield where we met Joe Mendiburu and his daughter, Jo Ann, at Wool Growers, a favorite Basque restaurant. It is decorated with pictures of all the original immigrants, including Joe's father, who came over as a sheepherder. I asked him how long it took his dad to start owning sheep, and he replied, "Two or three years." We enjoyed a tour, seeing Jo Ann's registered Beefmaster herd. They are some of our favorite customers. When the Mendiburus come to our sales, they buy the front end of the cattle, pay for them and are back at the airport, ready to go home, by noon the same day. Joe was roughly a contemporary of Dad's, and like Dad, recently died at about ninety years of age. Unfortunately, they did not mint any replacements.

Botswana and South Africa

I have mentioned that we sold 11,000 straws of frozen semen to Rhodesia out of top Lasater Ranch bulls in the 1970s. Some time later, we arranged a shipment of Casey Beefmasters to Sam Levy in that country. The semen was used also in Botswana and South Africa, and, being from outstanding bulls, the calves were good and the breed became well known and appreciated in Southern Africa. As in Latin America, Beefmasters fit the low-cost, grass-based beef production model. Over the years, we carried on extensive correspondence with cattle raisers from Southern African countries. We received visits from some twenty breeders between 1975 and 1999. At that time, there was no such thing as fax, e-mail, or cell phones. Business was conducted by airmail letter, telegram (mailgram) and limited telephone contact. In 1983, we made a shipment to Pieter Bosch, Martin Bam and Tony Brink of South Africa, ranchers who had used some of the original semen from Rhodesia. In some shipments, it is difficult to tell who is the actual buyer or buyers, but we received letters from these gentlemen detailing results from each bull used.

International business is very difficult because the currencies, government policies on imports and health requirements change daily. Wars and devaluations happen often. Some countries, such as Australia and Argentina, use bogus health requirements to keep out any competition by U.S. cattle. Fortunately, dishonesty is the exception rather than the rule. The customers involved are interesting, high-quality, educated people, who are making long-term investments in superior genetics for the future benefit of their families. The legacy we inherited of top cattle and honest dealing, as well as the good will the family enjoys, makes it possible for me to do business on a handshake basis all over the world. As long as it makes business sense, my policy has been to do whatever the customer wants, recognizing that no profit exists in cattle until something is sold at a premium. My strategy has been, "firstest with the mostest." What minor problems we have had with nonpayment could have been avoided, but I always realized that being more conservative, financially, in international business was counterproductive. Now, with cell phones, faxes and e-mails, plus increased sophistication on the part of everyone, we have come a long way since shipping bulls to the Guatemalan border, with no way to communicate with our trucks or the buyers' trucks coming from Costa Rica. It is fascinating now to call Brazil or South Africa and have the person answer his cell phone on the first ring. International business, with all the problems and rewards, fits my personality as a risker and an adventurer.

• • •

Letters received from people all over the world, commenting on current events and sending pictures of the calves sired by our bulls, have made for an interesting and gratifying part of my career. Johann Zietsman of Rhodesia (now Zimbabwe), in one of his numerous letters, described a nighttime attack by guerillas on his ranch home, which was destroyed. The military experiences in counter-terrorist warfare by the people I have known there are the equal of any in the annals of warfare. During those years, our friend Allan Savory was also heavily involved in that fighting. I have received numerous interesting letters from John Kempf of Botswana. In one, he described the problems of dealing with the Botswana Meat Commission in processing cattle for export to the European Union. In another, written pre-Mandela, he expressed concern about the possible collapse of South Africa. He wrote that a military airstrip had been built in Botswana, and he wondered if I knew why and who financed it.

• • •

We received our first letter from John inquiring about frozen semen for Botswana in 1984. He had seen the Casey cattle in Zimbabwe. I responded with a price quote, and about six weeks later, received another hand-written letter with a Botswana import permit. I will never forget making our first shipment to Sir Siretse Khama Airport, Gabarone, Botswana. John Kempf and Pieter Bosch would join Guillermo Osuna of Mexico as our largest customers worldwide. We have done business with Guillermo for over forty years and with John and Pieter over twenty. All are still active in ranching. John made his first A.I. breeding to Lasater bulls on July 20, 1985, and had his first purebred (⅞) calf born in May 1990.

The telephone rang in my office on October 19, 1989, and the caller said, "Mr. Lasater, this is John Kempf." I responded, "Mr. Kempf, where are you?" He answered, "My wife and I are downtown at the Best Western." I hurried to the motel and met them at the restaurant. At one point John left the table, and I asked his wife, Wilna, what had brought them to the United States. She replied that they had come to see me. I was incredulous and told her that it was a miracle I was even in town. She said that John never planned more than one day at a time. I knew then that I was meeting one of the most interesting people, and decided on the spot to take Lorenzo to Botswana the next year after he graduated from college.

John Kempf is an interesting man, very quiet, educated and literate. He has given me several fine books, which I have enjoyed. Somehow, the races in Botswana get along well and seem to have avoided the terrible racism that afflicted Rhodesia and South Africa. John told us that after their independence, his gardener took his place on the town council, and that the gardener was a better councilman. In one conversation, I said

The tree under which John Kempf camped.

that it amazed me that the old-time hunters did not take a woman or partner on their lengthy safaris. His reply was, "They were hunters," meaning that was their priority. If I were summing up John, I would say that he is a pioneer. His life and focus have been the acquisition and development of a great ranch. Like many quiet people, John has a dry humor. Several years later, he wrote that they had acquired various "gadgets," which meant that they could watch CNN News and had a GPS for their plane. He said having a GPS took the fun out of being lost in the Kalahari Desert.

The Kempf's Xumgai Farms consisted of approximately 150,000 acres and 7,000 cattle, and has since been expanded. Xumgai, pronounced Gum-Hi with a click in Bushman, means Plenty Thorn. John went to Botswana with the veterinary corps and took up a 20,000-acre tract when the country was still a British protectorate. Botswana on the old map was Bechuanaland. During the Patrice Lumumba war in the Congo, as the neighbors abandoned their ranches, John took them over. The ranch is now a well-developed, sophisticated operation on the Kalahari Desert near Ghanzi, Botswana. When Lorenzo and I visited, they walked their cattle 500 miles to town. His ranch, the largest in Africa, is now 240,000 acres with 12,000 cattle.

As a young single man, John camped for several years under the tree pictured here, and his present home is built around it. He shot the lions out before moving his cattle in, using a British Enfield .303 rifle from the Boer War. Ammunition was rationed, so he had many adventures while disposing of the lions. John Kempf and Bill Finan of Mexico, both still ranching, are the only men I have known who were the first to run cattle on their virgin ranches, which were approximately the same size.

When John decided to marry, he courted Wilna by driving her and her mother 500 miles in a Bedford truck to see the ranch. Wilna is an Afrikaner, and Africaans is the language spoken in their home. It is also the language of farming in Zimbabwe, South Africa, Botswana and Namibia.

• • •

A year later, as I had hoped, Lorenzo and I left San Angelo, bound for South Africa and Botswana. Because of the United States embargo, there were no direct flights to South Africa, so we traveled on American Airlines to Dallas, British Airways to London, Nairobi, and Johannesburg, then Air Botswana to Maun. The total trip was over 72 hours. In Dallas, we received a bonus. Since we have the same name, British Airways mistakenly had reserved only one ticket for the two of us and to correct their error, they upgraded both of us to business class. We had a long layover in London, so went from Gatwick Airport to the city to see Westminster Abbey and the Tower of London and then to Heathrow Airport for our evening departure. We had a good flight, arriving late at night at Jomo Kenyatta Airport in Nairobi. There is a Hemingway museum in the lobby of the airport, which I had looked forward to seeing. However, after we landed, a soldier with an AK-47 boarded the plane and ordered everyone to stay seated. Evidently, there was a revolution in progress, and no one was allowed to deplane.

At Nairobi, several hundred South African Muslims boarded, returning from their pilgrimage to the Holy Land carrying a five-gallon jug of holy water and a large carry-on. It took several hours to get them seated, with their belongings stacked in the aisle of the plane. (When we saw our baggage thrown off the plane and left beside the runway in Nairobi, we realized that we were far from home.) After takeoff, I dozed a few minutes, then awakened and opened the window blind to see Mt. Kilimanjaro, the symbol of Africa, silhouetted by the rising sun. It was a special moment. Lorenzo still jokes about my waking him to see it. We spent the night in Johannesburg and returned to the airport the next morning for our flight to Maun. Our checked luggage, still in Nairobi of course, had not surfaced.

Later in the trip, when I inquired at the airport about my suitcase, the lady behind the counter told me that it would arrive in San Angelo, Texas, on such and such flight and day, several days after my return. She had probably never heard of Texas or San Angelo, but her computer knew exactly where my suitcase was. I made the sixteen-day trip with my carry-on bag. Lorenzo's eventually caught up with us, but my bag did not. It arrived in San Angelo several days after I had returned home.

Maun, located on the edge of the Kalahari Desert and the jumping-off point for the Okavango Delta, is far from anywhere and is actually more of a village with tin-roofed houses. The airport is fenced with signs from the famous safari companies. The planes parked on the ramp were mostly Cessna 206s with luggage pods underneath. The 206 is also popular in Mexico, being a powerful six-place plane with large cargo space. As they say, "Africa belongs to the 206." I was glad John and Wilna and their two daughters, Frances and Willemien, were there to meet us.

The day we arrived, we toured Maun, had lunch at Riley's Hotel and spent the night at the Island Hotel. Lorenzo and I slept in a rondavel, a round stucco structure with a thatched roof. Everything was exotic and exciting. The next morning, the six of us boarded their 206 for the flight north to the Okavango Delta. As we flew north toward the Delta, the scenery became more like the Africa we had imagined. As we circled to land at the Kwai River Lodge, I almost had to pinch myself. I could see elephants drinking at a dam. We were met at the strip by a Land Rover driven by a friendly black man named Morgan, who drove us four hours through the Moremi Reserve to Okuti Camp. On that drive, we saw nearly every common African species except lion. The whole day was perfect, mid-winter (south of equator) weather, cold in the mornings, bright sunshine all day, then cool again after sunset. During the flight, we crossed the Buffalo Fence, which was built across Botswana, from east to west, to prevent the southward migration of Cape Buffalo carrying hoof and mouth disease. The ecological and economic pros and cons are still hotly debated. As a "black" nation, Botswana is given export preference to the European Union, and building the fence was part of their effort to comply with Europe's health requirements for Botswana's beef. The price of Botswana beef is tied to U.S. Select at Amarillo, Texas.

Okuti Camp is on a concession owned by a Botswanan of German descent. It is very elegant and set right on the edge of the Okavango, teeming with wildlife of all kinds. We enjoyed cocktails while watching the sunset, listening to the birds and animals, and had dinner on a white tablecloth in a roofed, open-air dining room. We were in a five-star hotel in one of the world's most primitive places. Early the next morning, I heard a lion roar for the first time.

After staying in another camp for one night, we flew to the Kempfs' Xumgai Farms, which is divided into "camps" that are rotational grazing units with a water well at the center, where a family lives with the cattle. Each camp is stocked with one class and breed of cattle. We saw good quality Hereford, Tuli, Bonsmara and Beefmaster Cross cattle. John had used semen from Lasater bull 9013, Lasater bull 9265, and Lasater bull 1703 to produce first and second cross cows, and Lasater bull 567 on the second cross females. The improvement in the cattle was unbelievable.

Photo by John-John Kempf

Xumgai after rains.

We went with John and his crew to brand and dehorn three-quarter Beefmaster calves in one of the camps. The Bushman living at the camp had the cattle corraled when we arrived. All the men knew their jobs, and not a word was spoken. There was no job for Lorenzo or me, so we were standing to the side feeling worthless when a short yearling heifer with three-inch horns escaped from the chute. I grabbed her and bulldogged her down with the help of the crew. John said later that it was good she did not escape; the Bushmen were watching to see if I could stop her. At Xumgai Ranch, we had seen the ultimate low-cost producer—no mineral or medicine. The burdizzo (a castrating tool) being used at the chute was so old that the engraving had worn off. Seeing excellent cattle and excellent pasture management was a perfect start for Lorenzo's career as a cattleman.

We left Xumgai Ranch in Cessna A2ACC (Alpha Two Alpha Charlie Charlie) bound for Sir Siretse Khama Airport in Gabarone, the capital of Botswana, where we met Derek Brink, another member of a pioneer family. There were no navigational aids as we flew over the Central Kalahari Game Preserve. About an hour from our destination, the VOR started to flicker as we came within radio range.

• • •

When Wilna drove us to the Tony Brink Ranch at Deerdeport, South Africa, we crossed the same checkpoint where the first frozen Beefmaster semen had entered into South Africa nearly fifteen years earlier. The

A sign featuring the bull head from my first book's cover and an FBA slogan.

terrain was dry and brushy like West Texas and there were many Brahman-type cattle. The ranch sign made us feel welcome with a bull's head copied from the cover of my book and the slogan of our Beefmaster Association. Tony is an early user of Beefmaster genetics in Southern Africa, and Tony and Pieter Bosch were the principal founders of the South African Beefmaster Association.

When we arrived, Tony and his wife, Annette, warmly greeted us. After a dinner of impala steaks, the talk turned to Beefmasters. Before we went to see the cattle, Tony opened his safe to bring out the empty straws of all the bulls he had used for over fifteen years and the brochure on each bull. He knew more about our cattle than we did. His main bull, Herman, was a descendant of Lasater 6136 (El Sultán) born in 1966, a bull I had helped Dad select at the start of my career. It was hard to believe that Lorenzo and I were standing together thousands of miles from home, seeing this bull. We had made the full circle. Tony was a fabulous character, cattle-trader and *bon vivant,* and he had the personality to go with it. In Africaans, the title of respect is *oum* which means uncle, and is equivalent socially to the Spanish *don.* Oum Brink certainly ranks as one of the more colorful people we have known and one who has helped us promote the Beefmaster breed. Their family also operated a hunting ranch and invited us to hunt. I declined, not knowing the etiquette of accepting a free hunt.

Our next stop was at Boschveld Farms. Pieter Bosch and his son, Mike, were establishing a herd of 400 Beefmaster cows by using embryo transfer, the largest undertaking of that type in the world at that time. Pieter has been the prime mover in legalizing the Beefmaster breed in South Africa, a difficult task as the nation is extremely bureaucratic and paperwork governs everything.

Pieter and his family had to leave Rhodesia because of the war. Pieter was heavily involved with the government of Ian Smith in interrogation of prisoners and procurement of arms abroad. He told me that his command of native dialects was such that a prisoner could not tell he was a white man unless the prisoner could see him. Pieter is also a hunter and was involved in elephant control. He took his elephant gun out of the safe to show Lorenzo and me.

> *"No, we are the lucky ones."*
> —*one of the sons*

That evening John, Pieter and I were standing in front of the fireplace, framed by 100-pound elephant tusks, enjoying cocktails with our three sons, when one of the men commented on how we were lucky to have our sons coming into the business. One of the sons responded, "No, we are the lucky ones." It was a meaningful moment. Pieter and Mike, like John, are some of our oldest friends and allies in the Beefmaster business.

The next day, we were given the grand tour in Pretoria. We saw the Beefmaster association office, the official bull-testing center and a packinghouse, and met many key people. The long-awaited field day took place. It was a beautiful day with many interesting people present.

Professor Cas Maree (Dr. Bonsma's successor) and Herman Venter, a cattle authority, contributed greatly to the proceedings. Seeing all those people and cattle, much like ours, haltered around the pavilion, I was so overcome with emotion that I could hardly give my talk. The Bosches had three young bulls in a pen nearby, so everybody adjourned to that pen, and Pieter asked me to rank the three bulls. I asked to see the records, but he said he wanted an eyeball evaluation. Fortunately, I "drew to an inside straight," and as I pegged them #1, #2, #3 in accord with their actual data, I saw an older Boer rancher smiling to himself.

Lorenzo and I took our leave of the Kempfs and the Bosches and drove with Paul Yiannakis to his ranch. Paul, an interesting man, came to South Africa as a refugee from Malawi and is a cancer survivor. He is a successful businessman, who is becoming a leader in the South African group and is an ally of Pieter Bosch. We saw his cattle, including one of the Lasater Ranch bulls he had bought. After touring, we drove to their home and met his wife, Mary, and their two young daughters.

We left Johannesburg the next evening for Heathrow Airport. Upon landing, we took the Speedlink to London's Gatwick Airport Hilton. After resting a while, we went downtown for dinner at the Chicago Meatpackers, which had a Texas and Southwestern Cattle Raisers sign on the wall. That evening, we saw Ibsen's play, *The Wild Duck,* in the theater district. The next morning, we enjoyed a $25.00 continental breakfast at the Hilton. Due to the time change, I would make it home the same day, July 25, ending another of our many trips together. I said goodbye to Lorenzo who stayed in Europe to travel for several more months.

Brazilian Adventure

"Everything we have already bought has been a mistake."

—*Alberto Rodrigues da Cunha, Jr.*

We had our first business dealings with Brazil when four brothers in the Rodrigues da Cunha family and their brother-in-law, Randy Spears, arrived in San Angelo on February 26, 1997, representing the father, Alberto, a cattleman and nation-builder in the state of Goiás. At the suggestion of

Randy Spears, who is married to their sister, Marta, the family had embarked on a large project to introduce the Beefmaster breed into Brazil.

The Brazilians, coming from the tropics to West Texas in the grip of severe drought, arrived in the dead of a bitterly-cold winter. We had our herd bulls pastured on a scenic ranch about sixty miles west of San Angelo. The brothers could not believe it was possible to live and ranch in such a hostile environment. They spoke in Portuguese, and Lorenzo and I spoke in Spanish, with Randy, an American, translating when necessary. When we arrived at the pasture gate, we all got out and the bulls started coming out of the creek bottom hoping to be fed cottonseed cake. These were the first of our cattle the Brazilians had seen, and they were impressed, to say the least. One of the brothers said, "Everything we have already bought has been a mistake." We saw some of our cows and had two days of heavy negotiations. They ended up contracting to buy thirteen cows for frozen embryo collection and a large amount of frozen semen. We agreed to work together to promote the breed in Brazil. On April 17, Marcos and Randy returned to San Angelo to select their cows before our breeding season. Lorenzo had gathered a significant number of eight-year-old cows with their seventh calf at side, many bred by Lasater 9510, in a big water lot at the McAfee Ranch. They selected thirteen cows with calves that were tops to be delivered to Bovagen at Seguin, Texas, where the frozen embryos would be collected. The cattle were paid for on schedule, and we bought the calves back at weaning. Marcos and I began having extensive communications by e-mail and telephone, and the future looked bright.

• • •

In April 1998, Lorenzo and I traveled to Brazil to give two talks at the livestock show at Londrina and at a field day at the ranch in Goiás. The flight from Dallas to São Paulo is 5,100 miles via Miami, Haiti, Caracas and Manaus. São Paulo is one of the largest cities in the world, so I expected the airport to be in proportion, but its size was more like that of the San Angelo airport. We were supposed to have a seven-hour layover, but the employees at the airline desk saw our hats and knew we were going to the cattle show. We had planned to exchange money and buy jewelry at the airport, but we could get on a flight leaving immediately, so instead, we arrived in Londrina six hours early.

THE LASATER RANCH
SINCE 1882 ═══════════════════════════ Matheson, Colorado 80830

April 2, 1998

Mr. Alberto Rodrigues da Cunha
Brazil

Dear Mr. Rodrigues da Cunha:

I am sending this letter with my son Laurie, and grandson, Lorenzo, who are very pleased to be doing business with you, and who are very enthusiastic about the prospects for the future.

My son has told me of the tremendous project you and your family have undertaken in introducing the Beefmaster breed to Brazil via embryo transfer. I am pleased that you are using genetics my family has been working on for over 100 years. It has been a rewarding endeavor for us, and we are thankful to be here to participate in the breed's on-going development both in this country and abroad.

More than seventy years ago, my father purchased Nelore breeding stock from Brazil, and that was one of the genetic sources that went into the creation of the Beefmaster breed. Now the circle is complete with your introduction of the Beefmasters to Brazil.

We have long recognized that Brazil is the greatest market for Beefmasters outside the USA and we are so pleased that you have undertaken this project. My family and I look forward to collaborating with you on matters of mutual interest, and to many years of friendship with your family.

My son, Dale, and I look forward to you visiting us in Colorado and we would like to take this opportunity to extend an invitation to you and all of your family to plan a trip here as soon as it is convenient for you.

Please accept my warmest good wishes.

Sincerely yours,

Tom Lasater

Tom Lasater

LASATER BEEFMASTERS — FOUNDATION HERD OF THE BEEFMASTER BREED
719-541-2855   Fax 719-541-2888   lasater@rmi.net

The letter Dad wrote to Don Alberto Rodrigues da Cunha

In Londrina, a city of 1,000,000 people, there was no money exchange, and traveler's checks and credit cards were not accepted, even at the banks. The cab driver had never heard of the Bristol Residence

Hotel where we were to stay. We finally found the hotel, and because the hotel staff knew Don Alberto Rodrigues da Cunha, we prevailed upon them to loan us enough money to pay the cab. We met Marcos and Don Alberto in the lobby and went to the fairgrounds where 2,000 cattle were on display. At the Beefmaster display, we met María Lopes Kireef, a director of the exposition, whose husband and son had visited San Angelo, and John and Kika (Cid) Carter, Lorenzo's classmates at TCU Ranch Management School. Kika and María would be in charge of our social lives and shopping for the next several days. Both the Cid and Lopes families own bus companies, so María took our group to a German dinner at the bus company pavilion. During our visit, it rained constantly. El Niño, which brought no rain to Texas, really hurt the livestock show.

Although Londrina is more of a farming area, many of those attending the show have big ranches in states to the north. At noon, María hosted an elegant luncheon in our honor at the Cattleman's Club at the fairgrounds. That afternoon, Kika took us jewelry shopping, which was quite an education. We walked into this beautiful store and the clerk showed us a counter filled with gems. "No, no, we are not interested in this trash, we want to see what is in your bank vault," Kika said. The clerk scurried across the street and brought back some of the most beautiful items I have seen. The negotiations were savage, and we were almost embarrassed by how low the final prices were.

We visited a fabulous ranch founded by Kika's grandfather, which is now a family gathering place and meeting ground for the power elite. They have on display skulls from the original Zebu cattle brought to Brazil from India. For the first time, Lorenzo and I saw the horn structure of the Gyr, Guzerat and Nellore strains, which are reflected in today's Beefmasters. We almost felt the presence of our ancestors there. That afternoon, Don Alberto, Lorenzo and I were interviewed by Brazilian National Television, and then the three of us gave our talks. Randy introduced the program and translated for us. Lorenzo's talk, along with historic slides, was excellent and showed a lot of creativity. Lorenzo and I hosted a dinner for fifteen at a *churrascaría* that night to thank our hosts for such hospitality.

We left for the ranch country on Saturday, driving 250 miles at 75-

Gyr (top), Guzerat (middle) and Nelore cattle.

miles-per-hour on narrow roads with heavy truck traffic. On the trip, we saw the remains of the Atlantic Forest where 25-foot-tall trees had been cleared by hand off millions of acres. We arrived at Fazenda San José, Don Alberto's main ranch, and after lunch, we spent time looking at their Beefmaster cattle, ranging from half-bloods out of artificial insemination to imported purebreds and toured the ranch, a fattening operation selling 1,100-pound steers for slaughter. As there is no financial credit, ranches must sell cattle every month to pay expenses. The cowboys sort the steers into groups to hit carcass weight and yield targets. The cattle to be shipped are lined up like stair steps in adjoining pastures, sequenced by month of shipment. The ranch was involved with intensive grazing based on the teachings of the Frenchman Voisin, who influenced Allan Savory. I have rarely seen such management skills as those we saw all over Brazil.

On one of the ranches we visited, I saw an amazing feat of skill. Two cowboys were artificially inseminating the cows "in heat" in a herd of 150 cows with calves. The cows had numbers branded on their ribs, and the cowboys knew the cattle from memory. While we were there, they bred the cows, remembering the numbers of the cows that had been in standing heat that morning. We were standing on the highway watching as the two men gathered the herd into a corner. While one held the herd, the other rode to the eligible cow and called "hoof! hoof!" to a group of lead steers, one of which would come in to escort the cow out of the group. When the "heats" were cut out, the cowboy took them to the corrals where they would be bred.

While at Fazenda San José, we visited several more ranches and we flew by twin-engine plane to Inocencia, Michael Corbett's ranch. His son, Roberto, met us at the airport driving a new Chevrolet pickup with an L Bar Beefmasters bumper sticker on it. We had never met, and when I saw the sticker, I asked where it had come from. Roberto did not know, but it pleased us to see it 5,000 miles from home. Years earlier, Michael had purchased semen from American Breeders Service from the Lasater Ranch bull, Tomás, and they had a large number of Beefmaster Cross cattle on the ranch, Vale do Sol. There were some 60 yearling bulls by Tomás and another bull in the pen. I asked the foreman, in Spanish, to separate them so we could compare the groups. Everyone agreed that Tomás' sons were better.

Next we flew to Chapadão do Céu, Goiás, where various Rodrigues da Cunha family members live. The town was founded and developed by Don Alberto. In the frontier days, his mother left her grandchildren 118,000 deeded acres and 300,000 acres undeeded. Dinner that night for forty was at the home of Don Alberto and Doña Nadir. The field day took place on April 21 on the ranch belonging to Randy and Marta Spears. Randy introduced the program and read Dad's letter. Those attending asked many good questions, and there were enough big ranchers present to carry the Beefmaster program in Brazil. One rancher, Sergio Capps, came from Goiania for the event and paid for in cash thirty-two frozen embryos, which Lorenzo and I divided to carry home.

After the program, we returned to the Spears' home overlooking the river, for another large gathering that evening. We said our goodbyes and left on a beautiful 400-kilometer drive to Campo Grande, a major cattle center, across the state of Mato Grosso Sul. It was obvious to us that Brazil could be one of the biggest future markets for our genetics. There we met another brother, Roberto, and visited an agricultural research station. We arrived at the airport early, having time to make a deal with Marcos and Junior, whereby they would pay us, payable as shipped, for Grade One and Grade Two embryos harvested from our cows. In effect, they were leasing the cows. We had a great trip to a terrific country, traveling 20,000 kilometers by airliner and 2,500 kilometers through four states in Central Brazil.

La Filosofía

Sometimes things happen in life that have an other-worldly quality. On our thirty-second anniversary (November 21, 1996), Marcos Giménez from Argentina came to San Angelo to meet us. Marcos, a rancher who was educated in the United States, had read my book, knew our friends in Mexico, and had been to the Lasater Ranch. Annette and I hit it off with him immediately, and all agreed that he should translate my book into Spanish. He not only did so, but wrote an excellent introduction to the Spanish edition as well as a Part II incorporating several of my talks. *La Filosofía Lasater de la Cría Vacuna* was published August 19, 1999. The book was so good that Marcos translated the Spanish edition back into English, and both of the books are in their second printing.

Speeches in the Nineties

I gave numerous speeches and talks around the nation and the world in the 1990s. By then my book had been widely circulated, and through our business, I had a lot of exposure in the cattle industry. In the spring of 1993, I was invited by Texas Tech University at Lubbock, Texas, to speak at the Beef Forum on September 17. I was to be the rancher response to two professors speaking on adaptability. Each speaker was to have equal allotted time, the talks were to be included in a handbook, and I was to speak last.

The Beef Forum was held in conjunction with The Ranching Heritage Banquet at which John Cargile was to receive The Golden Spur award for excellence in the livestock business. I put a lot of effort into preparing my talk, and the event was made richer by the presence of Lorenzo and Annette, Jay and J.D. Cage, as well as many industry luminaries. Lorenzo and Jay had just joined their families' businesses. The appointed day arrived. The professors ran over their time, and I finally gave my talk, making several strong points while taking great care not to make any radical statements that might embarrass John. After my talk, in the Questions and Answers session, Linda Davis, an industry leader from New Mexico, asked if she could obtain a copy of "Mr. Lasater's excellent speech," which was omitted from the handbook. Someone jokingly asked how much I had paid her.

After the program ended, I asked the professor in charge why the ground rules on time had not been followed. He replied that the university was paying the other two speakers, so they let them talk longer. I assured him that I would charge next time.

• • •

"You Yanks made us go metric."
—*a Canadian cowboy*

Through our friendship with Sherm and Claire Ewing, and their son, Charlie, of Calgary, Alberta, Canada, I was invited to speak there at the Western Stockgrowers convention in December. Because range adaptability is such a concern to ranchers, I chose that as my topic. The crowd was responsive and asked good questions afterwards. John Stewart Smith, whom I had met in San Antonio at the Ensminger School, was also there. John had left Southern Africa (probably Rhodesia) and was managing the Beefbooster program founded by Sherm Ewing and other area ranchers. They were raising composite bulls for specific uses, i.e., calving ease or terminal cross, and marketing the bulls cooperatively. John showed me the weaned bull calves that had just been placed on feed. I was impressed that they could put a fairly lightweight, weaned calf on feed in November and sell him as a bull in April.

It was very cold while I was in Calgary, and the thermostat in my room was in centigrade. I stepped into the hall just as a cowboy walked by, so I asked him if he could set it for me. He replied, "I can't read those damn things. You Yanks made us go metric." We had a good laugh, and he invited me into his room for a drink and to get acquainted.

• • •

In June 1997, I went on a bull-selling expedition that in retrospect was such a fiasco it is almost funny. On the way to visit Pearce Flournoy and Bill Boyd, I decided to go by Elko, Nevada, to see the area and visit Bill Maupin. After landing in Reno, I rented a car and drove 350 miles to Elko. Upon arrival, I checked into the Stockman's Hotel, where Bill had made arrangements for me to host a steak dinner for thirty area ranchers. When dinnertime came, not a single person of the thirty who had accepted, came to the dinner. Needless to say, there were only Bill and Wanda Maupin, the local extension agent and me to enjoy a $600 dinner. The Nevadans were mortified. There was, however, saving grace. I was able to shop at the famous Capriola's Saddle Shop and went to the Red Lion Casino. When I walked into the casino, I saw a high-stakes Texas Hold 'Em game in progress. The Nevadans could not believe their luck that a Texan had walked in, ready for shearing. I sat down at the table, and on about the fifth hand, rolled over four nines and broke the game. Without a word, I cashed in my chips and walked out, leaving them with tears in their eyes. That one hand nearly paid for the steak dinner.

The Boehme Ranch and La Casita

In 1998, I received a piece of property, the Dry Camp Ranch, that Dale had owned east of Colorado Springs as part of my withdrawal from the Lasater Ranch Partnership, which we were able to sell, setting up a need for a tax-free exchange. I began looking for ranches near San Angelo, and one of the properties was the Boehme Ranch near Eola, Texas, in Concho County. It was owned by the Krieg family. Mr. Krieg had bought the property after a heart attack as insurance for his wife. It originally had belonged to a German prisoner of war named Boehme who stayed in West Texas to work for the Henderson Ranch. On January 13, 1999, Lorenzo and I agreed to buy the ranch, making a tax-free exchange for the Dry Camp property in Colorado, and the deal was closed on February 25. This property, well improved but with no house, lies between the Middle and South Kickapoo creeks. Although we could ill afford it at the time, we installed a three-bedroom manufactured home, as well as welded pipe fence, grass and trees, which became the family gathering spot. We called it *La Casita,* and the whole family dearly loved it. We kept two horses there so I could take Isabel and the grandsons riding. Given how many ranches we had operated, it is surprising that that small place could mean so much.

L Bar 5502

"We feel good just knowing he is on the premises."
                                                    —Brad Cardwell

In August 1995, a bull calf was born that we named L Bar 5502. Now in his twelfth year, he is like a storied athlete who never has a bad game and lives his life with distinction. Appropriately, this great bull resulted from a family effort. His sire was selected by Lorenzo and me during Lorenzo's first year in the business. His granddam was one of Annette's original heifers, which eventually sold as a Brazil donor cow, and his dam was born on Bill Broussard's ranch in Florida.

This story starts at the sale in October 1997. As a policy, we do not top any bulls off our sale group, and we are the only breeders I know of who follow that practice. This always creates a lot of interest in our sale, which was especially true that year. In addition, we announced that we were retaining a one-quarter interest in 5502 as well as all semen collection rights. We thought this would discourage bidding, but in actuality, everyone attending bid on him. I had John Cargile set to buy him for us so there would be no mistake, and he bought L Bar 5502 as planned. Midway through the sale, I went to the lobby of Producers Auction and encountered Juan Sáenz, David Zambrano and their wives, who were attending from Monterrey, Mexico. They were upset because they thought they had bought the bull as they had not understood the bidding. I could see their point of view and I also realized that I did not want to alienate two 30-year customers, so I asked them what they would have paid for the three-quarter interest. They replied, "$12,000." I said fine, if they would

let me breed 5502 to a set of heifers, then collect him at Elgin Breeding Service, I would deliver the bull to the border on May 1, 1998, with the understanding that they would not collect him. They agreed to the proposal, saying it was a very gracious solution.

Photo by Elgin Breeding Service

L Bar 5502.

L Bar 5502 bred a set of heifers and the birth weights on his first calves, born in August 1998, were an extraordinarily-low 71 pounds. Low birth weights are very important in breeding cattle, and in my mind, this was his biggest hurdle. He was then collected for four months at Elgin, where he was their Top Across-the-Board Producer of all breeds, producing 1,000 straws of export-qualified frozen semen each month. By May, Sáenz and Zambrano realized he was too valuable to take to Mexico, so we agreed to keep him in Texas and to continue collecting him on the halves, with them having an exclusive in Mexico. In May 1999, we bred L Bar 5502 to thirty-five cows and he settled all of them. The next month, we had a field day at the Steen Ranch attended by friends and customers where he made his public debut. In addition to great semen sales, we donated straws of his semen to the Beefmaster Junior Association members. Our bull's progeny started winning shows, futurities and gain tests all over the world, continuing to this day. Not a month passes without a report of some new 5502 triumph. In 2002, at the BBU Beefmaster World Cup Bull Futurity on October 25, L Bar 5502, at seven years of age, placed third in the Senior Group in range condition, and we sold 1,000 straws of semen, a feat unequalled at any convention before or since.

We decided to syndicate L Bar 5502 in December 1999. After Mason Backus told me we could function as a small farm cooperative, with no tax returns if all monies were distributed each year, the partnership was structured for three investors to make a loan at six percent to the venture. Isa Cattle Co. would manage the L Bar 5502 Joint Venture and own a half interest after payout. Our friend Bill Richey committed on December 27, followed quickly by Peter Summers of Florida and San Pedro Beefmasters, Inc., of Texas. The venture was an immediate success, and the notes were paid off in short order.

In 2000, Beefmaster Breeders United entered into an arrangement with Texas A&M University to evaluate top sires for everything from birth weight to tenderness. It was a scientific program, with the university's commercial cows being bred A.I. to fifteen top bulls over three years. The results were reported in 2003, and when the professor-in-charge, Dr. Jim Sanders, reported the anonymous results at the BBU convention in Denver, Colorado, he said that the "B" bull (L Bar 5502) exemplified the "across-the-board" traits sought in beef cattle. In evaluation for six different traits related to desirable red meat production, L Bar 5502 stood alone at the top. No other bull, of the fifteen proven sires tested, was a close second.

Having such a great bull, while at the same time being in a severe drought, caused us to start sonogramming our cows for pregnancy, 30 days after our 60-day breeding season. This meant that we could use our bull four times a year, instead of twice, breeding him naturally to some 150 females per year, plus being bred to over 1,000 per year worldwide by artificial insemination. Dr. Charles Looney sonogrammed our first females for pregnancy which established that as a new technique that has been a valuable addition to our management repertoire. In spite of the drought, females bred to L Bar 5502 enjoyed good demand while other females bred to other bulls did not sell at any price.

Brad Cardwell, president of Elgin Breeding Service, took a great interest in this bull and in our program. Brad probably said it best in a telephone conversation, when he told me, "We feel good just knowing he is on the premises." It would be impossible for me to say what this great bull has meant to our family. Aside from influencing all of our established markets, L Bar 5502 is the first triple-trait leader in the Beefmaster breed, and his sons have carried us to new markets in Bolivia and Argentina.

Beefmaster Cowman magazine cover featuring the Breeder of the Year award.

PART III

CHAPTER 24

THE NEW MILLENNIUM

A new millennium occurs only every thousand years, and few members of the human race get to experience such an event. In 1999, the whole world anxiously awaited midnight on December 31 due to concerns about Y2K, which some predicted could cause the collapse of civilization. No one, however, predicted the disputed election of 2000, the attack on September 11, 2001, the war with Islamic fanaticism or the hurricanes of 2004–2005. These events showed us that the United States is over-populated and vulnerable to terrorist attack and natural disasters.

Milestones have always been important to me, and I felt that the new millennium would be important for our family and our business. It was more than a mark on a calendar. Some good stories have a happy ending, and this is one of those. However, on January 1, 2000, we still had nearly three years to go before seeing good times in business. We had one of the worst bull sales in 2002, and in the summer of 2003, we had to move cattle out of state due to drought. It was "the dark before the dawn." Thankfully, everything did turn around business-wise in October 2003, and this story ends in 2006. It seems that everything we had been working on for 42 years finally jelled, and we were more than rewarded for every single effort.

Cattle Associations

Breeder of the Year Award

October 28, 2000, was an important day in my business and association career. At breakfast, before the BBU convention in Farmers Branch, Texas,

Dale and I met and completed my withdrawal (begun ten years earlier) from the Lasater Ranch Partnership. Beefmaster Breeders United's highest honor, "Breeder of the Year," is given at the annual convention. The secret award is presented by a slide show in which the recipient is revealed. When the video started, I noticed that the corrals resembled those of Producers Auction. When our newsletter, *The Isa Informer,* designed by Isabel, appeared on the screen, I realized that our family was receiving the award. This honor was made richer by the presence of friends and business allies.

• • •

Life in various cattle associations has been challenging for me. I am the only breeder to have served on the board of all three Beefmaster associations: Beefmaster Breeders Universal, Foundation Beefmaster Association and Beefmaster Breeders United. The "Beefmaster Wars" absorbed a great deal of my time, energy and money over a 32-year period. I was again a director of BBU when Carl Hubble became president. While in office, he advocated using some of the association's cash reserves to establish a branded beef program. Although the company was not yet established, a significant amount of money was needed to keep the project afloat. To raise the required money, a conference call was made to the BBU board. Uncle Palo (Watt Casey) called me to say he had decided that he and I should invest and that he would finance our investment if I would serve on the board. The proposal was for those investing early to receive two units for each unit purchased. In the conference call, I spoke first and said that Watt Casey and I would buy two units—and the project was launched. In an interesting footnote, we had planned to name the new product Certified Beefmaster Beef, but when those starting the company went with our proposed name to the USDA, they were told that they could not use the name "Beefmaster" unless the parentage of blood was established. Our group asked, "What about Certified Angus Beef?" They responded that they were "grandfathered when the USDA had no requirements as to claims of parentage." Shortly afterwards, Nolan Ryan agreed to be part of the project and to loan his name. The company became known as "Nolan Ryan's Guaranteed Tender Meats."

On March 6, 2001, I was named to the board of managers (Beefmaster Cattlemen). I attended my first meeting on June 27, at the "300 Win Club" at the Round Rock Express Stadium in Round Rock, Texas. The members of the board represented every conceivable endeavor and brought valuable perspectives to the meeting. The company encountered every imaginable problem that a start-up company experiences. Nolan Ryan Beef is the only natural, branded-beef product that guarantees tenderness. At the time the company was established, BBU, along with the National Cattlemen's Beef Association, was financing a research project at Colorado State University to develop a camera that could identify beef for tenderness. When placed over the ribeye, the camera sees bands of color, not visible to the naked eye, that correlate with tenderness. The camera errs on the side of caution, so the product to be produced is measured objectively. Our former company, NewBeef, Inc., had clearly demonstrated, in significant numbers, that Beefmasters are superior feedlot and carcass cattle. Gary Smith of Colorado State University, one of the top meat scientists in the U.S., played a key roll in the design of our product and became a director of Nolan Ryan Beef. In 2005, Nolan bought out BBU's general partnership interest. My serving on the board of directors from 2001 to 2005 and the success of the company has been one of the highlights of my career.

Nolan Ryan and Lorenzo at an Isa bull sale.

• • •

In 2006, the Mexican Beefmaster Association celebrated its twenty-fifth anniversary and the South African group its twentieth. We made the first sales in those areas forty and thirty years ago respectively, and it is thrilling to be a part of the great success of Beefmasters in those countries.

Pasturing Cattle in the New Millennium

We saw difficult business conditions for most of the first three years of the new era. In April 2000, I noted in my diary that we shipped four loads of cattle to a different location. I do not remember what cattle they were or where they went, but I do recall that we kept the truckers busy for eleven years. We had had to move our Charolais cows to East Texas and 100 Beefmaster cows to Arkansas. Our grazing situation later improved in the new millennium, with pasturage being offered to Lorenzo on three properties in the San Angelo area—the McDowell, Turner and Ebeling ranches. These leases, combined with the Steen ranch at Christoval and our pasturage arrangement for the sale bulls with the Cages at Muleshoe, Texas, put us in a strong position regarding good homes for our cattle. It started raining in October 2003, commencing 24 months of the best conditions seen in West Texas. Our cattle, and their owners, recovered completely from the drought, and our cows finally had the nutrition to exhibit just how good they really are.

Bull Sales and Field Days

In August 2000, I made a deal with Tommy Mann to represent us in Florida. Tommy, like Lorenzo, is a graduate of TCU Ranch Management School, and is the head representative in Florida for the Superior Satellite Auction. His father was foreman of the Alico Ranch, so he knows the cattle industry in that state from the ground up. Our bull sale in October 2000 was a solid one with 200 bulls. The sale featured the first seventeen sons of L Bar 5502 to sell at an average of $5,500. Most of the cattle went to commercial ranchers in several different states and Mexico.

• • •

In July 2001, Pearce Flournoy and I put on a public relations event at Likely, California. The first day, I drove to Midland, Texas, flew to Reno, Nevada, (two flights) rented a car and drove 165 miles north to Likely. Upon arrival, we saddled up and began shuffling cattle around in preparation for the field day. It had been a 19-hour day since leaving home when finally, at 9:00 p.m. (California time) I told Pearce that if I did not get something to eat and go to bed, I might die. We had a successful event, joined by John Newburn of BBU, Don Biles of Oklahoma, and a good turnout of ranchers from Oregon, Nevada and California. It was there that I met Lonnie Schadler of Adel, Oregon, probably one of the toughest cowboys around. Pearce's one-line description of Lonnie is classic: "He rides horses most people couldn't get on."

Purchasing of Beefmaster Herds

From the time of our arrival in San Angelo over thirty years ago, John Cargile has been interested in Beefmasters and the Lasater philosophy. He developed one of the great herds, starting with the Musser heifer crop, using A.I. of our best sires, and buying the best bulls available. John did everything to save his herd, including moving them to Oklahoma, but finally, the killer drought of over ten years got the better of him. On Monday, June 24, 2002, he told me that he wanted to sell his registered herd and that he wanted to be done with the cattle by the time he left for Vail the following Friday. After seeing them and after careful analysis and consultation with J.C., Lorenzo and I agreed they should be bought, so we made a written proposal on Tuesday afternoon, which John, after consulting with his son, Johnny, accepted on Wednesday. Friday morning, we signed a contract for 244 head of Cargile Beefmasters and John flew to Vail, Colorado.

I then realized that the Marsh and Cargile herds could be rolled into one 50-50 partnership with the two Broussard herds (Beefmaster and Charolais), forming a new venture with strong equity and an established market. At Lorenzo's suggestion, I wrote a proposal for Bill, which he accepted as presented. Today, our partnership owns a spring-calving Beefmaster herd, a fall-calving Beefmaster herd and a fall-calving Charolais herd. Lorenzo runs the enterprise, and Bill's cattle interests will go to their family conservancy established by his wife, Margaret, and him, in memory of their son, Allen.

In December 2003, Lorenzo went to California to buy most of the cattle in the Vista Livestock herd dispersal, with financing from our partner Bill Richey. Like John Cargile's herd, these cattle were the same as ours genetically and on the same calving schedule. During the terrible years from 1990–2003, we bought six great herds of cattle that no one else wanted. Ours is a classic business story of having the nerve to push forward when all appears to be lost.

International Sales

For us, 2005 was the year of Brazil. In June 2002, Lorenzo traveled with Gary Frenzel to Brazil, and we began working systematically with Gary to open markets in Central and South America. In July, Randy and Marta Spears of Brazil bought the genetic material that her brothers had contracted earlier. On Lorenzo's third trip, he sold our original customer, Michael Corbett, a substantial amount of frozen semen. In 2006, we made the first sale of frozen semen to Argentina, another step forward in the opening of the South American market.

Ranch Land Company

Bill Pfluger and I had known each other for years and decided to learn to play golf together. We played our first game on June 11, 1993. Bill, a great athlete, did all he could to encourage me and suggested that I would get better if I would hit 100 balls every day, to which I replied, "Bill, I have a job." Along with golf, we had great business discussions, many involving diversification. Bill had diversified out of the livestock business and I had not. In the summer of 1996, after a golf game, I asked what he thought I should do business-wise to endure the drought. He answered, "Get your real estate license." Following his valuable advice, I attended real estate classes and three weeks later passed the exam for my license. The summer I received my license, we were four years into the Great Drought of the Nineties.

I was acquainted with Leon Nance, a successful real estate broker who owned Ranch Land Company, and in 1999, I joined his firm. I admired and attributed Leon's success in ranch brokerage to two things (in addition to hard work): his practice of always representing the client and that of giving buyers and sellers of big properties time to make up their minds.

In 2001, I made my first significant sale to Eudean and Terry Rice. Terry is the husband of Isabel's partner, Kay, in INK Design. I knew that he and his dad were looking for a hunting ranch, and the day we showed them part of the Buckle L Ranch at Childress, Texas, they committed to buy it. They have done a good job with the property, which has significantly increased in value.

• • •

Interesting people turn up when you are working in the large ranch brokerage business. One of those was Jeff Bezos, a fellow Princetonian and founder of Amazon.com. In 2003, Bezos called the office interested in ranches in West Texas. On March 11, 2003, Andy Smith, who had joined Ranch Land Co., Leon and I drove to Alpine, Texas, to show him the Cathedral Mountain Ranch located south of town. We drove to the ranch from the airport while the prospective buyers flew out, accompanied by Ty Holland, a local cowboy who had worked there. After seeing the headquarters, the buyer's group left in the helicopter to tour the ranch, and after a period of time, greater than the endurance of the Gazelle's fuel, I suspected that something had gone wrong and called the border patrol. They found the helicopter had crashed into Calamity Creek, which was

Wreckage from Jeff Bezos' helicopter crash.

in a canyon far from the road. Two rescue planes circling over the crash reported that all four persons were alive. Many law-enforcement and emergency personnel participated in bringing the four survivors out and taking them to the Alpine Hospital. When the copter crashed into the creek, Elizabeth Korrell, a young mother with small children, was pinned under water, and Ty, having injured both shoulders in the episode, pulled her out and saved her life.

Leon, Andy and I followed the cavalcade to the hospital and then preceded them to the Paisano Hotel in Marfa, where they were staying. When I went to the front desk about 4:00 p.m. to ask if they could open the bar, the bartender said, "No." When I explained that these were the people who were in the crash, he said, "We'll open the bar immediately."

When we last saw the survivors, they were drinking margaritas like cool water, and I am sure the celebration broke all records at the Paisano Hotel.

• • •

My real estate career shifted into high gear in 2004 when we listed and sold two ranches for Leon's friend, Cliff Bly, a financier in San Angelo. The first, the Red Cloud Ranch on the Colorado River, was an unimproved property consisting of 5,800 acres. The ranch, which we sold to Donny Linsey of Colorado City, needed a buyer who was not afraid to take on a project.

In addition to being our best year in the cattle business, 2005 was a great year in real estate. Frank Smith, a friend from my Laredo days and Andy's brother, listed his ranch, a beautiful property with great potential as a hunting ranch, with me. At the same time, my brother Lane and I bought a 1,340-acre hunting ranch, near Eldorado, Texas, and Bobby and Tracey Romatowski bought our beloved family retreat in Concho County, the Boehme Ranch. The fact that they loved the ranch as much as we did lessened the pain of selling it. My friend, Mason Backus, listed his property on the Colorado River, which we sold to buyers from Virginia.

In the fall, a broker in San Antonio called with a client, Joe Mach, for the former Dub Yarborough Ranch in Runnels County. Joe was an engineer who had made his fortune working in the oil industry in Russia. When I showed him the ranch, it was in fabulous condition and loaded with game and birds. Several days later, he bought the 5,129-acre property.

Nolan Ryan called me, interested in the Runnels County ranch that had sold, so Leon suggested that we offer him part of the Door Key Ranch. After seeing the 7,124-acre ranch, which is in the middle of San Angelo's future growth, Nolan bought it.

Like every other chapter in our lives, the real estate segment is a story unto itself. Someone once made a comment to me about the huge commissions in ranch real estate. I replied, "I don't know, I have not earned one yet." My first big commission came after seven hard years.

CHAPTER 25

SOUTH AFRICA—2006

n early August 2006, J.C., Lorenzo and I made our second trip to South Africa. As this was our second trip, we knew the ropes better and had established friendships there. The boys had progressed to a higher level of hunting and all of us were excited about what lay ahead.

On July 30, we began the 40-hour trip from San Angelo to Johannesburg. I never thought I would be flying an airline named "Luft." Lufthansa Flight 439 left Dallas at 4:00 p.m. for Frankfort. The 5,139-mile flight took approximately ten hours. Lufthansa Flight 572 departed Frankfort for Johannesburg around 11:00 p.m. This was another nine-hour, 5,392-mile trip. Upon landing, Justin Stretton of Stormberg Elangeni Safaris and Thami, his tracker, met us and took us to the Emperor's Palace Hotel and Casino. Later the boys went warthog hunting on Paul Yiannakis' ranch and shot two sows. That evening, we hosted a dinner for Manny and Johnny da Costa and Gideon Brits.

Beefmaster Field Days

As in 2004, the purpose was to attend the Beefmaster Alliance bull sale, to put on two cattle field days and to go on a safari. It rained a lot with a forty-mph wind blowing during our first night in South Africa. When we awoke the next morning, the wind, combined with very cold temperatures, made it the coldest weather there in twenty years. The field day was held at the sale facility. The suggested subject of my talk, "The Development of the L Bar Beefmaster Herd," included a lot of history as well as the methods we use. Afterwards, a sample of bulls was brought into the ring for Lorenzo to comment on, aided by Gideon. There was a *brai* (barbeque) after the presentation. We departed late that evening and when we arrived at a bird sanctuary where we were to spend the night, it was very cold, with the wind rattling the window blinds inside the house. We had to sleep fully clothed with the covers pulled over our heads. The next morning when we arose before daylight, there was still a cold, high wind howling and the chill factor was 20–25 degrees. We huddled around the oven drinking instant coffee and dipping rusks (hard bread for dipping) before departing for the da Costa Bros. office. Since our visit in 2004, they had built a conference room with a table 20 feet long made of indigenous hardwoods. Several Trevor Stretton paintings of L Bar cattle were hanging on the walls and the head of an L Bar

Photo by J.C. Hernandez

This AI son of L Bar 7499, a great grandson of Lasater 513, was the top-selling bull in the 2006 Beefmaster Alliance Sale.

5502 son was mounted over the bar area. The da Costa Bros. are second-generation immigrants from Madeira, Portugal. They inherited 375 acres of farmland and now own 15,000 acres of irrigated farmland, 20,000 head of cattle on feed and 1,000 registered Beefmaster cows, which they consider to be their best business. They have a company that processes food corn for export and feeds the by-products to their cattle. The brothers, who believe there is a worldwide shortage of protein, are active in several commodities and use the futures market (Chicago) for hedging.

The sale ring was first-class, round with floodlights directly overhead. The cattle looked good and flowed smoothly. The Beefmaster Alliance Sale, modeled on ours, was the largest production sale put on in South Africa as well as the second largest production sale worldwide, with ours being the largest. The sale was a huge success and turning point in Beefmaster history with the 176 bulls averaging $2,654. The top bull, an A.I. son of L Bar 7499, raised by the Manjoh Ranch (purchased by the Stretton and MacLean families), sold for $6,078. Beefmasters are second in registrations in South Africa, and will shortly be number one. When I was interviewed after the sale, the writer asked if we might be buying bulls there some day. I predicted that in the future, when there is free movement of frozen semen, the best bulls in the USA, RSA and Mexico will be collected with Isa Cattle Co. brokering the semen worldwide.

• • •

Our second public relations event was at the Stretton Ranch in the Stormberg Conservancy in the Eastern Cape, South Africa's principal cattle state, some 400 miles from Nigel. The Stretton ancestors came from England in the early 1800s. The conservancy consists of some 240,000 acres and is hunted exclusively by Stormberg Elangeni Safaris, in which three Stretton cousins are partners with two other families who control the Kat River Conservancy. The Lasater Cattle Day was hosted by the Stretton families and the Eastern Cape Beefmaster Club.

With Gideon Brits, Tony da Costa, Paul Yiannakis, Manny da Costa, Lorenzo, J.C., Trevor Stretton and Justin Stretton before the Beefmaster Alliance Sale.

Trevor Stretton, Justin's father, whom I met in San Angelo over twenty years earlier, welcomed us and introduced my talk. I spoke extemporaneously and many good questions followed. Afterwards, Lorenzo and Erwin Church, a cattle consultant, discussed several groups of cattle on display, including the top-selling bull in the Alliance Sale just held at Nigel. Manny da Costa and Gideon Brits had driven down for the field day the evening before in Manny's diesel Mercedes (making 125 mph on the straight stretches). They, as well as Graham Hart and Erwin Church, stayed with us at the Stretton's Branstone Lodge, so we had two late evenings together enjoying the fellowship and celebrating our breed's success in their country. The strength of the Beefmaster breed in South Africa is that there are numerous professional ranchers who put on their own annual sales.

The Safari

Hunting beckoned! We drove to the Hunters Moon Ranch in the "Great Karoo," which is geographically similar to West Texas and Northern Mexico. As soon as we drove through the gate, we realized we were seeing the future for ranching country worldwide. The ranch consists of 67,500 acres (with 80 miles of high fence; 300 miles of interior fence that had been taken up) made up of nine sheep ranches put together. It lies on the Seacow (Hippo) River at an elevation of 4,200 feet with an annual rainfall of some 15 inches. After culling 1,000 springbok, there were 5,500 head of wild animals. The ranch is owned and managed by the McAdam family, who developed and sold Bushmen's Kloof (Canyon), a five-star wildlife sanctuary.

The next morning, as we drove away from the lodge for a big day's hunting, Mark McAdam pointed out numerous animals and birds I would not have seen, including a mongoose, an aardwolf and a group of zebra about 1½ miles away, bedded down on a hillside. After the previous day's success of two record-book gemsbok and a springbok, it was hard to imagine that the day could be equaled, but Lorenzo and J.C. secured four trophies. J.C., shooting prone while lying on rocks, downed a zebra with a classic double-lung shot. After a terrific chase, Lorenzo shot a beautiful 36" Eland, the largest member of the Antelope family, a 5½" steenbok, and J.C. shot a beautiful 13¾" springbok. I could not believe the weight and body condition of the trophies.

• • •

Our next stop, halfway to the Stormberg Conservancy at Molteno, was at Duikie DeVillier's family's ranch, which has been in operation over 150 years and runs some 8,000 sheep on 40,000 acres. The Afrikaners (of Dutch descent) are interesting in that their language (Afrikaans) and modus operandi are unique. They are dedicated agriculturalists, and their language is the language of farming in Southern Africa (South Africa, Botswana, Namibia, Zimbabwe). Duikie, an excellent farmer, had double windmills pumping into concrete reservoirs to irrigate small patches of alfalfa for early-lambing ewes with twins. When he saw there were Blue Cranes (which are protected) on one alfalfa patch, he ordered J.C. to shoot his .300 Win Mag and was disappointed that J.C. did not keep firing "on the wing." The phrase "Balance of Nature" is not in the Boer vocabulary.

Duikie was ecstatic when Lorenzo got a black springbok and a white springbok buck, making a difficult running shot on the white. The next day, while hunting at the Stormberg Conservancy, it was about twenty degrees with the wind blowing. Justin had brought his 5-year-old son, Dylan, who stayed with "Uncle" Laurie at the pickup. He was dressed in a hunter's outfit from head to toe and carried a buck knife. After an hour, he asked if I had heard a shot. When I said, "no," he said he did, six or eight times. After a while, he said, "I think they got him." Finally Dylan said, "I think I hear blood dripping."

• • •

As we began the last part of our trip, Justin took us to see some Bushman art in a cave on his cousin Robbie's ranch. We then drove to the Graham Hart Ranch near Komga, north of East London. Driving toward the Indian Ocean, we passed through many beautiful climatic zones. The Harts are Beefmaster breeders, who have been in the area for many years and personify the small breeders we need in the U.S. Each of the Hart's three properties is different in rainfall and geography. Although the cattle are fleshy, they have to be dipped for ticks every fourteen days. That evening, our last in Africa, the Harts hosted a dinner party for Pierre Hart and family and another neighbor.

As we drove to East London and the airport, Justin took us on a small side tour to Morgan's Bay on the Wild Coast of the Indian Ocean, where the Stretton family has a beach cabin. The Indian Ocean is fearsome. The wind was blowing hard and the surf was hitting the rocks, splashing up 75 ft. Without warning, Justin drove us straight to the cliff's edge before slamming on the brakes. It was one of the worst scares I have ever experienced. After I finally shouted, "Stop, you *@*~!* idiot," he laughed all of the way to East London airport.

• • •

The trip home was hard, but uneventful. It was a fabulous adventure from first to last. Our cattle and program received powerful affirmation. We will always consider the Brits, the Yiannakises, the Harts, the Strettons and the da Costas as friends, and hope to see them again soon. As we celebrated the success of Beefmasters in South Africa, we renewed existing friendships and made new ones.

A Lasater Whitetail trophy buck, spotted during a helicopter survey.

CHAPTER 26

LASATER WHITETAIL LODGE

"This is the right move for our children and grandchildren."
                              —Annette Lasater

My second brother, Lane, and I always have been close. He kindly credits me with watching out for him as we were growing up. In June 2004, Lane decided to withdraw his interest from the Lasater Ranch Partnership and move his land and cattle to San Angelo to be managed by our family. This unexpected development took our family in three exciting new directions: land ownership, a commercial hunting business and a whitetail deer breeding business.

Although a family ranching enterprise is highly illiquid, thanks to favorable conditions in Colorado and Dale's stewardship over the years, it was possible for Lane and him to agree on a phased withdrawal. This method would not economically damage the Lasater partnership or do harm to the foundation herd of the Beefmaster breed, (a closed herd for 70 years). As was true when I withdrew, the values agreed to were fair to the withdrawing partner and attractive to the remaining partners.

"Go look at it, Dad."
                              —Lorenzo Lasater

It is difficult to find a good ranch for a tax-free exchange on a timetable. While we were looking at several properties, Andy Smith told me of a highly-improved hunting ranch, eight miles west of Eldorado in Schleicher County, Texas, 50 miles south of San Angelo and 20 miles from the Steen lease. When I told Lorenzo about it, he said, "Go look at it, Dad," so Andy and I met with Montie Turnbull, the owner. We went back the next day with Lorenzo, and Andy said that on the drive back to San Angelo we were already figuring out how to manage the ranch. A month of complex negotiations with Montie followed before we signed a contract on March 17 and closed on May 19, 2005. When I came home and told Annette that we were going to sell the Boehme Ranch, which she loved, to start a new business with a debt, it was quite a shock to her. After several days, she said, in the same brave manner as she had when we went to Mexico in 1964, "This is the right move for our children and grandchildren."

We bought the ranch with cattle and equipment and moved the Vista Beefmaster mature cows, purchased with Bill Richey in 2003, to the new ranch. Lane acquired them in December 2005 in another tax-free exchange, rounding out his herd and creating another infusion of valuable new genetics in our L Bar Beefmaster herd. After liquidating the cattle, Bill called me from Lagos, Nigeria, where he was trying a corruption case in court, agreeing to finance our new whitetail deer breeding venture.

• • •

The spring and summer of 2005 were especially beautiful, with ample moisture, making it ideal to move the cattle there. After all was finalized, we had bought a ranch in Texas that is very similar to the one we hunted on in South Africa in August 2004.

The reason we entered the commercial hunting and deer breeding businesses was that Lorenzo could see that they represent the future in West Texas. Lorenzo invited me to accompany him to visit the VLC Ranch at Hondo, Texas, a pioneer whitetail deer breeding establishment. Although we were only interested in buying one buck, the attentive treatment we received at VLC resulted in our purchasing 30 bred does to run in the facility we already had at Whitetail. Until then, I had no idea how big the deer industry is. Many of those investors are converting ranch land to recreation and are high-fencing and upgrading their deer herd's genetics. This is a worldwide movement, which will intensify as more individuals and corporations want private hideaways far from urban civilization. The high-fence phenomenon is an extension of the low-fence era, which started in Texas about 1880, with similar cultural and ecological ramifications.

When people look back on their lives, they can see patterns that have held throughout, while at the time, life seemed to be a series of surprises. In my case, since leaving home at thirteen years of age to go to Fountain Valley School, my life has been a long series of happy surprises.

• • •

An important event in our family history was May 25, 2006, when I flew to Newark, New Jersey, to attend our nephew Colin's graduation from the United States Military Academy at West Point. (Benedict Arnold's treason was selling West Point's fortification plans to the British.) Being a student of George Washington and having spent five years at school in New Jersey, this trip was meaningful to me. The drive north from Newark, through thick woods and along the tremendous Hudson River, passes the George Washington Bridge on the right and Trenton and Princeton on the left, where pivotal battles of the Revolutionary War were fought. When Lord Cornwallis, after the surrender at Yorktown, toasted General Washington, he said, in effect, "When these events are recorded, they will write not of Yorktown, but of Trenton and Princeton."

Each of the three graduation events involved heavy security with every car inspected. On Friday, May 26, we attended the graduation parade on the Plain. When the battallions that comprise the Academy's regiment marched out of their sally ports at the appointed second with the statue of George Washington, who had suggested establishment of a military academy, leading the way on horseback, the audience could see the crux of 230 years of American history. This event is where the seniors symbolically leave the corps and line up in front of the stands where a huge celebration takes place.

The speaker at the graduation banquet at the vast, historical mess hall (where 4,000 cadets eat two meals a day in 20 minutes) was General John Abizaid, Commander U.S. Central Command. His message (in effect) was memorable: "I can promise you three things—we will pay you poorly, you will sleep on the ground, and a year from now, you will be leading troops in battle and carrying responsibilities most people never dream of." This class was one of the few that had entered West Point when the nation was at war, and graduated as the war continued. A significant number of West Point men and women had already lost their lives in Afghanistan and Iraq.

The graduation on Saturday, May 27, 2006, was a memorable day for the graduates and guests, made special by the participation of President

With Colin before the graduation banquet at West Point in 2006.

George W. Bush. The day that began at 4:30 a.m. with early morning fog, which kept us cool, cleared just before the President's dramatic arrival in a black limousine, with all of the attendant security. As with the message of the graduation banquet the previous day, the words of the Commander-in-Chief were meaningful: "You are smart, tough and ready. You will lead America's most precious resource, its sons and daughters, in battle. You are the generation that will win the War on Terror." Seeing those enthusiastic young people who had elected to "pay the price," and listening to these dramatic words was a moving experience for the families and friends of the graduates. It was gratifying for me to see Colin, a protégé of ours, reach his goal.

CHAPTER 27

OUR GREATEST SALE

"You need to hire someone to handle your worrying."

— Leon Nance

I have always loved raising, developing and marketing bulls, and I have enjoyed the people who come to buy them. The sale of the bulls became the core of our business after we went to Mexico in September of 1964. From 1964 to 2003, the last year of the bull co-op, selling our bulls and those of others gave us the means of earning our living. The Beefmaster breed was in a growth mode from 1964 to 1989, and there was a need for someone to market a part of the annual bull production. Thankfully, no one but me wanted the job.

The business has evolved tremendously over 42 years since Roger Sanford and Bob Spence bought the first truckload of Lasater Ranch export bulls in 1964 for $200 per head. Arturo Siller and two friends bought our first bull calf crop in Mexico (minus El Gallo) in 1965 for $400 per head. From "The Bull Sale Nobody Came To" through our forty-fourth and greatest sale on October 1, 2005, it would be impossible to exaggerate the improvement in our cattle and in our selling methods— from selling volume bulls to commercial producers to a high-tech, highly-sophisticated production system, producing and identifying superior individuals. This system is also important for use in frozen genetics in an international business that is gaining momentum every year. It is in raising, identifying and marketing the outstanding individuals that I have found the challenges and financial rewards missing in other segments of the industry.

Central to the evolution of our bull business was the design and construction of our first Bull Test Facility in 1979. Although the facility was originally a child of necessity (due to the Brucellosis eradication campaign), the unexpected side benefits transformed our bull business, our ranching business and my career. We could handle any number of bulls (or other cattle) on short notice, and because it is much less expensive to develop cattle on a growing ration, we could get them in sale condition quickly and economically with financing on the feed. We could sort the cattle groups in different ways for pricing and marketing purposes and gather a vast amount of data easily and economically— thus our cattle were improving faster. Although we still follow Tom Lasater's principles, he would barely recognize the sophisticated catalogs that Annette and Lorenzo have created using large amounts of computer-generated data. The groups are handled five times, under ideal conditions, using a hydraulic chute-scale with plenty of time and energy to study the bulls and the data. The original facility and its successor, built in 1989, gave us a control over our cattle enterprise unknown in the ranching business. In 2006, we performance-tested our 45th group of bulls in the facility, and over the years, we have evaluated over 15,000 bulls in the same format.

The only negative in the evolution of our bull business was an unintended consequence of the Drought of the Nineties. We now have one smaller sale (200 bulls) a year, selling better bulls with higher profit margins and less risk. The downside is that our whole financial year takes place between 10:00 a.m. and 12:30 p.m. on the first Saturday in October. We have seen bull sales affected by drought, bad markets, high interest rates, hurricanes, terrorist attacks and stock market collapses. Leon Nance correctly told me that I needed to hire someone to handle my worrying during the two weeks before the sale.

From the beginning, I have evaluated our cattle business on two criteria only:

(1) Do I think the cattle are good before I sell them? (2) Are they selling to quality buyers? These criteria have been met from day one. Livestock breeding can become an art form—a search for perfection that is far-removed from food production. Our sale is a wonderful event with many of the same people, those who like our cattle and our hospitality, returning each year. We enjoy having them here with us for this

important event. After so many years, I have developed a ritual that I follow each year: Lorenzo and I load the bulls at 1:00 p.m. on Thursday for the short trip to Producers Auction and the sale on Saturday. When the trucks pull away from the bull facility chute, my job is done, and I relax and watch the event unfold.

Photo by Lorenzo Lasater

Loading cattle for a sale in 2007.

On October 1, 2005, we had our 44th sale, which was our greatest, with 192 Beefmaster and Charolais bulls averaging $2,987, bringing some $600 dollars more than any previous event. Normally, I keep track of how many bulls the buyers have bought to monitor whether or not we have enough buying power present. About fifteen minutes into that sale, I could see that something special was happening, so I closed my catalog and sat back to enjoy the show. One of the highlights, as always, was watching Lorenzo and our auctioneer, Joe Goggins, run the sale. Both are cowmen, and when they say something about the cattle, it connects with our customers.

• • •

I could feel the "Ghosts of Bull Sales Past" in the room that day. Roger Sanford introduced me to Arturo Siller in 1964, and Arturo's two sons and grandson were attending with other friends, including Sergio Siller (son of Humberto) who was buying bulls for Cornelia Múzquiz (Roger Sanford's granddaughter). Wayne Carlton of Florida, whose father, Reuben, bought bulls after I stopped the sale at Okeechobee, Florida, was the volume buyer. Wayne's son, Wes, is another third-generation customer. Jimmie Philman, representing A. Duda & Sons, twenty-five-year customers from Florida, was there and did his usual good job of selecting bulls. Tommy Mann, who represents us in Florida, was also a volume buyer. Dick Jones, from Hebbronville, Texas, a mainstay for twenty years, does not usually attend, but was present in 2005 with his wife, Ann. His grandfather and my grandfather were neighbors, and his son, Whit, will be the fourth generation of Joneses doing business with Lorenzo, who is the fifth generation of our family in ranching.

The westerners, including Goemmer Ranches of New Mexico and Nevada, and Pearce Flournoy of California, bought twenty-seven bulls.

Photo by Watt M. Casey, Jr.

Uncle Palo and Lorenzo at a 2005 Texas and Southwestern Cattle Raisers gathering.

The Goemmers bought bulls for nearly twenty years over the phone before we met personally. The extended Wedgeworth family from Carthage, Texas, whom we count on seeing every year, was present in force. John Cargile and Uncle Palo (who had not missed a bull sale of ours in Texas) were also present, as were J.D., Jay and Christopher (Jay's son) Cage, another five-generation friendship.

Selling bulls, like any other competitive endeavor, is about passion. It pleases me that I have two friends—Gary Frenzel of Temple, Texas, and Manuel da Costa of Nigel, South Africa—who share my passion for the business and who have used some of our ideas and genetics to create successful bull sales of their own.

CHAPTER 28

CLOSING

The most important things in this life are having a job to do and someone with whom to do it. As the oldest son of Tom Lasater, I was born with the opportunity to spread the Beefmaster breed and the Lasater philosophy to the four corners of the globe, which I have enjoyed doing. As this book has evolved since I began it in October of 2004, two sub-themes have emerged. First of all, I realized that I was writing as a witness to the decline of our greatest industry. During a time of prosperity unequalled in human history, sixteen of my closest associates in the cattle industry were forced out of business, quit in disgust or were disappointed in their careers. These men, and their wives, were and are the "best of the best." No other career in this era could have caused such heartbreak. I have been haunted throughout my business life by the realization that my friends were not able to achieve their ambitions. I have had four great competitors who pushed me to be better, who like me, operated without benefit of family ranches. All were destroyed by the economic circumstances described in this book, as well as by their own hubris. Our cattle have been recognized for their excellence, nationally and internationally, and it is only by the grace of God that we managed to survive and pay all the bills. To quote a Hollywood saying, we "took the big risk" leaving the family ranch, going to Mexico and operating for forty years on borrowed money.

Secondly, I realized that Annette and I had stayed with our beliefs, regardless of the circumstances. When we married, we wanted to live in a gracious manner and have good cattle. Each of our homes, including our first, the modest duplex on Calle Ocampo 540, has been a delight. All our hopes and expectations have been exceeded. Our children and three grandsons, the joy of our lives, are carrying us to new heights, and now we are excitedly awaiting the birth of Isabel and J.C.'s twins, an event that will grow our family beyond our dreams.

In September 1964, Annette and I drove from Colorado Springs to Sabinas for the first time. It was raining that day, and the landscape looked even wilder and lonelier than usual. We had no idea of the adventures that lay ahead, but we were young, strong and fearless. I know that today some young couple is starting a similar journey, and I wish them all the joy we have known.

I have enjoyed writing our story and hope you have enjoyed reading it. Godspeed! *¡Adios!*

Laurence M. Lasater
San Angelo, Texas
November 2006

You know with all your heart and soul that not one of all the good promises the Lord your God gave you has failed. Every promise has been fulfilled; not one has failed.

Joshua 23:14

Photo by Image Arts, Etc.

Annette with the sixth generation—Watt, Luke and Beau.

ACKNOWLEDGMENTS

I had the fun of writing this book. Others did the work of readying it for publication. I want to thank the following people:

- Sheila Alexander, our secretary for four years, for struggling through my handwriting and typing the first draft.
- Perry Gragg, retired chairman of the English Department at Angelo State University, for reading the first draft.
- Sally Lasater, my sister, for her insightful comments and reading of Part I.
- Watt Casey, Jr., my cousin, for the many great photographs that appear throughout.
- Rue Judd of Bright Sky Press for her good suggestions and for publishing the book.
- Dixie Nixon, my sister-in-law, the editor. Her enthusiasm and support for this project kept me going.
- Isabel Hernandez, our daughter, for her wonderful design and for all the pleasure her work on our public relations has given me.
- Annette, my *compañera* of 43 years. I invited her to be co-author, since I feel she did more on the book than I.